Doing Business in India

Doing Business in India

A Guide for Western Managers

Rajesh Kumar
and
Anand Kumar Sethi

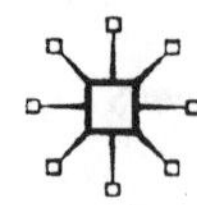

First published in 2005 by
PALGRAVE MACMILLAN™
175 Fifth Avenue, New York, N.Y. 10010 and
Houndmills, Basingstoke, Hampshire, England RG21 6XS
Companies and representatives throughout the world.

PALGRAVE MACMILLAN is the global academic imprint of the Palgrave Macmillan division of St. Martin's Press, LLC and of Palgrave Macmillan Ltd. Macmillan® is a registered trademark in the United States, United Kingdom and other countries. Palgrave is a registered trademark in the European Union and other countries.

ISBN 1–4039–6752–0

Library of Congress Cataloging-in-Publication Data

Kumar, Rajesh, 1954–
Doing business in India : a guide for western managers / Rajesh Kumar and Anand Sethi.
p. cm.
Includes index.
ISBN 1–4039–6752–0
1. Business etiquette—India. 2. Corporate culture—India. 3. Negotiation in business—India. 4. Industrial management—Social aspects—India. 5. Intercultural communication—India. 6. National characteristics, East Indian. 7. India—Commerce. I. Sethi, Anand. II. Title.

HF5389.3.I4K86 2005
395.5′2′0954—dc22 2005043432

A catalogue record for this book is available from the British Library.

Design by Newgen Imaging Systems (P) Ltd., Chennai, India.

First edition: October 2005

10 9 8 7 6 5 4 3

Printed in the United States of America.

Contents

Dedicated to the bright and
dynamic youth of India who stand
to inherit a new economic superpower

Preface

The Indian Tourism Board has a series of promotional advertisements with beautiful photographs of places, tigers, elephants, and various aspects of life in India, all with a highlighted expression of "INDIAAHH!." This sigh pretty much sums up India. An incredible country that can delight, thrill, fascinate, and yet drive people to exasperation. The expression represents the complete bandwidth of the sights, the sounds, the smells, and the colors that typify India, some great and yet some not so pleasant!

The British Broadcasting Corporation recently carried a television story about an English Lady who had just sold off her house near London but had missed out on booking her usual Christmas holiday. Seeing an advertisement about the Indian state of Kerala, as a holiday destination, she decided to try it out. Arriving in Cochin after having faced all sorts of travel-related hassles and a hair-raising ride from the airport, at the time of checking in to the hotel, out of sheer exasperation, she requests the travel desk to arrange for her to fly back home the very next day. Unfortunately, no seats were available for a few days. In the meantime, however, with each passing day she began to increasingly like the place and the people. She promptly canceled her return ticket and has now been in India for several years after having bought for herself a dream mansion in Kerala, for a fraction of the cost she would have had to pay in England.

Such tales abound. All around India there are former foreign managers and diplomats, who came to India as skeptics and critical of habits, mores, practices, and other things Indian, but in a reasonably short time started to love the country and its culture and got so assimilated that they now call this place home. We also personally know many people who having gone back from India have long pined to return for another stint.

There are of course those who, having been sanitized by long years of living and working in very orderly societies and corporations, hate most things about India and cannot wait to leave. It is those who assimilate, drop their "Imperialistic" attitude and become, what may be termed "Indianized," who like it and are liked. The others want out. This analogy applies equally well to companies setting up operations in India, as we highlight in this book.

Indian business history tells us that by the usual definitions, India in the past, with its active trading involvement with countries and peoples from all over the world, was the world's first globalized economy. India was also where the first confluence of the world's major religions happened. It therefore has a long history of cross-cultural relationships and an ingrained culture of tolerance, but demands assimilation. The Mughals came, were assimilated and stayed on as rulers.

The British were, however, different and, with notable exceptions, had clear Imperial and Colonial tendencies that generated strong antipathies, resulting in their departure from the subcontinent in 1947. Interestingly, observers also speak of strong evidence, although empirical, which seems to suggest that companies and entities from the old colonial countries are not as successful as those from the non-colonizers. Comparisons are made between the attitudes and performances of U.S. entities and British companies in India, Swedish companies versus those from Denmark (also an ex-colonizer), and German companies versus the Dutch.

In this book we attempt to provide Western managers with a background on and an understanding of India, its business culture, methods to deal with its people and its bureaucracy, and in general how to strategize success when operating in the country. We provide some case studies of companies that have done well and it is our hope that readers of this book will draw the relevant lessons from these successes.

We have deliberately refrained from covering the usual aspects of how to go about actually establishing local entities, laws, regulations, taxes, and government policies in general. All these are easily and readily available, and in this book we have provided some leads and links to relevant sources of information for the readers.

It is nobody's claim that India is a cakewalk and an easy place to operate in. Yet, it is well known that there are numerous success stories of companies doing very well indeed. In a June 2004 survey of multinationals operating in India, the Federation of Indian Chambers of Commerce and Industry, finds extremely high, and increasing levels of investor confidence, with a staggering 93 percent of respondent companies indicating attractive additional investment opportunities in their sectors of operations.

Also India is now rapidly becoming a favored investment destination. A.T. Kearney, the Japanese Bank for International Co-operation and the European Union are just a few of those ranking India among the top three investment destinations in the world. As far as Information Technology, Business Process Outsourcing, and other IT related services are concerned, India has already acquired an outstanding reputation.

The past few years have also seen a great surge in outsourced engineering and design services–related projects as well a phenomenal interest in the fields of Biotechnology, Healthcare, and Pharmaceuticals. But, with the recent announcements by the South Korean majors, the Italian company Piaggio, as also the Finnish companies, Elcoteq and Nokia of establishing large production units in India, it is becoming increasingly evident that India could well be the next good story as far as manufacturing is concerned.

It is, therefore, our fervent hope that this book will assist companies and managers from Western countries to understand and comprehend this great country, learn how to assimilate and thus, we hope, pave the way toward establishing successful ventures in India, restoring India to the global leadership position and the glory it once had in the past.

Chapter One

India: A Commercial History Perspective

To know my country, one has to travel to that age, when she realized her soul and thus transcended her physical boundaries, when she revealed her being in a radiant magnanimity which illumined the Eastern horizon making her recognized as their own by those in alien shores who were awakened into a surprise of life.

Nobel Laureate, Rabindranath Tagore on India

India: The Pioneer in Globalization

If we accept the conventional definition of the term "Globalization" to mean the movement of goods, services, and knowledge across geographical and political boundaries across large parts of the globe, or that goods, services, knowledge, and finance available in one part of the world are also increasingly made available elsewhere, then India would arguably qualify as the very first globalized economy in the history of the world.

Indian history records[1] that the Indian society of the fourth millennium BC was already dominated by traders who initiated the first Industrial Revolution in India subsequent to which it became a major industrial and exporting country. In the words of Professor H. Frankfort,[2] "It has been established beyond a possibility of doubt that India played a part in that early complex culture which shaped the civilized world before the advent of the Greeks."

Recorded history also indicates India's extensive export and import trade and commerce, right from the days of the Phoenicians (as noted by Herodotus) in the second millennium BC, when Indian natural products, textiles, precious stones, and a range of manufactured items were exported, usually taking the overland route by caravans or through a combination of sea and land routes. Imports were largely gold, silver, copper, and other metals as well as wine. There is also evidence[3] to show that King Solomon's trading ships regularly visited the Port of Cranganore (modern day Kerala) around 950 BC.

Tales and stories of India's fabulous riches carried by traders and merchants spread far and wide. Among those who were attracted by India's opulence was Alexander the Great of Macedonia who then planned and executed an invasion of India in 327 BC, not for the sake of establishing Greek rule but to monopolize the commerce of India.[4]

Alexander left a seminal effect on international trade linking his empire with Egypt, India, Syria, Persia, and the like. He established commercial cities at nodal points in the then Macedonian Greek Empire, some seventy of them called "Alexandria" (including at least four in then India).

After the Romans had become the dominating power in Europe, the first Indian ambassador was sent out by Hindu rulers from Madurai in South India who reached Rome in AD 26. A few years later, another ambassador was sent out during the reign of Claudius Caesar by which time the maritime trade between Rome and India had acquired very large dimensions.

In AD 45, a very important discovery was made. Admiral Hippalus serving under Claudius discovered the importance of the Indian monsoon winds and did an extensive study on them. This discovery enabled the Romans to send out very large trading fleets linking Alexandria with Indian ports. Every July a fleet of a hundred or so ships would leave from the Red Sea for Indian ports laden with wine, copper, lead, tin, and surprisingly, slaves. This fleet would then use the reversing winds of the retreating monsoon in November to take back cargoes of pepper, pearls, diamonds, and textiles.

While Europe, with its trade links with India, was transitioning from under the control of the Greeks to the Romans, a very important development was taking place in India. The great Indian emperor, Ashoka, Chandragupta Maurya's successor, decided in the year 262 BC to become a Buddhist after seeing the carnage and bloodletting caused by his many battles. During Chandragupta Maurya's time, India had already begun to propagate Buddhism in many parts of Asia. The process gained momentum with emperor Ashoka becoming an active Buddhist and many countries including China, Cambodia, and Thailand came into the Buddhist fold.

Xinru Liu in his excellent book[5] writes in considerable detail about the development of trade and commerce between India and China paralleling the spread of Buddhism from India to China and East Asia. The famous Chinese travelers to India, Fa Xian (AD 430–444) and Xuan Zhuang (AD 630–644) have written extensively about the then trade between India and China.[6]

After the Chinese conquered Canton in 111 BC, China acquired a very convenient port to expand their maritime trade particularly with India. The real breakthrough, however, came after AD 1000 when the Chinese started to develop reasonably accurate compasses for use on board their ships. During the reign of Yongle (AD 1403–1424), the third emperor of the Ming Dynasty, the use of these compasses on board Chinese ships became widespread and the Chinese were able to mount increasingly larger merchant fleets. At least seven major expeditions were sent to India from AD 1405 to AD 1433, most of them under the command of the famous eunuch Admiral Zheng He.[7]

But it was not all trade and commerce. Long before the dawn of Buddhism, India was already beginning to be a major center for learning. Writing in India goes back to the most ancient times. India's first prime minister, Jawaharlal Nehru, in his masterly book *Discovery of India*[8] writes that in ancient India, "The study of astronomy was especially pursued and it often merged into astrology. Medicine had its textbooks and there were many large hospitals."

However, it was in Mathematics that India made some really major contributions, which is discussed in chapter three, "A Brief History of the Indian Software Industry."

The development of Mathematics in India was not a result of basic philosophical meanderings but that which arose out of the existing demand of complex problems of trade and society such as taxation, debt, interest, exchange rates, calculation of the fineness of gold, and the like.

The study of Chemistry and Metallurgy were also quite advanced in India. Because of India's very large textile export market, special fast dyes termed "Indigo" were developed. The tempering of steel was a well-developed technology, and Indian metallurgical products were in great demand internationally, especially for weaponry. Testament to this is the iron pillar near Delhi, which was built before the fourth century, and has withstood the ravages of elements with no sign of any rust formation. It has been discovered only now by metallurgists that a thin layer of "misawite," a compound of iron, oxygen, and hydrogen, has protected the pillar from getting corroded. The protective film, formed catalytically by the presence of high amounts of phosphorous in the iron—as much as 1 percent as against less than 0.05 percent in modern day iron, started forming three years after the pillar was built.

Northern India, however, began to go into a decline toward the latter part of the fifth century AD, even though the Gupta Empire (fourth through sixth century AD), the so-called Golden Age of India, still existed. There were repeated invasions by the Huns from the northwest, who, for a period of 50 years actually ruled most of North India. This along with a rapidly fossilizing social and commercial structure, possibly because of the growing influence and rigors of the caste system, affected productivity as well as contacts and trade with the rest of the world. Basically, there was a large-scale decline in all the spheres. The southern part of India under the domination of the progressive Chola kings, however, remained by and large steady and prosperous and continued to maintain commercial relations with the outside world.

With North India going into decline, the way was open to all kind of invasions from Afghanistan, Central Asia and beyond. The Arabs and Islam were beginning to make their mark. Around AD 1000 Sultan Mahmud of Ghazni (Afghanistan) began his ruthless raids and occupied a large part of North India. While India for long had trade, commerce as well as knowledge interaction with the more moderate Islam of the Middle East, the barbarism of Mahmud and his harsh propagation of Islam brought a new dimension into India's knowledge of Islam and its culture. A succession of Islamic invasions saw the power base move to Delhi, the capital of their Sultanate.

The great Khans (Chengiz and Kubla) did not come to India; however, Timur the Turk and his armies ravaged and ransacked the North and pretty much denuded any remaining wealth and destroyed all commerce from the northern part of India. It was only in AD 1526 that the North came under the control of a somewhat better lot of invaders like Babar, from near present day Uzbekistan. Thus the Great Mughal Dynasty of India was born, which went on to rule a major part of India for over two centuries.

With the rise of Arab power (Caliphs of Baghdad), the Ottomans, and then the ascendancy of Genghiz Khan the overland trade between Europe and India came to a low ebb. European merchants did not like the stranglehold of other powers in the trade with India. It was in such a scenario that Marco Polo on his return from China by sea in AD 1292 stopped by in the much more prosperous South India. Marco Polo went back to Europe with great tales of India's fabulous wealth and trade potential and more importantly, about the "Spices" Europe had found in India.

Europeans Arrive in India: Confluence of the World's Major Religions

It was however not until the birth of the European renaissance after the Crusades and the defeat of the Arabs by Isabella and Ferdinand that the next chapter of India's globalization began. The technology of the maritime compass by then had spread to Europe and there were a few intrepid mariners who defied the church and believed that the Earth was round and circumnavigable.

One such mariner was the Portuguese Bartolomeu Dias who in AD 1488 sailed the Cape of Good Hope and sailed some distance up to the East Coast of Africa but inexplicably did not go on to India. Christopher Columbus was another such intrepid mariner and did manage to convince Queen Isabella in AD 1492 to proceed westward in search of India. The rest, as they say, is history. Although Columbus made landfall in San Salvador while searching for the prize that was India, he did kick off the great modernization of the world and globalized trade, as we now know it.

A few years after Columbus's historic voyage, another great sailor from Portugal, Vasco da Gama, sailed the Cape of Good Hope with his fleet of ships and with great navigational skills arrived at Calicut in India on May 20, 1498. Europe had finally found the invaluable sea route to India and its fabled wealth, safe from any interdiction by hostile Islamic elements that controlled the overland routes.

Significantly, although Christianity had been introduced into India in AD 52 by the arrival of St. Thomas in Madras (Chennai), it was only with the Portuguese that real Christian culture was introduced to India. Precolonial India thus had become a repository of the world's four greatest religions and cultures namely Hinduism, Buddhism, Islam, and Christianity. Little wonder then that, Indians are possibly the most adept in the world, in cross-cultural relationships.

The Portuguese in India: In Quest of Spices

The timing of the opening out of the two great all water trading routes, one to India and beyond and the other to the Americas turned out to be extremely fortuitous. As it later turned out, the Portuguese had more practical matters on their mind than pure plunder of India's fabled wealth!

In the early days, food in Europe was neither good nor palatable. There was no cattle fodder that could be stored so animals were killed for beef in the autumn and salted. There were no potatoes or corn or sugar or tea or coffee or lemons. A bit of pepper, ginger, cloves, cinnamon, and other spices could not only make the meat taste better but helped in its preservation with some health and medical related benefits thrown in for good measure. Medicines of those days used particularly large quantities of spices as reported by Hippocrates.

For centuries the Arabs controlled the spice trade into Europe with all its contingent profits. The Prophet Mohammed was married to a rich spice trading widow and when the Islamic missionaries traveled they also promoted spices. They kept their sources of supply—the Indian as well as the Chinese and Javanese traders who called into Indian ports—a complete secret. It was only after Marco Polo's travels that the secret was revealed.

With the availability of the safe, all water passage to India, the precious spices could now be obtained at much lower prices without the Arab middlemen. With increasingly larger ships, the cost of transportation to Europe also became considerably lower. Fortunately, with the simultaneous opening up of the Americas' trade, the tremendous expansion of European silver stock by the working of the Spanish American silver mines could easily pay for the Indian trading operations.

The Portuguese rulers of the fifteenth century looked with great envy at the riches of the nobility and traders of Venice and Genoa who controlled the distribution and sales of spices in Europe from being supplied by the Arabs. The arrival of Vasco da Gama in Calicut on an all-sea route was to change these equations irrevocably. The Portuguese were then well on their way to becoming the masters of trade with India, the Orient, and the New World with the consequent diminishing importance of Venice and Genoa as trading centers and the virtual destruction of the Arabian Empire of that time.

The Portuguese dominated trade with India for pretty much the whole of the sixteenth century. The control of India related operations was directly in the hands of the Royal trading firm "Casa da India" with the Indian side being handled by "Estado da India" headquartered in Goa. Under Governor Afonso de Albuquerque, a capital was set up in Goa in 1510, the very first piece of Indian territory directly governed by Europeans since the time of Alexander the Great. From here the Portuguese sent out ships to control all the strategic ports in the Indian Ocean and at the entrance to the Red Sea, effectively cutting off all the erstwhile spice and other trade including textiles, piece goods, horses, gold, and ivory, of the Arabs and their Gujarati partners. The Portuguese, after the capture of Malacca went on to establish the first ever commercial sea route by running the "Great Ship" from Goa to Nagasaki via Malacca and Macau.

The Portuguese, because of the priorities being accorded to their colony in Brazil, were unable to put together a genuine commercial and corporate infrastructure. Thus, when the Dutch and the English, two nations with greater resources, came to India, the Portuguese, having been weakened by their campaigns in Europe, Brazil, and Africa, were not only beaten and dispossessed of much of their settlements, but also had their commercial base in India ruined.

In September 1632 the Mughal Emperor of India evicted the Portuguese from their possessions in Bengal, and in January 1663, the Dutch under Ryckloff Van Goens defeated the Portuguese and captured Cochin. By 1665, Bombay went under English control, and the Portuguese were left with the small colony of Goa along with the small enclaves of Daman and Diu, north of Bombay, from where they were finally, and somewhat unceremoniously, evicted by the Indian Army at the end of 1961.

The Dutch and the English in India: The Birth of Modern Capitalism, the Establishment of the World's First Incorporated Company and Its First Multinational Corporation

By the middle of the sixteenth century, word of the exploits of the Portuguese had spread to England. Several business people in the city of London contemplated the possibility of business with India. It was however an explorer, Sir Richard Willoughby, who in 1553 formed what records indicate is possibly the world's first ever incorporated company. Willoughby set up, along with a set of merchants as other shareholders, a company with a really romantic name, "*The Mysterie and Compagnie of the Merchant Adventurers for the Discoverie of Regions, Dominions, Islands and Places Unknown*," later to be called the "*Muscovy Company*," to find and exploit an overland trade route to India. Yet, while it was for trade with India that the *Muscovy Company* was set up, the company made huge profits, but from trading with Russia, as their expeditions could not find an easy overland trade route to India.

The great English naval victory of Francis Drake over the Spanish Armada in 1588 kindled their desire for major maritime enterprise and particularly for a share in the sea-based trade with India and the Far East. At the end of 1600, Queen Elizabeth I granted a Charter with rights of exclusive trading to "the Governor and Company of Merchants of London trading into the East Indies." Thus was born the "Joint Stock" *East India Company* (*EIC*) constituted by a grouping of 218 knights, London merchants, ordinary city tradesmen, and Aldermen.

The Dutch

About the same time the Dutch with their strong mercantile tradition, especially in the spice trade, developed their own plans for trading with India and the Far East by the sea route. In 1602, a group of Burghers and traders from the Dutch towns of Amsterdam, Rotterdam, and Middleburg established the *Verenigde Oost Indische Compagnie* (VOC), the United Netherlands East India Company. The Board of Directors of the VOC was a set of 17 gentlemen (the Heeren XVII) who controlled the operations of the company, which at its peak included its huge network of factories and settlements in India, Sri Lanka, Indonesia, the Spice Islands, South East Asia, Africa, the Middle East, China, and Japan. Between 1602 and 1796, the VOC sent out almost a million Europeans to work on the Asia trade on nearly 5,000 ships, a number significantly larger than its nearest rival EIC, truly making the VOC the world' s first multinational.

Although the EIC was established a couple of years before the VOC, the Dutch beat their English rivals in reaching India. The first Dutch ships arrived in India at the Malabar Coast in 1604 under the command of Admiral Juris Van Spilbergen before going on to then Ceylon. By 1606, a trading station had been established at Surat in Gujarat, two years before the English were to arrive there.

By 1610 the VOC had established possessions in Pulicat (north of Madras) and Masulipatnam and expanded their trade considerably. The Dutch upgraded their presence by appointing Pieter Both as the first governor of their possessions in Ceylon and India. It was however the next governor, Jan Coen who not only consolidated the Dutch presence in India and Ceylon but also led the Dutch expansion into Indonesia. By 1619, Coen had captured Jakarta, and renamed it Batavia, which then went on to become for many decades the Dutch capital of the Indies and much like Goa for the Portuguese, the pivot of the Dutch trade of spices, sugar, textiles, timber, gems, and the like in the Asian region.

With the VOC getting increasingly involved with Indonesia and Malacca their activities in Malabar were largely confined to their factories at Kayamkulam and

Cannanore, and in Bengal to the factories at Chinsurah (Fort Gustavius) and Baranagore, until 1658 when with the weakening of the Portuguese in India, the Dutch under Ryckloff van Goens decided to strike. In 1658 they captured Tuticorin and in 1661 Quilon, Cranganore and Cochin in 1663 and subsequently all of Malabar. The Dutch established their capital in Cochin from where they controlled Malabar for the next 130 years, with the contingent advantage of the monopoly of the pepper and cinnamon trade of the region.

Surprisingly, neighboring Travancore did not come under Dutch control except very briefly. And it was here, off a small coastal town called Colachel on the route (the present day National Highway 47) from Trivandrum (modern Thiruvananthapuram) to then Cape Comorin (Kanyakumari) at the southern most tip of India, that a most remarkable event took place in 1741. In a major naval encounter, a squadron of the ruler of Travancore's navy defeated the invading Dutch fleet under the Command of Delannoy. For the first time ever an Asian navy had defeated a European power at sea. A feat not to be repeated until 1905 when Admiral Tojo defeated the Russians in the battle of the Yellow Sea.

The defeated Delannoy was so impressed that he switched to the service of Marthanda Varma, the ruler of Travancore and trained his forces for almost 30 years thereafter. Delannoy died in India and lies buried at the inland fort of Udaygiri, a name now proudly borne by a warship of the modern Indian Navy. The Dutch and the VOC never fully recovered from their defeat in this encounter.

From 1750 onward the VOC was in a state of decline particularly in India. The English by then had started to get stronger and more assertive. Industry and commerce in Holland had considerably diminished. On October 20, 1795, the Dutch lost control of their Indian capital, Cochin and on December 31, 1799 the VOC was finally wound up. The Dutch however kept control of Chinsurah in Bengal until 1825 when it was finally ceded to the English as part of the exchange deal for Sumatra.

Interestingly, the VOC was not the only Dutch effort in India. Merchants from Ostend, which had come under the control of Austria, with the support of some Dutch and Belgian merchants, set up their own enterprise for trade with India. They started the *Ostend East India Company* in 1722 (although some trading had begun as early as 1715) and established trade links with Mocha (Yemen), India, and China. The Ostend Company, to avoid conflict with the VOC, stayed away from South India and concentrated on operations in Bengal. In 1723, a trading station and factory was set up in Banki Bazar (now a suburb of Kolkata). However, in March 1727 the Charter of the company was suspended and finally in March 1731, after the Second Treaty of Vienna, the company itself was wound down and all its possessions were taken over by the Austrian Crown. The Austrians then ran the Indian colonies until they closed them down completely in 1744, except for a brief take over of the Nicobar Islands from the Danes between 1778 and 1784.

The English in India

The East India Company (EIC) in the start-up phase organized ship expeditions primarily to the Spice Islands. These were called "Separate Voyages" because each expedition was financed by a group of merchants within the EIC, who wound up the expedition on the return of the ships and divided the profits among themselves. The third such separate voyage called in at Surat in 1608 but was driven away by the then powerful Portuguese.

In 1610, the English did manage to establish a trading station in Masulipatnam in Andhra Pradesh. Meanwhile, a highly colorful character called Capt. William Hawkins had in 1609, arrived as an envoy of King James I to the court of the Mughal emperor Jehangir in Delhi. Capt. Hawkins rapidly became Emperor Jehangir's drinking partner and also an advisor to the Mughal army and commander of its cavalry.

In 1612, a group of English ships under the command of Capt. Best successfully beat off Portuguese counter attacks and established their first trading station at Surat. In 1613, the English received a formal approval from the Mughal emperor for full trading rights in the area around Gujarat and Surat became the first Presidency of the EIC in India, which with the efflux of time, developed into the Presidency of Bombay, and a major commercial center for the English in India.

In 1615, King James I sent out Sir Thomas Roe as the first official ambassador to the court of the Mughal emperor, who managed to obtain major concessions for establishing trading stations and factories around many parts of India. In 1625, Francis Day the English Commander in the southern part of the Bay of Bengal, managed to obtain from a local chief the grant of a strip of land north of the Portuguese settlement of San Thome with permission to erect a fortification. England had thus acquired her first property rights in India and the Presidency of Madras was thus established, with the fort being named Fort St. George.

As Nick Robins describes in his article "In Search of East India Company,"[9] "Asia played a great role in civilizing Europe. From the middle of the seventeenth century on, the growing influx of cottons radically improved hygiene and comfort, while tea transformed the customs and daily calendar of the people (in Europe). And it was in the huge five acre warehouse complex at Cutler's Gardens (London) that these goods were stored prior to auction at 'East India House' (Leadenhall Street, London). Here, over 4,000 workers sorted and guarded the EIC's stocks of wondrous Indian textiles, calicos, muslins and dungarees, ginghams, chintzes and seersuckers, taffetas, 'allibal-lies', and hum hums. Today, the company's past at Cutler's Gardens is marked with ceramic tiles that bear a ring of words: 'silks, skins, tea, ivory, carpets, spices, feathers, cottons.' "

By 1624, the English had figured out a great Dutch secret. It turned out that the Dutch used saltpeter from India as ballast for their ships returning home instead of plain rocks. Apparently Indian saltpeter was very rich in potassium nitrates and other alkaline salts essential for gunpowder in those days. The Crown put pressure on the EIC for their ships to bring back this high quality saltpeter from India for their guns. Failure to do so would result in the application of an export duty on all silver, the then trading currency, carried to India by the company's ships. Hundreds of thousands of tons of saltpeter was taken to England from all parts of India thus contributing enormously to the rise in the domination of English guns and weaponry of that time.

The EIC rapidly consolidated and expanded its Indian operations. Incredibly, except for a minor battle at Biderra (Chinsurah, Bengal) in 1759, there is very little evidence of large scale hostilities between the English and the Dutch. This enabled the EIC to gradually expand their trading portfolio. By the middle of the seventeenth century the EIC was shipping goods as diverse as cloth from Southern India to Sumatra and coffee from Arabia to India. Profits thus generated were put back into buying the spices required in the home country and hence were able to circumvent the Dutch stranglehold on the Spice Trade.

In 1661, the English in India got the equivalent of a "windfall." King Charles II of England married the Portuguese Princess, Catherine of Braganza, and Bombay ("Bom Baja") was gifted to him as part of her dowry mainly in order to secure English support to the Portuguese against the Dutch. The cash-strapped king leased Bombay to the EIC for a huge loan but with an annual rent of only ten pounds sterling per annum. One of the earlier governors of Bombay, Gerald Aungier (1669–1677) went on to develop this city and the Presidency into India's commercial powerhouse.

Indian Exports Lead to the World's First Protectionist Barriers. Nick Robins[10] further writes, "The lifestyle evolution (in England) was not without opposition. For hundreds of years, India had been renowned as the workshop of the world, combining great skill with phenomenally low labor costs in textile production. As EIC's imports grew, so local manufacturers in England panicked. In 1699, things came to a head and London's silk weavers rioted, storming 'East India House' in protest at cheap imports from India." Horace Walpole was famously known to have stated, "What is England now? A sink of Indian wealth, filled by Nabobs."

Shortly thereafter Parliament prohibited the import of all dyed and printed cloth from India, to be followed a few years later by a complete ban on the use or wearing of all printed calicoes in England. Such unique protectionist barriers were later to contribute enormously to the rapid progress of England's textile factories and the demise of India's handloom textiles business for years to come.

Meanwhile, the wealth being generated by the EIC led to considerable envy. Toward the end of the seventeenth century a rival company called The English Company Trading to the East Indies was set up and the future of the EIC was now seriously threatened. The directors of the EIC protested pleading that "two East India Companies in England could no more subsist without destroying one or the other, than two Kings, at the same time regnant in one Kingdom." After much quarreling an agreement was reached. Under the award of Lord Godolphin, who had the task of resolving the issue, the two companies were merged into one entity called *The United Company of Merchants of England trading to the East Indies.* This was then the company and not the old EIC, as is widely believed, which went on to control trade with India and ended up taking control of the sovereignty of India from 1757 to 1858. However, the moniker of the EIC has stuck in conventional history books and, for ease of recognition, is used in this chapter.

The English in India: Imperialism Replaces Capitalism. In 1743, a young man from an aristocratic family from Shropshire, England, by the name of Robert Clive, came out to India as a clerk for the company and ended up enrolling for military service with them. Clive was soon to distinguish himself in battle in 1751 and 1752 against the French (under Dupleix), who by then had also come to India, and were on the verge of achieving near hegemony, in the southern part of India. Shortly thereafter Clive was made the Governor of Fort St. George at Madras. From then on the history of India and the history of India' s business and trade were to be changed irrevocably.

Because of the continuing trade barriers in the textile trade, the EIC had to change tack. With increasing manufacturing activities in Europe, raw materials needed to be procured at very cheap prices. Also, there was great consternation in England about the huge outflow to India of precious metals, particularly silver, which was the principal "currency" acceptable to Indian traders. The EIC had to find other sources of financing their operations. The easiest way out was to diversify. And diversify the company did, and started a massive though dishonorable trade in opium that made huge profits but was to later lead to the infamous Opium Wars.

The other way of increasing finances was the military option of annexing territories and then taxing the local people. Gerald Aungier, the Governor in Bombay, wrote to the Directors in London advocating, "The time now requires you to manage your general commerce with the sword in your hands." Accordingly, Robert Clive, in 1757 on a not very convincing charge relating to the questionable "Black Hole of Calcutta" incident, attacked and defeated the Nawab of Bengal, Siraj-ud-daula, at the battle of Plassey and installed a compliant "puppet" Mir Jafar as the Nawab. This was then the defining moment and the turning point in Indian history. Imperialism had now replaced Capitalism.

The Loot of India's Wealth Finances the "Industrial Revolution." Within five years, revenues from tax at the rate of 67 percent on income went up by 300 percent, driving the people of Bengal to near penury. By 1769 such extortion, together with a period of drought, kicked off the great famine of Bengal. Over ten million people died and yet the company made no relief arrangements. Tax revenues were further increased and the EIC's monopoly textile trade was protected by some brutal measures such as the cutting off the thumbs of weavers who dared to sell to other traders. According to Nehru[11] "The English historians of India, Edward Thompson and G.T. Garrett, tell us that a gold lust unequaled since the hysteria that took hold of the Spaniards of Cortes' and Pizarro's age filled the English mind. Bengal in particular was not to know peace again until she had been bled white."

But Bengal and India can nevertheless take credit for the fact that its looted wealth paved the way for the Industrial Revolution. In the words of the American, Brooke Adams,[12] "very soon after Plassey, the Bengal plunder began to arrive in London, and the effect appears to have been instantaneous, for all authorities agree that the 'Industrial Revolution' began with the year 1770 . . . Plassey was fought in 1757, and probably nothing has ever equaled the rapidity of the change that followed. In 1760 the 'flying shuttle' for textile manufacturing appeared, and coal began to replace wood in smelting. In 1764, Hargreaves invented the Spinning Jenny and, in 1768, Watt matured the steam engine. Before the influx of the Indian treasure, and the expansion of credit, which followed, no force sufficient for this purpose existed. Possibly since the world began, no investment has ever yielded the profit reaped from the Indian plunder, because for nearly 50 years Great Britain stood without a competitor."

Needless to say, India's industry was devastated and its agriculture decayed. The economic development of India was completely arrested for the rest of the eighteenth century as well as for all of the nineteenth century. With Indian manufacturing and exports severely curtailed, the British started to flood India with their own products. According to Nehru,[13] "The Classic type of modern colonial economy was built up, India becoming an agricultural colony of industrial England, supplying raw materials and providing markets for Industrial goods." India was not to recover until late into the twentieth century.

Interestingly, among the increasing exports to India from Britain were such unique items as "India Pale Ale," a highly hopped beer to withstand the long and hot journey with large blocks of ice obtained from North America. Also at this time large quantities of gin and tonic (quinine water) used to be shipped out to India, "the Gin to keep the boredom (of the British expatriates) away and the Tonic Water to keep off malaria!"

The English in India: Imperialism gives way to Colonialism. All of these events, together with the constant envy at the wealth generated by those connected with the EIC led to great political pressure in England to carry out reforms, despite the interest to the contrary shown by King George III. In 1773, Lord North introduced "The India Bill" in Parliament providing for greater parliamentary control and placing India under the rule of a governor general. In 1784, Prime Minister William Pitt pushed through Parliament the "India Act" that effectively transferred the full management of the company to a board answerable directly to Parliament and thus according to Nick Robins,[14] "in the final 70 years of its life, the company would become less of an independent commercial venture and more a sub-contracted administrator for the English (later on the British) State, a Georgian example of a public–private partnership."

Warren Hastings came out to India as the first governor general and he vigorously pursued the expansion of British rule in India. The aggressive territorial policies of the subsequent Governors General led to the defeat or expulsion of the other European entities in India, as well as the defeat and annexation of any individual state that defied the British. By 1856, the British had total occupation of all of India. Imperialism had given way to Colonialism.

Unfortunately for the EIC though, its racial and administrative arrogance of the rule in India led to the Mutiny of India in 1857. This brutal war lasted two years and the victorious British sent the last Mughal emperor to prison and killed his two sons. While that was the end of the Mughal empire in India, the EIC itself, by a proclamation on November 1, 1858, was abolished and the direct rule of India by the Monarch and Parliament in London was established. This situation was to last until August 15, 1947 when India finally won its independence from British rule.

The Danes in India

According to Peter Ravn Rasmussen,[15] in 1615 two Dutch merchants, Jan de Willem and Herman Rosenkrantz, brought a proposal to King Christian IV, monarch of Denmark and Norway, a proposal for the establishment of a Danish trading company, that would compete with the VOC and EIC. On March 17, 1616, the King issued a charter giving *The Dansk Ost Indisk Kompagni* (DOIK—The Danish East

India Company), a monopoly on trade between Denmark and Asia for a period of 12 years. The DOIK was structured very much like the VOC and further, according to Rasmussen,[16] several of the Articles of Association were lifted in their entirety from those of the VOC.

However, it was only by 1618 that adequate finances could be raised to mount the first expedition. This voyage was originally to sail to the Coromandel Coast of India on the advice of Roelant Crappe, who was earlier in the service of the VOC. However, another Dutchman, Marselis de Boschouwer, claiming to be the emissary of the "Emperor of Ceylon," met King Christian IV and persuaded him to sign in March 1618 a "Treaty of Aid and Trade" between Denmark and the so-called Emperor of Ceylon (in fact just the Rajah of Kandy). The destination of the expedition was now changed to Ceylon.

On August 18, 1618 the Danish Ship "Oresund" under the command of Roelant Crappe sailed to the Indies from Copenhagen, followed shortly thereafter on November 29, 1618 by the main fleet of four ships under the command of Ove Gjedde. However, during the long voyage from Denmark, Boschouwer died, and shortly after arriving in Ceylon, the "Oresund" was sunk by the Portuguese, and Roelant Crappe captured and handed over to Raghunatha, the local ruler (Nayak) of Tanjore province in India. Thus, on arrival in Ceylon, Ove Gjedde did not find any satisfactory arrangements in place and decided to move on to India's Coromandel Coast. In October 1620, Gjedde, accompanied by Reverend Lutken, the Chaplain to King Frederik IV, arrived at the Court of the Nayak of Tanjore, and by November that year a treaty was concluded by him on behalf of the King of Denmark with the Nayak, and permission obtained for establishing a fort ("Dansborg") at the village of Tarangambadi, later to be called "Tranquebar."

By 1621, with "Dansborg" well established, the ship "Kobenhavn" (Copenhagen) sailed out from Tranquebar to Tenasserim (Mergui) on the western coast of Thailand and returned with a large cargo of pepper. In 1622, Gjedde sailed back to Denmark leaving the now freed Crappe in charge of Tranquebar. In 1624, the Danes expanded their trade by sending expeditions to Macassar in present day Indonesia to bring back cargo loads of cloves. With these initial successes, the Danes felt emboldened to expand their Indian operations and in 1625, a Danish possession was established in Masulipatnam on the Andhra coast and subsequently similar operations were set up in Pipely and Balasore in Orissa.

However, it appears that the finances of the Indian operations of the DOIK were poorly managed and by 1627, the Danes were reduced to running their ships on third party neutral charters for the Portuguese and the Dutch. Worse, Roelant Crappe was unable to pay the agreed upon royalties to the Nayak of Tanjore and was promptly put on notice. Crappe tried to negotiate with the VOC for them to take over Tranquebar but the Dutch were not interested. Crappe decided to return to Denmark to seek financial assistance and left the operations in India to another Dutchman, Pessart, who made the financial situation worse by mismanagement, and by 1638 he along with his family were finally held hostage in lieu of outstanding Danish payments.

The major shareholders of the DOIK petitioned King Christian IV to wind up the company in view of its deteriorating finances but the king clearly had other ideas.

In 1639 two more ships, the "Solen" and the "Christianshavn," were sent out to Tranquebar along with William Leyel, the designated new governor of Danish possessions in India. On arrival in India the "Solen" managed to seize a ship belonging to a wealthy local businessman and Pessart and his family were released in exchange for this ship.

Unfortunately, serious differences arose between Leyel and Pessart. Pessart finally ran off on a Portuguese ship taking with him all the remaining money, gold and silver and some of the best guns, and to top it all, the books of account. With no money left the Danes in India had to abandon conventional commerce and unfortunately resorted to privateering and piracy in the south of India as well as off Pipely and Bengal. Worse was to follow. In 1648, a number of the Danish officers led by Poul Hansen Korsor, successfully rebelled and Leyel was sent back to Denmark and the privateering activities further intensified with the DOIK now virtually bankrupt.

DOIK—The First of the European East India Companies to Wind Up. In 1648, King Christian IV died and Frederik III became the new king of Denmark. However, with the ongoing wars with Sweden at that time, Frederik III was not particularly interested in DOIK's Indian operations. In 1650, the king, at the request of its majority shareholders finally dissolved the DOIK, the first of the European East India Companies to wind up. Attempts were made to sell Tranquebar to the Dutch as well as to the Elector of Brandenburg[17] but nothing came of these efforts.

Poul Hansen Korsor died in 1655. By then the Danish population in the Indian possessions had substantially dwindled and operational control was passed on to a chief gunner called Eskild Andersen Kongsbakke. The Nayak of Tanjore, disgusted by the Danes who had settled their dues, decided to attack Dansborg in Tranquebar but Kongsbakke and his small force of two remaining Danes and a few Portuguese mercenaries beat off the attacks with the help of the local population. Kongsbakke, obviously a loyal Dane, then went on to fortify all of Tranquebar with revenues from increased privateering and set about improving the finances of his territories. By 1660, it is reported, he was the only Dane left in India but continued to send regular reports to Copenhagen where they were received with considerable disbelief. Finally in 1668 he managed to send to Copenhagen a personal representative, Geert van Hagen, a Sergeant from a nearby Dutch enclave. The Danish government promptly despatched a warship, the "Faroe," to Tranquebar and in May 1669 the long isolation of the Colony was lifted. Kongsbakke married a local Indian girl, received a Royal accolade, and stayed on to help develop and govern Danish possessions in India. He finally died and was buried in Tranquebar in 1674.

On November 20, 1670 a second DOIK received a Danish Royal Charter from the then king, Christian V, for exclusive trade with the East Indies for 40 years. The new company[18] consolidated the Indian operations and expanded its trade connections (reportedly including slavery) to Malaysia, Malacca, Sumatra, and China. Tranquebar enjoyed great prosperity from 1687 to 1714 through export of sugar, spices, saltpeter, and textiles.

In 1698, Danmarksnagore was founded at Gondalpara in Bengal and an additional trading station was established on the Malabar Coast for trading in pepper. In 1699, a colony called "Frederiksnagore" was set up in Serampore, Bengal.

However, the same year the then Nayak of Tanjore besieged and ransacked Tranquebar and left it in ruins. As a result of this attack, and with the growing recession in trade, the second DOIK was also wound up in April 1729 after the then King, Frederik IV, refused further aid to the company.

A new company, the *Dansk Asiatisk Kompagni* (*DAK*), was established in 1732 with a 40-year-monopoly on Asian trade. In 1752, DAK established a major pepper trading center at Calicut. In the same year two Danish warships arrived at Tranquebar to reestablish the colony, and to protect it from the impact of the Anglo-French wars. It was also decided to reopen the Bengal trade by resettling Frederiksnagore in Serampore.

The principal items of trade were textiles, saltpeter, salt, pepper, soft brown sugar, rattan, indigo, and tea, amounting to several million "Rigsdalers." The traded "tea" was largely smuggled from Denmark into Britain, an aspect that caused great concern to the directors of the EIC.

In 1756, a Danish expedition was sent from Tranquebar to the Nicobar Islands, which were then occupied in the name of the Danish king and named "Frederiksoerne" (The Islands of Frederik). A trading station called "Ny Danmark" was established on Greater Nicobar Island. The commercial activities out of Nicobar, however, never really took off as a result of large-scale deaths of the expatriate Danish community due to tropical diseases and also because of the several battles with the Austrians, who actually managed to colonize the Nicobar Islands briefly between 1778 and 1784.

Upon the outbreak of hostilities between Britain and Denmark in 1801, Tranquebar and Serampore were captured by the British but were restored to the Danes under the Treaty of Amiens. Six years later, when war resumed, both places were again taken possession of and were occupied by the British from 1808 to 1815, and subsequently returned to the Danes in a somewhat miserable condition.

Finally in 1845, all Danish territories on mainland India were sold to the EIC for 1.25 million rupees (1.1 million Rigsdaler). The Nicobar Islands remained under Danish control and Frederikshoj was built on Nancowrie Island and another outpost on Polo Milo Island north of Little Nicobar. With further outbreaks of tropical diseases decimating the Danish population in Nicobar, the islands were finally handed over, free of charge, to the British in 1868 ending 250 years of Danish commercial and colonial activity in India.

The French in India: The World's First Corporate "Wars"

The French, who competed with the English on many grounds, also took to exploring trade with India and the East. In 1611, Emperor Louis XII granted a monopoly to a French company to pursue their quest of trading with India. Nothing much, however, came of this venture. In 1664, the then Emperor, Louis XIV, granted another permission to a company established by Jean Baptiste Colbert and chartered by the emperor to begin trade with India.

Colbert's *Compagnie des Indes* (CDI—French East India Company) first managed to establish trading stations on the islands of Bourbon (Reunion) and Ile de France (Mauritius) off the East Coast of Africa. The French landed at Pondicherry, south of

Madras, and established their first colony in India. By 1719, they had established themselves in the southern part of India and established additional factories and settlements (*Etablissements Francaises dans L`inde*) in Masulipatnam, Karaikal, Mahe, and even one in Chandernagore in Bengal.

Like the DOIK, the French operations in India were not successful initially and remained so until 1741. At this time, the French colonies in India received a new and ambitious governor called Joseph Francois Dupleix. He pursued a very aggressive policy both toward the Indians as well as with the British. Dupleix's efforts at undercutting the EIC trade and commerce, and political machinations involving local Indian rulers, brought him into direct confrontation with the British.

This led to the clash of the two multinational companies. It was the first of the world's greatest "corporate battles," except in this case, unlike the modern age, the battle was fought with real guns, cavalry, and infantry. Three wars were fought in India between the French and the English during the period 1746 to 1763, the last of which was to result in the rout of the French by the English under Clive and the loss of most of the French trade and many of their possessions in India. Dupleix was recalled to France but a few of the French possessions, including their capital of Pondicherry, remained in their control until 1949 when they were ceded back to Independent India. The CDI, never really financially successful, went bankrupt and was finally dissolved in 1769.

The Other Europeans in India

The Portuguese, Dutch, British, and the French were not the only ones coveting a piece of Indian trade and commerce. By the end of the seventeenth century and the beginning of the eighteenth century, almost all the West European maritime nations with the exception of Spain (who were preoccupied with the Philippines), large and small, were in one way or the other involved in trade with India.

The Swedes, for example, established in Gothenburg the *Svenska Ostindiska Companierna* (SOC) in 1731 at the initiative of an enterprising Scotsman, Colin Campbell, who had his own axe to grind against the English. He and a few other partners, including the British—Charles Graham, Charles Morford, and Charles Irvine—wanted to take advantage of the trading space left after the closure of the Ostend East India Company in March 1731 after the Second Treaty of Vienna. The SOC had also learnt its lessons from the activities and problems of the other East India Companies and decided to concentrate purely on trade without recourse to any colonization. This policy was to bring the SOC huge profits without the liability of supporting any colonies in the East. It has been stated that the relative success of Swedish companies in modern India may have something to do with the non-colonial policies of the SOC in the past and certainly a bearing on traditional Swedish neutrality.

The initial Swedish activities are chronicled in Colin Campbell's "A Passage to China"—a diary of the first Swedish East India Company Expedition (1732–1733). The good ship "Friedericus Rex Suecia" built at the Terra Nova shipyard in Stockholm set sail in 1732 for India and China, under the command of Captain Georg Herman Trolle. It docked at Surat in Gujarat before going on to Bengal and

Canton in China. Between 1731 and 1813 the SOC sent out 38 ships ("EastIndiamen") to the East with a large majority of the later expeditions more focused on China and its ceramics. Interestingly, the SOC has recently been revived recently, more as an historical project to reconstruct a new "EastIndiaman" called the "Gothenburg" at the new site of the Terra Nova Shipyard at Eriksberg, and to sail the ship to Canton later in 2002.

In 1647, the *Compagnia Genovese delle Indi Orientali* (The Genoese East India company) was set up. Not much is known about the activities of this company except for a few references relating to trade in Bengal. In 1754, the Prussians established the "Prussian Bengal Company" at Emden and again very little is recorded of their activities. In 1779, Haider Ali, the ruler of Mysore, during the period of his problems with the British, invited as a counterpoint, the Germans to establish an East India Company and establish operations in Nandangade in present-day Karnataka. This German company was wound up in 1789. In 1780, the "Philippines-Spanish East India Company" was set up but this carried out only some minor trade between the Philippines and Bengal. The Austrian interest in India came through the Ostend East India Company established in 1722 in Austria controlled Ostend. As earlier, this company was wound up in 1731 after the Second Treaty of Vienna and its possessions in India taken over by the king of Austria. Although the Austrian colonies in Bengal were formally closed in 1744, the Austrians still made their presence felt by capturing the Nicobar Islands from the Danes in 1778 before they were finally defeated and driven out by the Danes in 1784.

The (North) Americans and India

As we know, Christopher Columbus set out from Spain in 1492 to find the western sea route to India and fortuitously hit America. It was, however, only after the British were well entrenched in India that the first contacts between North America and India were established. The Portuguese by then had already established commerce between South America (Brazil) and India (Goa).

The EIC had established significant trading links between the two large British colonies by 1625. Directors and officers of the EIC as well as administrators of the British Government were actively involved in this activity. Prominent among them were Lord Baltimore (founder of Maryland and a Director of EIC in the 1620s) and Elihu Yale (founder of Yale University and a former governor of Madras for the EIC from 1687 to 1692).

It was also common for senior functionaries of the EIC "to invest in a few servants or slaves, which they resold at a profit. The slaves were subsequently taken to the colonies in the New World."[19] Francis Assisi, in his extensively researched work,[20] identifies a "Peter Fisher" (name obviously changed from his original Indian name) as possibly the very first such Indian slave brought into America by Lord Baltimore. He subsequently married a white Irish servant girl, Mary Molloyd, and their first child, Mary Fisher, born in 1680, is recorded in history as the very first Indian American. In fact there is evidence to suggest that the first real slaves in the United States were from India.

The first direct American contact with India was however established in 1784 by the sailing of the ship "United States," from the Port of Philadelphia and arriving in the Indian city Pondicherry in December 1784 with a cargo of "Madeira, Tobacco, Copper, Lead and Iron."[21] This and few subsequent voyages were financed by Thomas Willing of Philadelphia, who entertained visions of establishing an "American East India Company" but was unable to do so because of subsequent events in history.

According to Bhagat,[22] because of the war between France and England, American merchants who were neutral made enormous profits from trade with India at that time. Elias Hasket Derby of Salem (Mass.) became America's first millionaire. Between 1795 and 1805, American trade with India exceeded that of all the European nations put together.

However with the escalation of hostilities in Europe, attacks on American ships by both, the British and the French increased so much that President Jefferson's administration imposed an embargo on all foreign trade that had a significant negative impact on the economies of the prosperous coastal towns.

Although the embargo was repealed in 1809, the declaration of war by the United States against Britain in 1812 brought further restrictions on international trade especially against British-controlled India. These restrictions led to the unforeseen benefit of a rapid industrialization of America, which got further impetus when in 1816, the U.S. Congress introduced a prohibitive tariff against the import of inexpensive products from India, especially textiles, thus more or less putting an end to Indian imports into America for several years to come.

More interesting, however, was the effort by an enterprising American from Boston, Frederic Tudor, to export ice from the United States to the British in Calcutta in the year 1833. The ice, cut from fresh water ponds in New England, was sent out by ship to Calcutta, insulated with thick layers of sawdust from Maine. Nearly two-thirds of the ice survived the long journey without the use of refrigeration. The grateful British built an "ice house" in Calcutta to store the imported ice. Tudor made about $ 200,000 profit from the Calcutta trade alone. This enterprise is well chronicled in "The Frozen Water Trade."[23]

> So far as I am able to judge, nothing has been left undone, either by man or nature, to make India the most extraordinary Country that the Sun visits on his rounds. Nothing seems to have been forgotten, nothing overlooked. (Mark Twain)

Indian Business—Coming of Age

Indian Enterprise and Industry in the Days of the "Raj"

> *The Governments of an exclusive company of merchants is perhaps the worst of all Governments for any country whatsoever.*
>
> Adam Smith in *The Wealth of Nations*, referring to the East India Company

For centuries prior to the arrival of the Europeans, Indian business was largely in the hands of a few business communities (e.g., Marwaris, Parsis, and Gujaratis, etc.) endowed with traditional business skills. However, the establishment of the domination of British business interests with the East India Company enjoying a trade monopoly guaranteed by the British Monarch, worked to the enormous detriment of local Indian enterprise, particularly in the period starting from the later half of the eighteenth century. As noted earlier, this British domination was a result, not of market forces, but of non-economic, legal, punitive taxation and other coercive factors.

Fortunately, while the Indian business communities were made totally subordinate, they were not completely decimated, primarily because Indian merchants and moneylenders proved useful to the British. In Bengal, for instance, Indian merchants were essential as middlemen for the procurement of items such as silk, fine cotton cloth, and indigo. With the substantial increase in industrial output in Britain after the Industrial Revolution, middlemen all over India were also increasingly used for marketing and trading of imported products manufactured in Britain. The local moneylenders, on the other hand, extended short-term credit to producers of commodities and also supplied cash with which land revenues could be paid to the British Indian government.[24]

A few of these middlemen and land holding (Zamindars) financiers particularly in and around Calcutta, won the confidence of the British and were encouraged to form interracial trading and agency houses in partnership with the British. The first agency was formed by Dwarkanath Tagore, Nobel Laureate Rabindranath Tagore's grandfather. He formed the Agency House "Carr, Tagore & Co." in 1834 and went on to become a pioneer in the mining, banking, insurance, shipping, plantation, and export–import trading businesses.

British policies during the "Raj" in India clearly promoted the export of agricultural products, minerals and raw materials from India for factories in Britain with a substantial percentage of the finished goods exported back for sale and consumption in India. Industrialization of India was certainly not on the agenda. Even the noted economist, John Maynard Keynes[25] wrote in 1911, "specialization among nations was a good thing and, though the Indian educated class seem to desire, with patriotic fervor, industrialization of their country, such industrialization was neither desirable nor likely."

Sabyasachi Bhattacharya writing in "A Pictorial History of India"[26] notes that "British capital investment in India did not play a significant role in nineteenth-century industrial development with the exception of jute mills, coal mines and tea plantations, followed by some investment in tobacco, hydrogenated oils, electrical machinery, pharmaceuticals, and petrol." Thus India's industrial and commercial development was left primarily to the fervor of patriotic educated Indians belonging to the traditional business communities.

Because of the very substantial quantum of import and export trade, predominantly controlled by the British, amongst the first corporate enterprises established during the "Raj" were banks and insurance companies starting with the "General Bank" that opened for business in Calcutta in 1773, during the time of Governor General Warren Hastings. In 1793, the "Calcutta Laudable Mutual Insurance Society" opened for business and the "Bank of Calcutta" was established in 1806. The "Bank of Calcutta," in 1809 changed its name to "Bank of Bengal" and in 1921 merged with the "Imperial Bank of India" which, after India's independence in 1947 morphed into the "State Bank of India," currently India's premier bank.

The first Indian Companies Act was instituted in 1850 (subsequently amended in 1856 to include limited liability companies) and the very first Indian company, "The New Oriental Life Insurance Co. Ltd." was registered under the act in 1851.

It was however the Parsi business community in the western part of India that pioneered the establishment of Indian-owned manufacturing companies, with the first textile mills being established in the middle of the nineteenth century, after the removal in 1843 of all restrictions on the export of textile machinery from Britain. On July 7, 1854, Cawasji Nanabhai Davar set up the "Bombay Spinning and Weaving Co." followed a month later by the establishment of "Oriental Spinning & Weaving Co." by Manekji Nasarvanji Petit. Jamshedji Nasarvanji Tata, the founder of India's highly acclaimed conglomerate, the Tata Group, established the "Empress Mills" in Nagpur in 1887 and followed up shortly thereafter with the "Swadeshi Mills" in Bombay.

The Indian business community in other parts of India was somewhat slower to start their own enterprises. The east, with the colonial capital in Calcutta was under close British political and administrative control. Also, business in the east as well as the south, was under the near total domination of British owned or controlled "Agency Houses." The north, on the other hand, until the first Indian war of Independence (referred to as the "Indian Mutiny" by the British) in 1857, was still largely under Mughal rule.

In eastern India the breakthrough came with the jute industry. In 1855, Bysumber Sen, a Bengali entrepreneur, joined hands with George Acland to set up the country's first organized jute mill. After the Crimean War in the 1860s, hemp which was then the packing material of choice, was in short supply giving a big boost to Indian jute exports. A few years after Bysumber Sen's effort, G.D. Birla (who was subsequently to become a doyen of Indian business and industry) set up an even larger unit, the "Birla Jute Mills," in the face of the strongest possible opposition and obstructionism from British Agency Houses and the Government.

It was however during World War I, when a large numbers of British businessmen from Bengal were called out for military and other duties, that several of the British jute interests were bought over by Indians who then proceeded to establish additional capacity. Indian owned jute mills made enormous profits during World War I with dividends of over 100 percent annually and this is what largely helped create the wealth of the Marwaris (the traditional business community from Rajasthan) who had migrated in large numbers to Calcutta.

Because of the extreme conservatism of the south Indian business community and the relative lack of adequate infrastructure in the south, compounded by the overwhelming influence of the British Agency houses (Parry's, Binnys, Arbuthnots, Best & Co. etc.), in that region, Indian commercial enterprise in South India was also a late starter. Even the initiative for the establishment of the first textile mills in Madras also came from Bombay-based industrialists.

The engineering business in India started in 1823 when the "East India Company Ordnance Company" was set up in Bombay, but the first recorded private initiative was the establishment in 1830 of the "Porto Novo Steel & Iron Co." near Cuddalore by Josiah Marshall Heath.[27] This company, later to become the "East India Iron Co.," Madras, was inexplicably closed down in 1866. Because of the availability of iron ore and coal in the region, The "Bengal Iron Works" was set up near Asansol in 1874. But these were British-owned enterprises.

It was the genius in Jamshedji Tata and his vision that really set India on the path to industrialization with the establishment of the "Tata Iron & Steel Co. (TISCO)."

As Dwijendra Tripathi writes in "A Pictorial History of Indian Business"[28] "His (Jamshedji Tata's) dream of launching steel production in India must have seemed impossible to anyone familiar with past attempts in this direction, and the prevailing situation in India. But Jamshedji persevered in the face of ludicrous prospecting regulations, an unhelpful government, financial stringency and paucity of technical hands. Regrettably, he did not live to see the consummation of his dream project, but if TISCO finally became a reality in 1907, it was due to his vision and dogged determination. From the far off United States where he had gone in search of technicians, he continued to send elaborate instructions to his son Dorabji back home, about every aspect of the project in Bihar."

It is said that when Jamshedji Tata approached Lord George Hamilton, the then secretary of state for India in the government in London, he was told that Lord Hamilton was prepared to eat every ounce of steel that Tata could produce. Within a few years TISCO began to produce tons of the finest quality steel. The London financial markets rebuffed Jamshedji Tata when he tried to raise 1.6 million pounds sterling. Not willing to take this lying down, Jamshedji Tata appealed to the patriotism of Indians and within a few weeks raised this amount from 8,000 Indian shareholders. The British, to paraphrase Queen Victoria, "we are not amused." TISCO was "ironically" (pun intended) to become the only dependable source of supply of high quality steel, rails, and other products to the British rulers of India during the period of World War II.

In 1909, Laxmanrao Kirloskar, a teacher of "Engineering Drawing," at the Victoria Jubilee Technical Institute in Bombay, resigned his job in protest as he was passed over for a promotion, ostensibly on racial grounds, and went on to set up a unit to manufacture plows and other agricultural implements in Belgaum (in present-day Karnataka), the first such industry in the country. After a few years[29] the unit moved to Kirloskarwadi (Kohlapur) and additional products such as diesel engines and centrifugal pumps were added.

Subsequently, the Kirloskar empire grew substantially with additional units set up to manufacture machine tools, electric motors, transformers, compressors, industrial combustion engines, and the like. In 1945, the Kirloskars were to enter into the first ever recorded Indian joint venture with a British company, the "Associated British Oil Engines Export Ltd." Today, apart from a host of items, they also manufacture passenger cars in a joint venture with Toyota of Japan.

Meanwhile, the Tata group went on a major expansion program, especially during and shortly after World War I when transportation and supplies from Britain were severely disrupted and British enterprises in India were deprived of financial and manpower resources.

The Tata Hydroelectric Power Supply Co. was set up in 1910. The origins of this company are interesting. In 1902, the state of Mysore established the "Kolar Goldfields Power Company"[30] at Sivasundaram Island near the Cauvery falls (providing the city of Bangalore with modern electricity), in association with General Electric of the United States. This is the first officially recorded active U.S. corporate activity in India (although as early as 1882, Thomas Edison had incorporated in England a company called "Edison's Indian and Colonial Electric Light Co." to promote power projects in India and other British colonies). Harry Parker Gibbs, was sent out to India by General Electric of the United States, as the Chief Engineer of this project. Gibbs was subsequently employed by the Tata group to establish their power companies including the "Andhra Valley Power Supply Co." in 1916 and the "Tata Power Co. Ltd." in 1919.

The Tatas had also, early in the 1900s, started the world famous and celebrated, "Taj Mahal Hotel" in Bombay, and in 1912 set up the first cement company with another one added immediately after World War I. To put up these large projects the Tatas had established another entity called the "Tata Construction Company." In 1920, the Tatas invited a young entrepreneur, Walchand Hirachand, to become a partner in this company and to manage it. In 1923, Walchand[31] purchased large tracts of land near Nasik to grow cash crops and which was to later become the supply base for the establishment of "Ravalgaon" a large sugar, candy, and confectionery complex, and subsequently for the manufacture of cardboard, paper, edible oils, and alcohol.

Meanwhile as in the other sectors, patriotic fervor had begun to stimulate Indian businessmen and industrialists to challenge the monopoly of British shipping interests. Mafatlal Gaganbhai, a textile manufacturer from Ahmedabad, after making serious inroads into British jute interests in Bengal, had set up a small coastal shipping operation called the "Ratnakar Steam Navigation Co." But, it was Walchand Hirachand who was determined to really challenge the British monopoly. He, along with three partners, established in 1919, the "Scindia Steamship Navigation Co." and also merged the "Ratnakar Steam Navigation Co." into it, much to the chagrin of the British. The story is told of Walchand angrily telling Lord Inchcape, the then head of "British India Navigation Co." that "Indians had the right to run our own steamers on the coast of our own motherland."

In December 1940, Walchand went on to establish on a site in Bangalore gifted by the Maharaja of Mysore, the "Hindustan Aircraft Company" in collaboration with the "Intercontinental Aircraft Company" of the United States to assemble the Harlow trainer, the Curtiss Hawk fighter, and the Vultee attack bomber aircraft. He also set up in 1941, "Hindustan Shipyard" in Vishakapatnam, the first Indian-owned modern shipyard. Both these companies were, after independence, taken over by the Government of India and today are at the very heart of India's Defence production.

Not only did the luminaries of Indian business and industry resolutely challenge British monopoly interests, several of them actively participated in the Indian freedom struggle either by direct financial assistance or by taking active part in protests and other programs, such as the Quit India and the Non Cooperation Movements initiated by Mahatma Gandhi, which, in some cases, led to their incarceration. This spirit of patriotism and nationalism soon spread from leading industrialists to professionals, merchants, traders, and small businessmen.

Efforts to challenge British interests were soon being made in diverse areas such as paper, tea, coal mines, and the like. In Calcutta, P.C. Ray armed with a Doctorate from the University of Edinburgh, and with a worldwide reputation of pioneering work on the synthesis of mercurous compounds, decided that the people of India should have access to cheaper medicines and be free of British pharmaceutical domination. In 1899, he established India's first pharmaceutical manufacturing company, the "Bengal Chemicals & Pharmaceuticals Works." It is little wonder then that by the time of India's independence, local enterprise had captured over 70 percent of the domestic market and controlled over 80 percent of bank deposits and was close to self-sufficiency.

British Companies in Pre-Independence India

As mentioned, British commercial interests in India were predominantly based on trading. The typical capital investment in these ventures was small and usually made by individuals and directed by managing agency firms such as Andrew Yule, Bird-Heilgers, Jardine Skinner, Rallis, Killick Nixon, Brady & Co., British India Corporation, and so on. Though they controlled some manufacturing units like jute and cotton mills, basic engineering units, mining companies, and tea plantations, the agency houses were primarily exporters of jute, jute goods, tea, raw cotton, shellac, and the like, and importers of manufactured goods such as cotton textiles and yarn, paper, various other consumer goods, and production equipment.

With Calcutta as the then capital of British India, it became important to provide the city with electricity. The city had its first demonstration of electrical lighting on July 24, 1879, courtesy P.W. Fleury and Co. It however took almost 20 years before the company, "Calcutta Electric Supply Company Corporation," with its head quarters in London, secured the license for lighting the city in 1897. In 1899, when the city was electrified it was merely 12 years behind New York and 11 years behind London, a testimony to the importance of India and Calcutta.

This nature of British investment in India however began to change in the period after World War I. This war stimulated policies to enhance India's industrialization to make it less dependent on imports, and the great depression of 1929–1933 again boosted incentives for industrial growth by reducing prices of agricultural commodities compared to manufactured goods. As a result, industrial output in British-ruled India grew steadily from 1913 to 1938.

The years between the two World Wars also saw the rise of the British transnationals based on the momentum generated by the Industrial Revolution and postwar growth of demand. Thus were born such world famous companies as Imperial Chemical Industries, Unilever, General Electric Company (United Kingdom), Guest Keen Nettlefolds—partially owned and managed by Joseph Chamberlain, father of Neville Chamberlain, prime minister to be, of Great Britain—and the like. With the protection provided to industries in India, especially those of British parentage, many of these transnationals began to set up operations in India. Although Edward Dwyer had established Dwyer Breweries (later to be called Dwyer Meakin) in Solan in 1855 and Lever Brothers had set up a basic import and sales operation for their "Sunlight" brand of soap as early as 1888 in Calcutta, the first real industrial corporate to be set up was that of GEC for electrical machinery and fans at their unit in Calcutta in 1911.

In 1911, a British company called Brunner Mond set up sales operations in Calcutta for dyes and alkalis. This company was one of the four that were to later, in 1926, merge to form the Imperial Chemical Industries. In 1929, the Indian entity was renamed Imperial Chemical Industries India Ltd. and full-scale manufacturing started in 1939 in Rishra, West Bengal, under the name of the subsidiary, "Alkali and Chemical Corporation of India."

Other major British transnationals followed into Calcutta shortly thereafter. These included, Britannia Biscuit (Subsidiary of Peak Frean & Co.) in 1918, Dunlop (1926), Metal Box (1933), Guest Keen Nettlefold (in 1931 as Henry Williams India Ltd., later to be renamed Guest Keen Williams), and British Oxygen (in 1935 as Indian Oxygen & Acetylene Co.). By the time India achieved independence in 1947, about half of British private capital holdings in India was Foreign Direct Investment in the subsidiaries of British Companies.[32]

However, as a prelude to the fight for Independence in 1947, Indian businesses had already begun to challenge British business interests in India and had made great inroads into their market shares. Postindependence, many of the British companies sold out their companies and their managing agencies to big Indian business interests. Along with the "Union Jack," British businesses in India were in decline and it was not until the 1980s, would there be any significant revival.

U.S. and European Companies in Pre–Independence India

The earliest known mention of modern U.S. business in India, outside of the "Frozen Water Trade," relates to the power sector. As noted earlier, the maharaja of Mysore roped in General Electric to establish a modern power station in the state. In the same year, an American financial institution, "International Banking Corporation," established a banking operation in Calcutta and provided finance for the trade and export of jute, silk, and cotton textiles. On December 15, 2002, this institution celebrated its centenary in India under its current name, "Citibank."

In 1910, the "Singer Sewing Machine Company" set up a company in India to assemble and sell basic sewing machines and in 1912, became the first real multinational manufacturing operation in India. Singer is still a known brand entity long after control passed into Indian hands.

History records that the first automobile was introduced into India in the year 1900, but it was only in 1928 that "General Motors" established an assembly operation in the city of Bombay (now Mumbai) for 11,000 cars and trucks annually under the Buick and Chevrolet marquees. This operation would be followed by the Dodge DeSoto and Plymouth brands in 1946 in collaboration with Walchand's Premier Automobiles. Walchand, as already noted, was also to go on to establish an aircraft assembly operation, "Hindustan Aeronautics" in Bangalore, in collaboration with "Intercontinental Aircraft Company" of the United States.

The very first of the European continentals in India was the Swiss company, "Volkart Brothers," who in 1851, established a large trading operation with headquarters in Bombay (now Mumbai), and traded in coffee, cotton, and industrial goods. They opened their first coffee venture "Volcafe" in 1857 and went on to set up a facility in Tellicherry, near India's coffee growing district.

The Danish company, "Dumex" established a baby food venture in 1920 and followed it up with a pharmaceutical operation in 1928. Others were to follow. Swedish Match AB (as Western India Match Company) set up operations in 1923, the Czech/Canadian venture "Bata Shoe Company" came to India in 1931 and set up their first modern shoe factory in Batanagar, Calcutta in 1936. Sweden's "Vulcan" (Alfa Laval) set up shop in Poona in 1937, while Philips established India's first electric lamp factory in 1939.

Business in Post-Independence India: Advent of Socialism

Business in India underwent a sea change after attaining independence on August 15, 1947. Even before independence, the doyens of Indian business, including luminaries such as J.R.D. Tata, Walchand Hirachand, Padampat Singhania, and the like had in the 1940s formulated "The Bombay Plan," which was a "blueprint adopted by the leaders of the Indian capitalist class who, in their nationalistic fervor, had decided to 'eclipse' their individual interests and favored a largely state led revival of India's industry."[33] The Federation of Indian Chambers of Commerce and Industry (FICCI), the chamber favored by Mahatma Gandhi, comprising of India's prominent capitalists, strongly endorsed the policies of the ruling political party, the Indian National Congress, "in its strategy to make India a strong and self-reliant economic power."[34]

It is said that when economic policy for development is being formulated for the governments of newly independent nations, policy making gets heavily influenced by their experience under the previous colonial rule and the inequities and deprivations suffered through colonial history. As Abid Hussain, a famous Indian diplomat, writes eloquently[35] that "at the time of independence after a long period of subjugation, its land and people were a picture of distress, removed from great events of its past glory and splendor. A whole creative side of Indian civilization had shrunk under foreign rule. The common man, burdened by poverty, hunger and ignorance, had lost the will to exercise its productive might. Out of the dust, they had to be raised by men of great vision like Gandhi and Nehru."

Abid Hussain goes on to say that, "India was a stagnant economy at the time of independence. The economy was predominantly agrarian with little industrial development. Most people lived in villages, in hunger and despair. Bullock carts, wooden plows, spinning wheels and thatched huts—life made of small things, unimaginatively hard, dull and cruel. Agricultural growth was around 0.3% per annum in the first half of this (20th) century. The colonial government took little interest in the improvement of the cultivation practices, except in the case of export crops like cotton, jute and tea."

As far as industry was concerned, the British were not interested in increasing the industrial base of the country as their policies were primarily targeted toward taking out raw materials and intermediates from India for their own large factories for processing and exports to the rest of the world. So jobs were created in Liverpool and Manchester based on Indian raw material while Indian manufacturing and job creation was substantively ignored.

It was in such a scenario that Nehru assumed office as India's first prime minister. Nehru, already influenced by the socialistic ideals of William Morris and George Bernard Shaw while at Cambridge University, and equally impressed by the Fabian socialism of Britain's Labor government in 1945, looked upon the then Soviet system of centralized planning, as the ideal way forward in governing the newly independent country. Such centralized control, as noted, also had the support of India's leading industrialists and businessmen.

Consequently, in 1948, shortly after independence, India's "Industrial Policy Resolution" was formulated, giving prominence to heavy industries and the public sector. Under its dispensation, governmental monopolies were created in most of the important industrial segments including, for example, iron and steel, telecommunications, and mineral oils. Eighteen other industries were brought under central government and control.

Other controls on the economy namely, Imports and Exports, Foreign Exchange, Industrial Licensing, and Capital Issues were, unfortunately, already in place, being a legacy of the wartime controls introduced by the colonial government. These controls then just got incorporated into the industrial policy of the new government. Soviet style "Five Year Plans" were to be formulated and oversight given to a "Planning Commission."

Things were to get worse. In 1955, at its annual meet, the ruling Congress party passed a resolution stating that, "planning should take place with a view to the establishment of a socialistic pattern of society, where the principal means of production are under social ownership or control" and further that steps should be taken to, "check and prevent evils of anarchic industrial development by the maintenance of strategic controls, prevention of private trusts and cartels." These sentiments were incorporated into a new "Industrial Policy Resolution" in 1956 and additional draconian measures introduced in 1961 and 1969, including the controversial "Monopolies and Restrictive Trade Practices Act."

The Indian private sector, which had initially supported centralized controls, were now in a real "pickle." All their enterprise and activities were now under strict political and bureaucratic control. Private sector "profit making" was seen as a social sin. Survival was possible only by satisfying the greed of rent-seeking politicians and bureaucrats, and by cornering hard-to-come by industrial and import licenses, in what came to be termed the "License-Permit Raj." In the words of Amit Mitra, current secretary general of FICCI, "Private sector manoeuvered and meandered to simply remain functional at the cost of low economies of scale, over employment, low productivity, poor quality, obsolete technologies, inevitable rent seeking practices and global isolation in a regime of import substitution."[36]

This state of affairs continued during the period 1977–1979, when the first non Congress government led by the Janata Party came to power. This period is, more regretably, noted for the expulsion from India of the multinationals, such as IBM, ICL, Coca Cola, and others.

India's Economic Liberalization

However, by the time the Congress party led by Mrs. Indira Gandhi, returned to office in 1980, it was abundantly clear that Indian business and industry could no longer continue under rigid socialism influenced controls. Policy changes were introduced in 1980 but as Amit Mitra writes,[37] they were "measured and introspective, focusing primarily on delicensing of two major groups of industries, access to imports for manufacturers of exports, and a change in mindset towards acquiring higher order technologies. The result of, even these halting steps, towards decontrol were almost spectacular. The growth rate of the economy wrenched out of the 3 percent record to an average of 5.5 percent in the 1980s and there is strong evidence that productivity too improved significantly. India was at the door of a new vision of political economy driven by markets and private enterprise. The days of the

'License-Permit Raj' were now numbered, the period of atrophy over, and India was entering a brave new world".

With the easing of restrictions and the gradual removal of licensing, subsidies and other political and bureaucratic roadblocks, many of the old established industrial houses that had survived by playing "the game" within the rules and rent seeking of the old order were now in serious trouble and within a few years the more inefficient of them had started to crumble and close down. The public sector, especially in the states, with their inherent inefficiencies was in serious trouble. First generation entrepreneurs such as Dhirubhai Ambani of Reliance Industries and others, with new concepts, modern management, economies of scale, and a more international approach had now arrived on the scene. The high technology sector, particularly IT, biotechnology, and telecommunications, had been provided a boost by the modern thinking prime minister, Rajiv Gandhi, and his extraordinarily talented advisor, Sam Pitroda, and had spawned the likes of Infosys, HCL, Biocon, and Bharati Telecom, Dr. Reddy's, Ranbaxy, among others. It seemed to be the beginning of a new dawn. The wealth creators had arrived.

However, some of the inefficiencies and controls of the old order continued especially in terms of foreign exchange controls. The economy, by the late 1980s, was struggling to globalize and there was a growing dependence on imports. The economy was also affected by the pressures and vicissitudes of the international financial system. This led to a more significant vulnerability of India's balance of payments and reliance on debt. Surely enough, in 1991, India found itself in situation of a "debt trap" leaving India with no alternative but to go in for full-scale reforms. Thus, in 1991, under the stewardship of Mr. Manmohan Singh, the then finance minister and, at the time of writing, the prime minister of India, a massive economic reform process was initiated. Licensing was abolished, the Monopolies and Restrictive Trade Practices Commission was disbanded, imports and exports were almost freed of restrictions and most importantly, foreign exchange rates rationalized and important fiscal house cleaning put in place. The rest, as they say, is history. India was now set on the path to becoming an economic super power with the target of becoming the world's fourth largest economy by 2020.

Chapter Two

The Rise of India: India and the West—Institutional Contrasts

India is now emerging as a major player in the world economy that is increasingly dominated by the ascendance of knowledge-based activities. It is the second fastest growing economy in the world, with an expected GDP growth of 8 percent during 2005–2006. The rapid growth of the information technology sector alongwith globalization, and deregulation, created new opportunities as well as new challenges for firms in an environment that is ever changing at an accelerating rate.

In the changed scenario, India is becoming an active participant in the global economy, while at the same time drawing increasing interest among foreign investors as well as national governments in Europe, North America, and Asia. A number of factors indicate the growing integration of India in the world economy and is reflected by a number of different indicators. To begin with, there has been a significant increase in the flow of foreign direct investment to India. It is estimated that foreign direct investment increased by 66 percent in 2001.[1] More broadly during the decade 1990–1991 to 2001–2002 foreign direct investment inflows increased from US$103 million in 1990–1991 to US$5.9 billion in 2001–2002.[2] During the period 1991–2002 India is estimated to have received a total amount of US$24 billion in foreign direct investment. This figure, of course, does not include that of Foreign institutional investment that is considerably larger.

There are other indications that an economic transformation may well be underway in India. A study by Goldman Sachs suggests that India is expected to be the world's third largest economy in 2035, after United States and Japan.[3] A ranking by Forbes of the world's best corporations included nine Indian companies such as Indian Oil, HLL, Infosys, Reliance, and WIPRO.[4] By 1999, India had become the third largest car market in Asia.[5]

The intense competition in the Indian market due to the entrance of foreign competitors, has led domestic firms to upgrade the quality of their products, and these firms often give the multinationals a run for their money. India has become a haven for foreign companies seeking to outsource their business operations. General Electric is reported to have garnered cost savings of US$350 million a year by outsourcing to India.[6] The decision by IBM to buy Daksh (see chapter three), India's third largest back office services firm, in an acquisition that is valued between

US$150–200 million is a good example of India's increasing attractiveness as an investment destination.[7] Overall, it is estimated that there are several hundred call centers in India with a turnover of US$2 billion and employing about 150,000 people in India for companies such as Citibank, Deutsche Bank, HSBC, Dell Computer, SAS, and Compaq.[8]

India's resurgence as a major economic player is not without historical precedence. It is estimated that in the early nineteenth century, India accounted for about 16 percent of the world's GDP.[9] As noted in chapter one of this book, as early as the second century BC, India was a major trading nation and it was perhaps the reputation earned as a commercially oriented country that led Alexander the Great to invade India in 327 BC,[10] Indians exported products to the Roman Empire, and after its fall had developed ties with their successors both in that part of the world as well as South Asia. The active involvement of the Indians in trading suggests a strong entrepreneurial spirit among Indians, a spirit that was curtailed (although not eliminated) initially by overseas invasions, as well as the advent of colonial rule, and post independence, by a regulatory regime that created impediments to innovative ideas.

That this entrepreneurial spirit still exists can be seen not simply by the rapid growth of the information technology industry in India (see chapter three), but also by the fact that the Indians who have migrated overseas, have utilized their entrepreneurial spirit for considerable gain for themselves as well as the larger community. It has been suggested, for example, that a third of the engineers in the Silicon Valley are of Indian origin while 7 percent of the high tech firms are led by Indian CEOs.[11] Similarly about one third of Microsoft employees, a quarter of IBM, and a sixth of the scientists of Intel are said to be of Indian origin. There are other examples as well. Consider the case of the Jain community, who have carved out a dominant position in the lucrative international diamond trade. It is estimated that they control about 50 percent of the market for gem quality diamonds.[12] The Tatas and the Birlas, two of the leading business groups in India developed under British occupation and fortified their position in the post-1947 regulatory regime. The global Indian diaspora is estimated to be about 25 million people and their importance seems to be on the rise.

What are the implications of the potential emergence of India as an economic superpower for foreign investors seeking to do business in this country? This is the central theme that we attempt to address here. Although the resurgence of India as an economic power is a view that is now widely held by scholars and business people, India is still a country in the process of economic transition. It is our belief that while the Indian market does offer huge opportunities, the opportunities have to be utilized in the right way.

A prerequisite for such an endeavor and a deep understanding of the Indian business environment. This calls for a keen knowledge of the Indian political, cultural, and economic realities that govern economic transactions in this country. Although each business opportunity is unique, tailoring that opportunity for creating a win–win solution for all, requires a sophisticated understanding of environmental realities.

We begin this chapter by providing a broad overview of the differences that exist in the institutional environment between India and the North American and European environments and the implications that they may have for the practice of business in these countries. A more detailed analysis of the political and the cultural environments follows in the subsequent chapters of this book. The institutional environment comprises the economic dimension, the political dimension, and the sociocultural dimension. These dimensions are not entirely independent of each other but for expositional purposes we will be dealing with them as separate entities. We also recognize that not all European countries are the same, and are equally cognizant of the fact that the European business environment is different from the North American one. Therefore, the institutional gap is likely to be far greater between India and the Western world than is the case between Western European countries and North America.

The Institutional Contrast between India and the Western World

"The nineteenth century belonged to Europe, the twentieth went to America, and many believe that the twenty-first century is likely to be Asia's."[13] This comment highlights the great optimism that is felt by some experts about developments taking place in this region. Some experts are even suggesting that within Asia, it is India that may have the edge over China, given the strong tradition of entrepreneurship in the country.[14] Indeed, the Global Entrepreneurship Monitor of the London Business School has rated India second in entrepreneurship globally.[15] It is evident that there is considerable potential in this country, and indeed, one of the implications suggests that the institutional gap between India and the West may diminish over time, and that there is a possibility of a two-way knowledge flow, as opposed to a one-way flow, that traditionally existed between the West and India.

(a) Political Dimension

"India is a modern state, but an ancient civilization," writes Stephen Cohen in his 2001 book *Emerging Power: India*.[16] As a modern state, India came into existence in 1947 when it attained independence from the British. As an ancient civilization, contemporary India had its origins in the Indus Valley civilization. This civilization was at its peak around the third millennium BC. This was an extraordinarily sophisticated civilization in which commerce played an important role. The geographical extent of this civilization was huge, spreading as it did from the eastern border of Iran till eastern India. The decline of the Indus Valley civilization was followed by the rise of the Indo-Aryan civilization, which provided the spiritual foundation of India as a civilized entity. It was during this period that some of the most sacred Indian texts (e.g., Vedas) were written.

A unique feature of the early Indian political order was its chronic instability. The idea of a state as an agency that could exert power to change society was notably lacking in this period.[17] The stability of a society rested less on the political order than on the social order that was shaped by the cultural ideology of *Brahmanism*. The *Brahmins* exchanged political power for social power by creating a set of cultural rules that everyone in the society had to follow. A notable example of this is the caste system, which drew a distinction among different segments of the society, and provided a hierarchical ordering of the society. The Hindu ruler was constrained by caste obligations and his duty was to preserve the integrity of the Hindu social system.[18]

It is the disjunction between political power and social power that was the hallmark of the earlier Indian civilization. The greater emphasis laid by Brahmanism on social conduct rather than on issues of governance was also to have a number of significant implications. This was in contrast to the developments in Europe where the onset of reformation and the birth of renaissance during the period 1450–1670 created a situation where the political rulers started to extend their control over territories, carving out their own spheres of influence. The impetus for this was both economic as well as political.[19] This was the immediate precursor for the emergence of the nation-state in Europe in the mid-nineteenth century.

British colonialism undoubtedly left a deep imprint on the Indian society and commentators still remain sharply divided as to its impact on Indian development. Whatever be the merits or the demerits of the different arguments in this domain, it was the British who introduced India to the notion of a state as a sovereign entity with definable territorial boundaries.[20] However, a vast cultural gap between the British and the Indians, with the British relying on the local Indian elite to maintain control remained. Although pragmatically expedient, this policy continued to maintain the cultural gap between the parties, and generated its own counterreaction in the form of a nationalist reaction. This manifested itself in the formation of the Indian National Congress, a political party that was founded in 1885, and was the precursor of the post-independence Congress party.

The impact of colonialism on the Indian mind-set should not be underestimated. It has shaped India's attitude toward foreign investment, played a role in stressing the importance of self-reliance and autonomy in the country's developmental strategy, and more broadly, it has traditionally made the country more cautious when engaging with the outside world. After the liberalization of 1991, this mind-set has begun to change, and there is less now less suspicion of foreign capital than at any other time in India's history, but remnants of this fear probably still exist, and it may take a little more time before the ghosts are finally laid to rest. This is only understandable given that nationalist feelings are not entirely absent even in the industrialized world. Consider the case of Norway where foreign investors such as Danske Bank, of Denmark, Fortum of Finland, Elf Aquitane of France, and Telia of Sweden have been thwarted by nationalistic pressures in acquiring local companies.

With India gaining independence in 1947, Jawaharlal Nehru became India's first prime minister. A charismatic politician who was deeply involved in India's struggle for independence, Nehru embarked on a process of rapid modernization of the country. Although the economic policies pursued by his government, proved to be counterproductive in the end, the early years of his government were crucial in both extending and enhancing state capability as well as firmly embedding the principles of democracy in India. Indeed, one of the most remarkable things about India is that democracy has taken firm root, even though some of the preconditions for the establishment of a democratic state in Western Europe and the United States such as the preexistence of a nation-state, high literacy rate, a vibrant middle class, high levels of industrialization were absent in 1950.[21] Perhaps it is also worth mentioning that while in the West democracy arose as a result of a contest between aristocrats and commoners, in India democracy was the by-product of the Indian fight against colonialism. A further point of contrast is, while in the West the growth of democracy limited state authority, in India, it led to an increase in the power of the state.

India is now the world's largest democracy with a voter turn out that is often higher than in many industrialized countries. The most recently concluded election in the summer of 2004, in which the voters decided to vote against the Bharatiya Janata Party (BJP) led coalition, against all expectations, is clearly indicative of a thriving democratic culture.

During the first 50 years of independence, India was primarily governed by the Congress Party, with a brief interlude, during which, a coalition the comprising of the Janata Party, the BJP, and other opposition parties, was in power in the late 1970s. If there was opposition, it existed within the party, rather than from other competing parties. All of this began to change in the late 1980s with the rise of BJP, a party that focused its appeal on reviving Hindu nationalism or "Hindutva." This ideology had many dimensions to it. One was rediscovering and/or recreating, the greatness of India, which had been crushed during the era of colonialism. The other point was that the state should seek to favor the interests of the Hindus as they constitute the majority of the population.

The nuclear tests conducted by the BJP in 1998 were a dramatic illustration of recreating India's past glory and making its mark as a major power. The BJP was quick to capitalize on the weaknesses of the previous governments, and in conjunction with a moribund economy, extended its electoral base from the trading community to the middle and the upper middle class. In 1996 the BJP emerged as the single largest party although it was not able to retain power for any significant period of time.

Although BJP has undoubtedly, of late, been a major player in the Indian politics, its ability to fully realize its nationalistic aspirations are constrained by its necessity to rely on coalition partners who do not necessarily subscribe to its "Hindutva" plank. The BJP's first extended run of power came in 1999, when it formed a coalition government. When it called for elections six months before its term in 2004, it was expected it would return to power in conjunction with its coalition partners. This did not happen and it has surprised both the ordinary public as well as political commentators.

The emergence of coalition politics in recent years is another theme that is gaining prominence in the Indian political context. The new Congress-led government is also a coalition government. Some have voiced concern that because the government is dependent on communist support it may not be able to vigorously pursue reforms to the extent desired, as the communists are not keen on liberalization. The current prime minister of India, Dr. Manmohan Singh dismisses these concerns and suggests that his government will have no difficulty in implementing the reform measures.[22] Although the ultimate proof lies in the actions taken by the government it needs to be noted that even the communists have been promoting reform and liberalization in the state of West Bengal where they are in power.

In recent years there has been an increase in the number of regional political parties, and they are now likely, in the foreseeable future, to decisively shape the pattern of Indian political development. The increase in the number of regional parties, and in particular, the growing mobilization of the lower castes in the electoral process, has imparted a new dynamic to Indian political development. The new groups are trying to maximize the benefits more for their own particular group. At the same time they are opposed to the narrow nationalistic vision inspired by BJP, which is primarily an upper caste based, predominantly Hindu party.

The emergence of coalition politics does impart a certain degree of unpredictability to the political dynamics, but this unpredictability is not unique to India. Many European countries such as Denmark, Italy, or Germany have had coalitions. The fact that coalition governments may not necessarily be detrimental to sustaining growth is also illustrated by the fact that in the 1990s the Indian GDP grew at an annual rate of 6.3 percent, but this was also the period characterized by political instability.

As stated earlier, a core constituency in support of economic reform has now emerged in India with the resulting implication that while the pace of economic reform may not consistently accelerate, it is at the same time, unlikely to be reversed altogether.

(b) Economic Dimension

Without question, there is still a vast gap between the GNP per capita in India and that in Europe and North America. World Bank 2002 statistics suggest that GNP/capita in India is US$480, US$35,060 in United States, US$26,220 in France, US$26,180 in Germany, and US$25,870 in UK.[23] Nearly a third of the country's population is below the poverty line. In the IMD' s annual ranking of world competitiveness in 2004, India was ranked 34 whereas in 2003 the country had been ranked 50. Although this represents a considerable improvement over previous years, the study also suggests that Indian growth and development is constrained by the poor quality of infrastructure and ineffective management of public finances.

There are numerous infrastructure bottlenecks in power, transportation, ports, and telecommunications sectors. An infrastructure survey by the World Economic Forum in 1999, ranked India 55 out of 59 in terms of the adequacy of the infrastructure. Inadequate infrastructure has without question hampered the growth of the Indian economy, with some estimates suggesting the cost is about 3 percent of the annual GDP.[24] One gets additional perspective on the nature of the problem by looking at more micro level data. For example, it is pointed out that the cost of industrial power in India is 8 cents per Kwh, which compares unfavorably with other countries where the cost is estimated to be only between 4–6 cents per Kwh.[25] It has also been pointed out that given the unreliability of the power supply more than 70 percent of the Indian firms possess their own generating sets.

The Indians were cognizant of the problem and in 1991 opened the doors to foreign investors in power generation, but the results have been disappointing. The Indian government expected to add new generating capacity of 10,000 MW during the period 1991–2000 but in actual fact the net increase was only 2000 MW.[26] A number of foreign firms decided to pull out of potential projects that they were seeking to develop. Although there are a number of reasons for their exit, the common problem centered was the lack of certainty of payment by the State Electricity

Boards, who were to buy the power generated by these projects. It is widely acknowledged that the State Electricity Boards are in poor financial health either due to excessive subsidization of electricity and/or due to theft. The first example of privatization of distribution of electricity took place in Delhi in 2002. In Delhi theft of power accounted for a staggering 50 percent of transmission and distribution losses.

The inland transportation costs are also said to be high thus adversely affecting the competitiveness of Indian industry. For example, the freight costs from Gujarat to Chennai are said to be around US$40 per MT whereas the comparable costs from China to Chennai are around US$20 per MT. The Indian ports are also not noted for their efficiency. It is estimated that in 1999 in India it took about 4.7 days to turnaround a ship whereas in Singapore it was 6–8 hours.[27] This adversely affects the competitiveness of Indian exports and has a cascading effect on inefficiency throughout the system. Although a new policy designed to encourage private investment in ports has been announced, the conditions surrounding the investment have not made such an investment a very attractive one for the foreign investor, at least not yet.

The reforms in the telecommunications sector have progressed more smoothly vis-à-vis the power sector. Although much has been accomplished compared with the situation in the early 1990s the pace of movement needs further acceleration. It is estimated, for example that in 1997 India had 18.6 telephone lines per 1,000 people compared with 444 in Korea, 107 in Brazil, and 96 in Mexico. Ten years ago the information technology structure in India was on par with China. However, in 2000, the "teledensity" in China was 112 telephone main lines per 1,000, whereas in India the figure was 32. Likewise China had 15.9 personal computers per 1,000 Chinese whereas India had 4.5 per 1,000.[28] However, it may be noted that at the time of writing, the mobile phone user base in India was already nearing the 45 million mark, crossing the number of fixed line subscribers, usually seen, particularly from the experience of China, as a critical inflexion point in the growth and modernization of a country.

Although there is clearly much that remains to be done, India has made considerable progress in recent years and there is an underlying dynamism that is now increasingly being exhibited by the Indian economy. It would also be fair to say that India is now at a stage where the logic of the economic reforms has gained widespread consensus within the country. This means, there is no going backward, the only choice is to move forward.

To understand the full magnitude of the transformation that has occurred and is happening in India, one must examine the current pattern of Indian industrial growth and development in the context of the period after independence in 1947. In 1950, the Indian per capita income was estimated to be around US$95.[29] The country was primarily agricultural with over 70 percent of the population being engaged in agriculture and with just less than 50 percent of the GDP from agriculture.[30] Scholars remain divided as to the impact of the colonial rule on the Indian economy. While the British created the institutional foundations for a functioning market economy, India still remained largely non-industrialized at the onset of independence (see chapter one).

As seen in chapter one, the then prime minister, Jawaharlal Nehru decided to embark on a policy of import substitution led industrialization. This policy had acquired ideological respectability at that time in history and many countries sought to follow this model. The underlying rationale to pursue this policy in the Indian case was a deep sense of pessimism about increasing the country's exports, a desire to industrialize rapidly, and a romantic attachment to the fundamental tenets of Fabian Socialism, so deeply ingrained into some of the new India's ruling class under the influence of, amongst others, The London School of Economics.

In practical terms this policy meant that some industrial sectors were to be the sole monopoly of the state, others could be jointly developed between state and the industry, while the other sectors were reserved for the private sector, and all this in a regime of licenses and exchange controls. In practice, this "well-intentioned" policy, led to a cumbersome system of controls in which the bureaucrats and the politicians reigned supreme. Many commentators described this period as "license raj," during which business firms were subject to extreme forms of micro management by the bureaucracy. Naturally many of them, sought to evade these controls, and in doing so, furthered the practice of corruption (see chapter five, "Understanding India").

Internal constraints on entrepreneurial activity were also reflected in India's declining share of world trade. In the period 1947–1990, India's share of world trade declined from 2.4 percent in 1947 to 0.4 percent in 1990.[31] What is interesting is that in 1948 India's share of world merchandising exports was 2.2 percent, a figure that exceeded China's 0.9 percent, and Japan's 0.4 percent.[32] The consequences of this introspection were profound. During the period 1950–1980, India's GDP growth rate was around 3.75 percent per year, a rate that often came to be pejoratively called the "Hindu rate of growth."

By the late 1970s or the early 1980s it had become reasonably clear that the existing growth strategy was producing suboptimal outcomes. Analysts classified India as a "low income, slow growing economy."[33] When Rajiv Gandhi came to power in the early 1980s, the first attempts to liberalize the economy were made but the reform agenda was never implemented wholeheartedly for a variety of reasons including the debilitating effects of a weapons purchase scandal involving Bofors of Sweden.

It took the balance of payments crisis in 1991 to refocus the government's attention on removing the shackles on the Indian economy. While the economic imperatives for reforming the economy were clear, it was the collapse of the Soviet Union, and the emergence of China as a major actor on the world stage, that impelled the Indian government to initiate bold and decisive action. The reform process of 1991, was spearheaded by Dr. Manmohan Singh, the then Finance Minister and the current Prime Minister. He initiated a series of first generation reforms, that is, reforms covering industrial policy, trade and exchange rate policy, and financial markets. The government for all practical purposes abolished industrial licensing, allowed automatic approval for foreign investors to gain 51 percent equity in their ventures in India, and lowered tariffs and quantitative restrictions on imports. Prior to the liberalization the average tariff rate in India was 125 percent.[34]

The impact of the first generation reforms has been, without question, positive. Analysts estimate that the poverty levels in both the rural and the urban areas have declined by a third.[35] It has also been pointed out that in absolute terms, the number of poor people has declined by 60 million with the poverty rate declining from 55 percent in 1973/1974 to 26 percent in 1999.[36] This has also been accompanied by an increase in the literacy rate, which rose from 52 percent in 1991 to 65 percent in 2001.[37]

This is in large part a consequence of the higher growth rates experienced by the economy in the post-reform period. The reforms have also helped to alter the sectoral shares of agriculture, industry, and manufacturing, in the GDP. The share of agriculture as a percentage of GDP has declined from 40 percent in the 1971–1980 period, to 28.3 percent in the 1991–2000 period. At the same time the share of the services sector in the GDP has increased from 34.4 percent in 1971–1980 to 44.4 percent in 1991–2000.[38] Furthermore, the opening up of the Indian economy has also helped to create new opportunities for the Indian exporters.

Finally, the growing opening up and integration of India in the world economy has also strengthened the impression among foreign investors that India may be a good place to do business. This intangible benefit is of vital importance because investor sentiments are crucial in attracting foreign direct investment. In India's case this is doubly important as prior to 1991, the Indian trade and investment regime was very restrictive.

Although much has been accomplished, there is clearly more to be done. Policy makers need to focus their attention on second generation reforms like reforming labor laws, which would make it easier to lay off workers. However the focus on privatizing inefficient public sector enterprises that are a drain on the national treasury remains a controversial issue, and the newly elected coalition government may have to fight some battles in moving this process along. They have already disbanded the Ministry of Privatization, but that by itself may not necessarily be a negative omen.

Mr. P.C. Chidambaram's appointment as the Minister of Finance is an encouraging sign as he is considered to be an ardent supporter of reform. There is an urgent need to deal with the overall government deficit (central and state combined), which is estimated at about 10 percent of GDP. This deficit is a consequence of excessive subsidies given by the central and the state governments, as well as a low tax yield, stemming from the fact that only few people pay taxes. The free distribution of power to farmers, as well as transmission and distribution losses due to theft, are additional contributing factors. As we have pointed out earlier, an emphasis on the improvement of infrastructure is an absolute must if higher rates of growth are to be sustained. An improvement in government finances will provide an opportunity for the government to undertake substantial investments in this area.

In our view, there is now an increasing recognition in European countries as well as in the United States that India is fundamentally committed to the process of economic reform, although there is a clear understanding that in a democratic framework, the reform process may not necessarily proceed smoothly. But this greater interest in India that is now being demonstrated by the United States and the European countries is likely to further strengthen the Indian enthusiasm for engaging with the outside world. The visit of the then U.S. President Bill Clinton to India in 2000 generated a very positive response. This openness means that the reform process is unlikely to alter its fundamental direction, even though its pace may accelerate or decrease, depending on circumstances.

What are the implications of this economic contrast for the European and the North American investors who seek to do business with India? The first point to be noted is that there is a new spirit of openness in India with the Indian populace recognizing that integration with the world economy can produce significant benefits. This spirit of openness has been reinforced by the dramatic growth of the information technology industry in India (see chapter three). This industry has become one of India's major exports and also a major advertiser of India's strengths. Consider the fact that India's software exports increased from US$128 million in 1990–1991 to US$8.3 billion in 2001.[39] The industry has been experiencing 50 percent annual growth since 1991 and constitutes about 8 percent of total Indian exports. Most Western companies now consider India as their first option in outsourcing software development.[40] This is particularly true of American companies.

In the year 1997–1998 total software exports from India totaled US$1.8 billion, and of this figure 58 percent went to the United States, 21 percent to Europe, and 8 percent to South East Asia. The industry has gradually moved up the value chain with Indian companies now engaged in high value-added work. A study by McKinsey and Company suggests that the output of the Indian software and services industry is expected to increase to US$87 billion by 2008, of which US$50 billion may be exported. NASSCOM, the industry association, predicts a turnover of over US$20 billion for the current fiscal year with US$16 billion to be exported.

In addition to the success of the Indian software firms in the global market, foreign firms are also taking advantage of the local talent that is available here. Intel has reportedly invested about US$25 million in software development in Bangalore, India. This investment appears to be paying off handsomely. In 2003, the Indian subsidiary of the U.S.-based company Intel filed 63 patents. Intel is not alone in reaping the benefits of operating in India. More than 100 multinational firms have established research and development centers in India including companies like General Electric, Bell Labs, Du Pont, Caterpillar, Microsoft and IBM. One of the largest R&D centers has been established by GE in Bangalore. This is a US$100 million center that was set up in 2000 and has already applied for 17 patents. Texas Instruments, which was one of the first companies to set up operations in Bangalore has realized 225 patents while Cisco systems has 120.

There are many other companies that have attained comparable level of success. The development of this industry has undoubtedly been greatly aided by the presence of a large and skilled manpower that is fluent in English. India annually produces about 75,000–80,000 software professionals, and perhaps more interestingly, there are about 140,000 professionals who work in Bangalore, a number that is 20,000 more than in Silicon Valley. Analysts predict that foreign firms are likely to use India as a base for R&D even in industries such as biotechnology and pharmaceuticals.

The demographic profile of the Indian population is also becoming younger and this has implications for the marketing strategy of firms as well as for a country's rate of growth and development. Estimates suggest that more than 500 million Indians are below the age of 21 and the median age of the Indian population is 24.[41] This is in sharp contrast to the median age of 36 in the United States and 30 in China.

The implications of this demographic transition are many. A more youthful population that has grown up in the Internet age and in era of globalization may have higher levels of aspiration, and may also seek to realize their higher aspiration levels in different ways. It is now widely believed that well over 600 shopping malls in the American style, may now be created in India. Malls have already been established in Gurgaon, a town on the outskirts of Delhi. These malls contain outlets of the likes of international brands such as Nike, Benetton, and Pizza Hut, among others.

The growing number of young consumers is also forcing multinational firms to tailor their marketing strategy to a new market segment. Motorola has developed cheap phones primarily for the younger consumer market segment. Citibank has observed that the average age of a mortgage holder has declined in India from 41 to 28. The company is developing new programs to attract an increasingly younger crowd. The youth are part of an emerging middle class in India. Estimates of the middle class vary but a study by the U.S. Department of Commerce suggests that India has 20 million people with annual incomes in excess of US$13,000, 80 million people with annual incomes in excess of US$3,500, and 100 million people with incomes in excess of US$2,800.[42]

A shift in the age distribution of the population also has implications for the rate of growth that a country can hope to realize and sustain. Scholars note that when the percentage of people who are working in a given country increases, the saving rate increases correspondingly. Increased savings, in turn, will enhance the growth rate.

The heightened interdependence between India and European and North America also implies that there are many more foreign investors active in India and likewise there are Indian companies that are increasing the scale and scope of their international operations. Foreign companies are operating in India in a wide range of industries such as the automotive, consumer electronics, food processing, telecommunications, financial services, infrastructure, engineering, information technology, biotechnology, entertainment, retail, and healthcare sectors. Ford has made an investment of more than US$350 million in India. The company currently exports cars from India. At the other end of the spectrum, Marks & Spencer, a well-known U.K.-based retail chain has set up franchisee outlets in Delhi and Mumbai.

In the era of control it would have been unthinkable for Indian companies to operate overseas. As Indian firms venture overseas, they are likely to absorb the capitalist ethos to a heightened degree, and may seek to reshape their corporate culture to conform to the demands of the international environment. This can only but strengthen the Indian integration in the global capitalistic environment. There are several indications to suggest that this process is already underway. India has already become the eighth largest investor in the United Kingdom. At the same time Indian companies are reported to have acquired about 120 foreign firms during the period 2001–2003 with a combined value of US$1.6 billion.[43] Indian pharmaceutical companies, for example, have sought to acquire overseas firms. Dr. Reddy's laboratories acquired Trigenesis, a U.S.-based company, for US$11 million to enter the speciality drugs market. Ranbaxy acquired the French generic drugs maker, RPG Aventis for about US$70 million. Hindalco has acquired an Australian company, Straits (Nifty) Pty., for a value of AD$79.80 million. Seven Indian companies are reportedly listed in the New York Stock Exchange while three are listed on NASDAQ.

India is a country comprising 29 states and 6 union territories. There is considerable interstate variation in economic performance. In 1998/1999 the Gross State Domestic Product per capita was highest in the state of Maharashtra (US$657) and lowest in the state of Orissa (US$238).[44] Since the start of reforms, highest growth has been recorded in the states of Karnataka, Maharashtra, Tamil Nadu, and Gujarat, and lowest in the states of Uttar Pradesh and Bihar. Andhra Pradesh, Karnataka, Maharashtra, Tamil Nadu, and Gujarat have also been the most pro-reform states, whereas Bihar and Uttar Pradesh, with very large populations, can at best be described as reluctant reformers. The implications of this state of affairs are fairly clear.

The five pro-reform states have accounted for two-thirds of private investment inflows, even as these states constitute only a third of the country's population. To put it in more concrete terms, Tamil Nadu has become a major hub for companies in the automotive sectors with firms such as Mitsubishi, Ford, and Hyundai having a presence in the state. Karnataka and Andhra Pradesh have staked out their claim in the information technology sector by attracting companies such as Microsoft and Sun Microsystems while Maharashtra has been a home to Mercedes Benz and Siemens amongst others.

Differences in the regional performance of states has a number of different implications. First, it clearly suggests that some states are much more attractive destinations for foreign investors than others. The differential economic performance of the states may be attributable to the differences in the quality of governance and that of the infrastructure, as well as differences in their motivation and ability to create an investment climate that is attractive to foreign investors. The area around Delhi, the southern states in India and the western region of the country are by far much more attractive destinations for foreign investors than states such as Uttar Pradesh, Bihar, or Orissa.

As foreign investment gets localized in the more promising states, the differences between the high growth and the low growth states are likely to widen. Regional inequality is likely to increase and this may create some interstate tensions as the less well-performing states demand greater allocation of resources from the center. Although these tensions may cause some hiccups they are highly unlikely to fundamentally threaten the integrity of India as a nation-state.

We are also seeing the emergence of regional centers of excellence within India. Thus the southern states, and in particular, the city of Bangalore in Karnataka, has become the hub of the Indian information technology and biotechnology industries. These centers, if we can call them as such, are often much more integrated with the global economy and the operating routines within these segments conform to global norms. Finally, the clustering of foreign investment within certain regions may also have the additional potential of creating synergies among the foreign investors.

(c) Cultural Dimension

Many scholars have often debated as to whether India belongs to the East or to the West, but a consensus seems to be emerging that the Indians are closer to Europeans/Americans than they are to the Asians. A renowned German scholar of India, Max Mueller, once noted "India for the future belongs to Europe, it has its place in the Indo European world, it has its place in our own history, and in what is the very life of history, the history of the human mind."[45] A good example of this observation is the close linkage that exists between *Sanskrit*, the language of the Aryans of India, and *Greek*, *Latin*, and *Anglo-Saxon*. Scholars have shown that all of these languages have a high degree of commonality about them with this commonality being indicative of a shared Aryan culture. The Aryans who are supposed to have migrated to India around 1500 BC spoke Sanskrit and this provides the foundation for languages currently spoken in India.

Even if we move from the realm of shared knowledge to the realm of action there are similarities. The Indian, for example, is aggressive, argumentative, emotional, and analytical. These are traits that set the Indian far apart from the model of the "Confucian gentleman" that is so revered in Asia. A Japanese anthropologist, Chie Nakane, described the Indians as being very logical and noted that their thinking was much more similar to the Westerners than it was to the East Asians.[46] An ABB manager who has done business in India for more than 20 years once indicated to one of the author/s that it was extremely difficult to win an argument with the Indians.

Similarities aside, there are without question, some differences between the Indian and the European/American cultural realities. Cultural differences are rooted in ideas/practices that originated in ancient times, but it needs to be noted that all societies evolve and adapt continuously. Culture is, therefore, both stable as well as malleable, and for this reason its potential impact cannot be overlooked. At this point we would like to draw attention to some aspects of the Indian culture that have exerted a significant impact on practices from ancient times till the present. The aspects that we will focus on are the caste system and the family.

(i) Caste System. No aspect of the Indian social system has probably attracted greater attention than the caste system. Although both Indian and foreign observers have been, and continue, to be critical of it, it is still very much a part of contemporary life in modern India. The caste system represents a hierarchical ordering of the society and stands in opposition to the norm of social equality, so characteristic of Western societies in general and of Scandinavia in particular. Although hierarchy is a universal feature of all societies, the hierarchical ordering implied by the caste system had extreme rigidity, and it was this rigidity, that has most fundamentally attracted the opprobrium of many commentators past and present.

The term *caste* is derived from the Portuguese word "*casta*," which refers to family strain, breed, or race and was first employed by Portuguese traders in their interactions with the Indians in the sixteenth century. The Sanskrit word for *caste* is "*jati*." The *jati* was broken down into four varnas, which in a hierarchical order were *Brahmins* (priests), *Ksatriyas* (warriors), *Vaishyas* (merchants), and *Shudras* (workers). Each group in this hierarchical order had an important role to play in promoting the well-being of the society. The *Brahmins* at the apex of this order were the intellectual guardians of the society; the *Ksatriyas* defended the society from external or internal threats; *Vaishyas* provided the commercial lubricant for the society, while *Shudras* performed the menial tasks in the society.

Each *caste* has its own *dharma* or a set of behavioral norms defining what is acceptable and unacceptable behavior. The *Brahmins* are expected to be vegetarians, teetotalers, and spiritual; the *Ksatriyas* must be strong and brave and it is acceptable for them to drink alcohol and be nonvegetarian; *Vaishyas* are your conventional businessman; while the *Shudras* were considered to be seen as behaving in a less than desirable manner.

The caste system in India originated more than 3,000 years ago when the Indo-Aryans migrated to India. Deepak Lal has made the interesting argument that the caste system developed in India as a response to problems of political stability that was endemic in the early Aryan civilization.[47] There was an urgent need to ensure a stable supply of labor for the labor-intensive agriculture that was practiced by the Aryans in the Indo-Gangetic plain. Given the lack of an effective centralized state, which could maintain control over labor through coercive means, only a decentralized control mechanism could ensure this option. Within the rubrics of the caste system, it was not possible for any individual or group to flee, because they would lack the complementary skills necessary to function autonomously.

Although the origins of the caste system may have been benign, and while the caste system may not have been very rigid in the early Vedic period, it is a system which continues to exist, notwithstanding governmental laws and regulations which explicitly forbid caste discrimination. It is believed that there are around 2,000–3,000 subcastes today as a consequence of the subdivision of the original fourcastes.

It is also worth noting that there is some, although not a perfect correlation between status and income, implying people of higher status are overall more prosperous. It is interesting to note that the Indian information technology industry, in which India excels, has been primarily dominated by *Brahmins*. One commentator made the observation that "There have never in Indian history been so many entrepreneurial *Brahmins* as seen in the software industry now."[48] This is a remarkable development, but in some ways not surprising because the *Brahmanical* emphasis on knowledge goes well with the development of the information technology industry, in that the latter is also knowledge intensive. The political elite has also, for the most part been dominated by people, who belong to the upper castes and the unstated goal of the now-ousted BJP was to strengthen the position of the upper caste groups.

What is the role of caste in modern India, and especially in the business sphere? Undoubtedly, caste has less relevance in the urban domain than it has in the rural domain. In the urban domain, business transactions are anonymous and professional identities may be more salient. However, it is worth noting that while caste barriers may not negatively shape interaction, caste similarity may certainly induce the actors to be more motivated to cooperate with each other. In this context caste is not intrinsically important, but it is important only because it helps to draw a distinction as to whether a person is a member of an in-group or a member of the out-group. Most often members of in-group are trusted more than those of the out-groups making it easier to enter into transactions with the former than the latter.

(ii) Family. The family represents the fundamental building block of the Indian social system. It has been the "*joint family*," that is, a family in which two, three, or four generations all live together, that has been the normative ideal in India. The Indian system, by and large, is a patriarchal one, which brings together many generations under one common roof. Although the *joint family* may be undergoing some changes, and especially so in the urban areas, it would be fair to say that the family is revered by most Indians, even today. The basis for this strong identification lies in the strong mother–son relationship as well as a deeply internalized set of obligations that are inculcated in early childhood. Parents are willing to make sacrifices for their children and vice versa, a norm far different from that of contemporary Western industrialized societies. The family structure is hierarchical with key decisions being made by the head of the family. Such hierarchy is usually accepted by the younger members of the family, as it is accompanied by benevolent paternalism.

The strong sense of interdependence that exists among the members of a family does not imply that there are no conflicts. Often, there is an attempt to paper over or avoid these conflicts, but should either of these prove unsuccessful, conflicts can certainly escalate in an unrestrained manner. Most importantly, it is hard to overestimate the impact that family has on social life and on business practices in India. In other words, without a sufficient grasp of the role played by the family in an Indian's life and world, it is often difficult to explain the Indian employee's commitment to the organization, or to the strategic decisions made by Indian organizations.

For an Indian, the primary loyalty and commitment lies with the family rather than to the work or organization. Scholars have maintained that it has been the narrow loyalty to the family or to the caste grouping that has historically prevented the development of a broader loyalty toward the nation. This does not imply that Indians cannot transfer their loyalty to the larger organization; only that such a transference requires a communal corporate culture and a nurturing leadership style.[49]

The strategic significance of family in a business context can best be gauged by recognizing that much of Indian business is still family owned. It has been estimated that 71 percent of India's market capitalization can be attributed to the Indian family business. The Indian family businesses are said to employ 75 percent of Indian citizens.[50] In the post-independence period the Indian business firm grew in a protected and a closed environment. The key to success was good relationships with the bureaucrats and the politicians. Analysts have noted that Indian family business has often suffered from a lack of clear focus, short-term thinking, weak marketing skills, and often an inability to separate the interest of the family from that of business.[51] It has also been pointed out that very few (3 percent) of Indian family businesses are able to survive in their present form beyond the third generation. One of India's largest family owned businesses, the Reliance Group, witnessed a major power play between two brothers who inherited the business after the demise of their father.

Post-1991, the Indian family business firm is facing new challenges as a number of multinationals have entered the Indian markets and tariffs/quantitative restrictions have been eased, thus permitting foreign firms to export directly to India, after a long time. How are the Indian family businesses doing in the changed scenario? By all accounts, it has not been an easy ride for them and there is often still a reluctance to thoroughly professionalize management by bringing in "non family" members in positions of control.

A recent study on family businesses conducted by Grant Thornton found that 46 percent of Indian business people felt that their successor should come from their family whereas only 24 pecent of Europeans and 22 percent of North Americans subscribed to this view.[52] Indeed, even in the Indian pharmaceutical company as dynamic as Ranbaxy, it appears there are pressures to re-exert managerial control from within the company. The sudden departure of their professional CEO raised concerns within the larger financial community in India.

There are Indian family business firms that have made a mark in the Indian business environment. The three largest owned family businesses in India are Reliance Industries with an estimated value of US$9.63 billion; the Tata Group with an estimated value of US$7.9 billion; and the Aditya Birla Group Industries that has an estimated value of US$6 billion. These are companies that have been bold and innovative in coping with the changing environment, although as we have noted above, the Reliance Group is now confronted by sibling disputes.

We began this section by making the argument that culturally speaking India is closer to Europe and North America than it is to Confucian Asia. Although in subsequent paragraphs we have identified some key differences between the Indians and the European/Americans, these differences have to be viewed within the context of an overriding similarity. The Indians and the European/Americans have an analytical bent of mind and an abiding desire to know more about the world, although there may well be differences in how they have made, and make use their knowledge about the world.

Commonality in language (English), the annual exodus of many Indians to study in the United States and Europe, and external events, most notably the end of the Cold War, and more recently the terrorist attacks of September 11, 2001 have only heightened this natural affinity. This shared sense of unity is, of course, also accompanied by differences, and it is this bridge that Western expatriates will have to build to succeed in the Indian environment. As pointed out in the earlier part of this chapter, the Indian environment is now becoming an increasingly attractive one for Western firms. The next few chapters will discuss the best methods to operate in such a challenging environment.

Chapter Three
A Brief History of the Indian Software Industry

"I.T."—"India's Tomorrow"

A.B. Vajpayee; Former Indian Prime Minister

The West created wealth through the Industrial Revolution and then West Asia through Oil. Now, it is India's turn. They created it by using wealth that nature offered to man, but we (Indians) will create it by using what's within ourselves—in the human mind. In the 21st Century, which will go down in history as the "Century of the mind," India has the rare opportunity to earn back its pride of place among the nations of the world.

Rajendra Pawar, Managing Director of the leading Indian IT Company, NIIT, quoted in *The New Nirvana, India Today*'s Special Issue (2000)

India's software history perhaps can trace its origins from within the ancient Indian texts, the "Vedas" (derived from the root "vid," meaning "to know"). These texts, which lay stress on abstract, logical, and rational thinking, form the basis of all Indian learning and education. Vedic mathematics is based on sixteen "sutras" or word formulae that describe the way the human mind naturally works, and direct one to the appropriate analysis and solution, often with only mental calculations.

The Vedas have an adage that states "knowledge is wealth." This concept is viewed as fundamental in most Indian families who perceive learning and education as the most important investment of all. Thus, steeped as they are in vedic values with an extraordinary facility for lateral thinking and mental abstract hypothesizing, and with ancient Indian history replete with extraordinary contributions to mathematics, the software exploits of Indian "humanware" or "wetware" should come as no surprise.

The late Jawaharlal Nehru, India's first prime minister, writes in his book, *Discovery of India*,[1] that ancient India laid the foundations of modern arithmetic, geometry, and algebra and that the so-called Arabic numerals originated in India. Further, arguably India's greatest contributions to the world have been the concept of "zero" as well as the decimal place-value system that are integral concepts in modern software and in all calculations.

Mathematical contributions from India also came in the form of fractions and their multiplication and division; the rule of three; squares and square roots and their respective signs; cube and cube roots; the minus sign; calculation of the value of "pi" as well as the origins of trigonometry.

According to T.R.N. Rao and S. Kak of the University of South West Louisiana, in their fascinating book *Computing Science in Ancient India*,[2] traditional thinking has it that the first software programs, if defined as logical statements for complicated problem solving, were written by the great Indian mathematicians and astronomers, Aryabhata (in AD 476) and Bhaskara (in AD 628).

The modern Indian Information Technology industry came into existence when the government of India invested in Defense, Nuclear and Space, Research and Development, and invested heavily in the various public sector undertakings during the many years of socialistic, centralized, planned "command economy." The first digital computer was introduced into India as early as 1956, at the Government's, Indian Statistical Research Institute, in Calcutta (now Kolkata).

The early history of the so-called software development in India was closely interlinked with the growth of the computer hardware sector. Until the mid-1960s, computer hardware as well as supporting software was largely provided by two multinational companies with operations in India namely IBM and ICL (United Kingdom). All the software to run the systems as well as the basic programs had been developed overseas and more often than not, was provided as a thrown in item at little or no cost, as an adjunct to the sale of the main hardware. This of course was the prevalent international practice.

However, the needs of India's strategic R&D establishments, the defense services, and some of the leading public sector undertakings, required more than plain vanilla software. Since it became increasingly difficult for the multinational computer hardware companies to respond to these demands and also in a few cases where national security considerations required confidentiality, local engineers were required to write out such special software. Such software development was mainly carried out by in-house developers, writing programs for their own organizations.

From the mid-1960s onward, partly due to dwindling foreign exchange resources, and largely due to restrictions imposed on India by the developed countries after India had conducted its first underground nuclear test explosion, the Government of India at that time embarked on a major indigenization program in the strategic electronics sector. Accordingly a policy of locally assembling computers at an Indian public sector company, Electronics Corporation of India Ltd. (ECIL), was initiated, based largely on technology cloned from IBM systems, and sourced from the then soft currency trading partners from the erstwhile USSR and other COMECON countries.

Further, some of the larger hardware systems were imported as completely built units from these countries, using an Indian public sector electronics trading entity as an intermediary. Unfortunately, for obvious reasons, all such technology and hardware procurement came with only the very rudimentary software and it was left to local Indian software engineers to make up the deficiency. Thus by the 1970s, government and academic computer users relied very marginally on imported software bundled with the hardware, and increasingly Indian software engineers were called on to develop IBM compatible software for the IBM-360 series computer clones sourced from USSR and the COMECON countries.

At about this time, the French came forward to offer their own IRIS range of computers and technology, developed at their company CII (later to become a part of Honeywell-Bull). A cooperation agreement was signed with ECIL, and initial systems and technology was transferred. Unfortunately, the IRIS machines were not quite IBM technology compatible and hence some special software tweaking was needed, again, to be carried out by Indian software engineers. With the increase in domestic hardware production, either of Indian design, or under license from France, USSR, Poland, and Bulgaria, an increasing number of Indian commercial organizations as well as research and educational institutions, started using computers for which development had to be contracted out because of the lack of in-house expertise. A fledgling software industry had been created in India.[3]

The continuing difficulties in obtaining computers and the very high cost of hardware, led some entrepreneurial companies and computer professionals to set themselves up as computer bureaus, to provide services to private companies. In some cases, the computers in these bureaus, were imported and the principal method of acquiring the precious foreign exchange to pay for them was to provide an undertaking to the Government of India to earn substantial sums of money through exports. The first such firm to set up operations was Tata Consultancy Services (TCS) in Bombay (now Mumbai) in 1974, thus initiating the Indian software exports industry. At the time of writing, TCS is a "billion dollar" plus turnover IT Company, India's largest software entity, and one of the world's premier software companies.

In the late 1970s, the data processing departments of some of the larger companies and the software groups of some of the hardware companies began trying to sell the software developed in-house. As they came to recognize the revenue generating potential of software, several of these firms made their software units as profit centers while a few others hived their software groups into separate companies within the same business group.

An interesting aspect of the history of the Indian software sector, is highlighted by Professor Howard Rubin of the City University of New York in an article entitled, "The US, IT workforce shortage" (*Dr. Dobbs Journal*). Professor Rubin states that "Due to the import restrictions and foreign currency shortages during the 1970s and 1980s, Indian engineers had to make do by connecting low cost PCs and work stations into a "network" which though at that time was a make shift solution, turned out to be India's major contribution to international computing. The world now had "Computer Networking," an unintended consequence of Indian expertise and propensity for practical and adaptive solutions, locally described as "Jugaad" (see chapter five, "Understanding India").

In 1977, the first non-Congress Government formed by the Janata Party was in power. The minister of industries decided that all the large multinationals operating in India were not really required and in an extraordinary development, the government of the day decided to "expel" multinationals such as IBM and ICL, and Coca Cola, among others, from the country. Unwittingly, and unintentionally, this action, a quirk of history, became the trigger for the rapid growth of the Indian software industry.

Most of the 1,200 plus ex IBM India employees and many others from ICL were now out of work. A few managed to get jobs overseas and some of the hardware specialists were recruited into a new public sector company grandiosely called the "Computer Maintenance Corporation Ltd." All the software engineers who could not readily get jobs overseas were left to fend for themselves. Several of them teamed up together and set up their own software operations, often beginning as computer services bureaus but then graduating into software development for local clients. Thus, by 1980, India had the kernel of an IT industry, albeit small.

Two very significant developments, however, took place. A young man, Azim Premji, all of 21 years old was studying at Stanford in 1966, when his father, who headed a vegetable products (Cooking Oil and Soaps) company, called "Western India Vegetable Products Co." (WIPRO), passed away. Azim left Stanford without completing his degree to come back to India to take charge of the 20-year-old family business and promptly started a program of modernization and diversification, first moving into the manufacture of electrical bulbs. With the exit of IBM and ICL from India, Azim Premji sensed an opportunity in the IT hardware business and so in 1980 obtained a license for WIPRO, from the Sentinel Computer Corporation of the United States, to make and sell Minicomputers in India. Shortly thereafter, in 1982, WIPRO entered into a tie-up with Sun Microsystems and several other international companies to address the Indian hardware market. At one stage WIPRO had become India's leading computer printer manufacturer. With the decline in the IT hardware business and the rise of software in the late 1980s, WIPRO's focus also shifted toward software and designing. By 1992, WIPRO's software activities had grown to such a level that they established their Global IT Services Division. The company has now grown to be a "Billion Dollar" IT entity with worldwide offices and working with world leaders including Nokia. And, because of the market capitalization of his shareholding, Azim Premji, at least on paper, is now the richest Indian.

Meanwhile, in 1975, another young man, N.R. Narayana Murthy (NRNM), with a postgraduate degree from the Indian Institute of Technology, Kanpur, one of the world famous Indian Institute of Technology, returned to India after working for three years with SESA in Paris on projects such as designing a real time operating system for air cargo handling at Charles de Gaulle airport, and took up a lowly research assistant's post with a small institution in Pune. NRNM was, even at that time a bit of an idealist and at the very first meeting with his father-in-law to be, confessed that he "wanted to become a politician in the communist party and wanted to open an orphanage."[4] The venerable "In-Law-to-be" promptly declined to let his daughter, a qualified engineer with a good job with the Tata Group, marry this young man unless he got himself a proper job so as to be able to support a family. At that time NRNM was already financially indebted to his wife-to-be.

So, at the end of 1977, NRNM took up the assignment of general manager in a small IT start-up company in Mumbai, Patni Computers, which had just been appointed as the Indian representative of the U.S. Minicomputer company, "Data General." Shortly before being sent out to the United States for training, the young couple finally got permission to get married. In 1981, Narayana Murthy, at the age of 32, "being passionate about creating good quality software,"[5] together with six colleagues, all software professionals, and with the equivalent of US$250 borrowed from his wife as initial capital, set up "Infosys Technologies." The fledgling company started operations out of a tiny two-room residential flat in Pune, acquired after the Murthys sold off all their jewelry to raise the margin money for obtaining a housing loan.

For Infosys, business was initially slow and there were also the then prevailing formidable Indian bureaucratic hurdles to be overcome. *The Times of India* of April 28, 2002, carried a story that, to obtain permission (only available from Delhi in 1982) to import a computer costing $15,000, NRNM had to make 25 visits to the capital, spread over a period of 18 months, involving costs exceeding that of the computer. It was only in 1983 that Infosys got its first client, MICO (a Bosch associate) in Bangalore. The little flat in Pune was sold and the Murthys and the Infosys headquarters moved to Bangalore into a rented house.

Within a short span of nine years, Infosys had already begun to acquire the reputation as a competent Software company within India and overseas. Yet, when the company came out with a public issue in 1992 for a listing on the Bombay Stock Exchange, it barely managed to get fully subscribed. NRNM and his colleagues however kept up a relentless pace of growth and began to pick up clients like Reebok, Nortel Networks, Nestle, Cisco, and Nordstrom. Infosys, like its peers such as TCS, WIPRO, and Satyam, had come of age.

In March 1999, Infosys became the first company with an Indian registration to get listed on the American Stock Exchange and during the stock market mania of 1999–2000, the share value of the company reached unheard of highs. Today, Infosys is a "billion dollar" company, but more than that, the company as well as NRNM, have now become Indian icons and a great inspiration to many youngsters who for the first time can visualize the "Indian Dream" of first generation entrepreneurs from modest family backgrounds, becoming millionaires by sheer talent and hard work.

Although the growth of the software industry in the 1980s was slow and erratic, exports of software began to grow after 1981 because of increasing export awareness, largely arising out of the need to earn foreign exchange for meeting the commitments given to the authorities in lieu of being able to import computer systems. Further, at this time, in the international market, the cost of hardware had dramatically dropped and software, especially application software, as a cost factor had started to gain prominence. This increasingly required low-cost, highly skilled, software expertise, which by then was available in India in reasonable measure.

With the advent of modern and "forward looking" policies introduced during Prime Minister Rajiv Gandhi's tenure, the IT scenario in India underwent a quantum change. The government now actively promoted software exports for the first time, by providing concessional financing, export incentives, improved infrastructure, legal regulation, and export marketing assistance. Furthermore, in 1984, import of computer hardware was liberalized for the first time and large quantities were imported, principally small mainframes, PCs and minicomputers, as that was pretty much what could be afforded at the time. A large number of software companies then set up operations to meet the large market created by the companies who had imported these computers.

Many of the then software exporting entities thus had their origins in the domestic market, either as data processing centers of large companies or as software developers for domestic hardware installations. However, under the new dispensation, with the active encouragement of the government and with the provision of incentives, the focus rapidly shifted to exports. Also, as noted later in this chapter, by this time, Indian engineers and managers, who had gone overseas to study, particularly to the United States, and stayed on in jobs there, had now started to reach positions of considerable influence in their companies and some had also ventured out as successful entrepreneurs.

Thus, in the 1980s, multinational companies also began, for the first time, to take a serious interest in India as a source of software development and also as a potential market for software "products." Companies like Unisys and Burroughs even entered into Indian joint ventures with equity participation. Some of the world's leading airlines including British Airways and Swiss Air outsourced IT, ticketing, and fare reconciliation activities into dedicated "virtual" software operations set up in Indian entities.

In 1985, Citibank established a 100 percent foreign-owned, export-oriented offshore software company in the Santa Cruz Electronics Export Processing Zone (SEEPZ) in Bombay (now Mumbai). Indians working at Citibank's Indian operations were particularly keen on creating this subsidiary, which initially undertook software development work for the parent company and later diversified into other activities. This activity spawned the Indian company I-Flex, which developed, Flexcube the world's leading banking software product and other products such as Microbanker and Reveleus a business information tool for financial institutions. "I-Flex" is now a world leader. Soon thereafter, the U.S. companies, Texas Instruments and Hewlett Packard established subsidiaries in Bangalore, in 1986 and 1989 respectively.

With these significant initial multinational software commitments in India, worldwide attention was drawn to the possibilities for offshore software development in India. This increased awareness coincided with the severe shortage in the supply of programmers and software developers in the international software industry, particularly in the United States.[6]

In 1991, the Government of India, as part of the overall economic liberalization regime, established "Software Technology Parks" (STPs) in the major cities of the country. The STPs provided the software export industry with international quality, satellite-based telecommunications infrastructure as also the possibility of importing hardware and software products free of import duties. Further, profits from exports of software were entitled to claim zero income tax. The STP scheme became enormously successful and was the real facilitator for India's software export boom. Now, STPs have also been established in the smaller towns of India with the same facilities as in the larger cities.

The reforms of 1991 also brought about some other very significant policy changes, which were to really benefit the Indian software sector. First, with the introduction of currency convertibility on the current account, it was now possible for companies to hire the services of international consultants to assist in global branding. Second, foreign companies were now freely allowed to set up 100 percent owned software companies in India providing appropriate competition and "benchmarking" for the healthy growth of Indian IT companies. Third, with the abolition of controls on Capital issues, companies were now free to enlist shares both on Indian as well as overseas stock exchanges and also offer stock options to their employees. But the greatest benefit came from the abolition of wealth tax, which for the very first time brought about the possibility of attractive wealth creation for entrepreneurs and shareholders alike.

The 1990s also saw two very interesting situations, which went a very long way in establishing India's software prowess on the international scene. First, and possibly the more significant event happened in Switzerland. The Swiss Railways, famed for their precision and demanding performance, wanted to completely revamp and modernize their software and integrate all their disparate systems. Despite international competition, the Indian company TCS was awarded the contract. They not only delivered excellent service to a very demanding customer, but also finished their assignment well in advance. This shattered two long held negative beliefs. First, that, Indian software professionals were just "techno coolies" fit only for low-grade software work at "sweat shop" wages. Second, that Indians, given their casual attitude to time, could never finish or deliver an international project in the time allocated, and to the desired quality standards.

The more knowledgeable U.S. companies, particularly those in California, with link to India through engineers and managers of Indian origin as also through work done for them by Indian entities, were aware of the skills of the Indian software professionals. It was a revelation and eye opener for the rest of the world. And it came at just the right time! The world was heading toward a change of the century. The long awaited and dreaded "Y2K" was soon going to be upon us, and companies and users had not reacted fast enough. Worse, there was not enough local talent to fix this potential nightmare. So, the word was now out. Call in the Indians and let them fix it.

Thus, in the second significant event, Indian software engineers, passing out in thousands from excellent universities and colleges and professional software training institutions, were filling the aircraft of the world's leading airlines, traveling to the corners of the developed world fixing the "Y2K" problem. The Indian companies did themselves proud by responding appropriately to the challenge and delivering.

Shortly after the "Y2K" situation, another peculiar situation arose. A large part of the European Union was going to convert to their new, unified currency, the "Euro." This again needed massive software inputs not readily available within Europe. So once again the Indians were called in. Countries such as the United Kingdom and Germany even relaxed their visa regimes. The Indian software companies, aided and abetted by their highly professional and effective association, the "National Association for Software and Services Companies" (NASSCOM), were now on a roll. There was to be no looking back from here.

IT and the Indian Diaspora in the United States

The great Indian poet and Nobel laureate, Rabindranath Tagore, eloquently said:

> To study a Banyan Tree, you not only must know its main stem in its own soil, but also must trace the growth of its greatness in the further soil, for then you can know the true nature of its vitality.

This extraordinarily philosophical statement is appropriate for an understanding of the international growth of India's software business. It also leads us to study and analyze the extraordinary contributions to global IT made by the phenomenally successful Indian diaspora in the United States, particularly those from the so-called Silicon Valley in California.

According to Professor Anna Lee Saxenian[7] of the University of California, Berkeley, "the origins of the high skilled immigrant presence in the U.S. date back to the mid 1960s," when an amendment was made to the U.S. Immigration and Nationality Act repealing the national origins quota system allowing for graduating overseas students to extend their residency in the United States. At about this time some of the graduates of the initial batches of the then recently established and now famous, Indian Institutes of Technology (IITs), had just started to finish postgraduate studies in the United States.

This was also the time when the Silicon Integrated Circuit had just been developed in the San Francisco Bay area, and Stanford University, the Xerox Palo Alto Research Center, Hewlett Packard, and others were anchoring a massive development of the electronics industry in the geographical area now called the "Silicon Valley." The skills of the enormously talented, English-speaking, Indian engineers with fresh postgraduate degrees from leading U.S. universities such as Stanford, University of California—Berkeley, MIT, Carnegie Mellon, and so on could now be used by the high technology companies in Silicon Valley. The success of these pioneers led to a clamor by both universities as well as high technology companies for more Indians, and they came in increasing numbers. In December 1998, the prestigious U.S. publication, *Business Week* in a report said that, "a full 30% of the graduating classes (from the Indian Institutes of Technology) headed to the U.S. for graduate programs and better job opportunities in 1998. In the more popular computer science programs, nearly 80% leave for Silicon Valley. So routine is the exodus that at the IIT—Madras, the local campus postman and bank clerk provide unsolicited advice on the best U.S. schools to attend."[8]

Over the years, U.S. companies derived great benefits from the skills and talents of this great diaspora, but for the Indian engineers the path up the technical management ladder was slow and limited. It was only in the years following the Vietnam War, with California rapidly becoming a multicultural society, that the "glass ceiling" of senior management was finally broken and several Indians such as Vinod Dham, the "father" of the Pentium chip at Intel, almost reached the top rung. A June 1999 study by Professor Anne Lee Saxenian,[9] indicated that at that time, India and Taiwanese Chinese constituted over 35 percent of the Silicon Valley region's scientific and engineering workforce. Further, Saxenian notes that by 1998, these Indian and Taiwanese had become senior executives at about one quarter of Silicon Valley's new technology businesses.

However, by the 1980s, with cuts in the defense and space budgets, several U.S. companies started downsizing. By then the entrepreneurial bug had bitten the Indian diaspora in the U.S. and several of them in senior positions decide to strike out on their own. Among the first few was Kanwal Rekhi, an alumnus of IIT—Bombay and a postgraduate from Michigan, who in 1981, along with two other Indians, set up "Excelan," the first Internet company. Shortly, in 1982, Vinod Khosla (IIT—Delhi) established Sun Microsystems and in 1984, Suhas Patil (IIT—Kharagpur) set up "Cirrus Logic." These organizations became highly successful multi-million dollar businesses and inspired other Indian professionals to follow suit.[10]

The start up of the Internet was now to provide great entrepreneurial opportunities. Technology leaders such as "Exodus Communications," "i2 Technologies," "Sycamore," "Juniper," "Junglee," and so on, all set up by Indians later grew to become great wealth creators. The Internet technology domain was now rapidly dominated by people of Indian origin. Michael Lewis in his book *The New Thing* quotes Jim Clark of Silicon Graphics and Netscape fame as saying "The Internet had acquired a predominant flavor of curry!"

But the "big one" was yet to arrive. Smitten by the Internet bug, the then 28-year-old, Sabeer Bhatia, quit his job after just nine months at Apple Computers to join a start up company, "Firepower Systems" which in a few months, went under. Along with an ex-colleague from Apple, Jack Smith, Sabeer sat up one night and wrote a business plan for a software company that would enable the users to send e-mails from any computer, anywhere in the world. This concept was named as "Hotmail" derived from "html" the programming language used to make web pages. But venture capital was required to start up the company. Following 19 rejections, Sabeer reached the offices of Draper Fisher Jurvetson who, in 1997, impressed by the concept, put up $3 million as venture capital. By the end of the year Hotmail had a million customers and in a year's time, when Microsoft paid $400 million to buy out Hotmail, they had over 10 million customers.[11]

With the great success of the Indian diaspora in Silicon Valley, as far as India was concerned, many possibilities now opened up for outsourcing work, establishment of delivery centers in India, and the setting up of new high technology ventures in India by Indians who returned from the United States (described as "brain circulation" by Professor Saxenian) for all kinds of IT work from IC chip designing to animation of Hollywood blockbusters. What was needed was an institution that would somehow bring all this together along with advisory functions, venture capital facilitation, networking, political and bureaucratic contacts and most important of all, nurturing of the entrepreneurial spirit. The more experienced among the diaspora, led by Kanwal Rekhi, formed just such a non-profit institution, "The Indus Entrepreneurs" (TIE), 1992 with its headquarters in Silicon Valley, with chapters in several U.S. cities as well as in India and other countries of the world. With an active membership and with a wealth of experience being made available by the driving forces at TIE, the two streams of Indian IT, the home-grown one and that of the diaspora are now rapidly converging to make India the great information technology powerhouse, in the process completely transforming cities such as Bangalore, Hyderabad, Gurgaon, and Chennai.

IC Chip Designing/Electronic Design Automation (EDA) Services

While the story of India's software exports prowess was being written about and highlighted in the world's media, some other IT-related activities were beginning to gather momentum in India. Although these were technical enough, they required different skill sets and were really not mainstream software activity.

In 1985, Texas Instruments (TI) established a small export oriented IC design facility in the city of Bangalore to leverage the local engineering and design talent.

At that time there were no guidelines or regulations (particularly related to customs) in place, regarding design exports over satellite telecommunication channels. Technocrats from the Indian Government's Department of Electronics had to be positioned in the TI facilities in Bangalore to be the virtual customs authorities.

Over the past few years, the TI facility grew from strength to strength in their IC chip designing capabilities. Today they are engaged in several full product development including, for example, a world class Digital Signal Processor (DSP) as well as DSP Systems on a Chip (SOC) for Controllers and Audio and Video functionality for broadband communications and 3G telecommunications. Their success was a pathbreaking endeavor that induced others to follow suit.

Today, India is considered the IC chip design capital of the world.[12] There are at least 70 companies of a significant size engaged in chip designing in India. Over 50 of these are located in Bangalore. Many world leaders such as ST Microelectronics (see Case Study on ST Microelectronics in this book), National Semiconductor, Sage, Motorola, Sanyo-LSI, Lucent, Analog Devices, Alliance Semiconductor, Cypress, Cadence, Cirrus Logic, AMD, Zilog/Qualcore, Intel, to name a few, now have large chip design and "System on a Chip" (SOC) design capabilities in India. Integrated Circuit design export billing now exceeds US$300 million and employs almost 10,000 VLSI engineers, software engineers, system and complexity engineers, to design chips for products ranging from i-PODs, to DVD players and advanced telecommunications systems.

IT Enabled Services (ITES) and Business Processing Outsourcing

While the Indian IT and EDA sectors were making their mark in the international sphere, an interesting sector that is the subject of a raging international controversy which has even been brought into focus in the U.S. presidential race, with India facing some backlash. This sector covers the whole gamut of IT enabled services (ITES) and Business Processing Outsourcing (BPO), ranging from simple Back Office Operations, Medical Transcriptions (for the U.S. medical sector), financial services, engineering design services, architectural services, Geographical Information Services, technical support centers, through to plain vanilla Call Center Services.

From a near nonexistent presence as recently as the 1990s, the ITES/BPO services today are a $4 billion revenue earner for India, employing over 200,000 Indians, with skill sets ranging from raw young graduates to highly qualified engineers and scientists, some with Ph.D. degrees. And more are being added every day, to the consternation of many countries, who see this development as a massive transfer of jobs from the developed world to India and even became a major issue in the 2004 U.S. presidential race. But how did it all start?

The Indian ITES/BPO story starts in 1984 when Raman Roy, described as the "Father of the Indian BPO Industry," joined American Express in India to help set up its automation services and accounting operations. From a small beginning, Raman Roy went on to establish a global, centralized, accounting facility in India, providing services to American Express customers in Europe, United States, Japan, and Australia. Today this center has grown to about a thousand employees and provides all aspects of accounting and other services to the global offices of American Express.

In 1992, Swiss Air established a joint venture company, ATS, in India, with the Tata group to work on airline back office assignments. In 1997, British Airways, as also American Express also started to outsource some routine back office and reconciliation work of India. By the mid-1990s some entrepreneurial Indians had also managed to get medical transcription work from the U.S. medical sector. Not much IT or technology was however involved in such work.

The real fillip however came in 1998 when the Indian subsidiary of GE Capital, GE's finance arm, set up a small eight-person team to do elementary address changes for the group companies. This experiment was so successful, that it was not too long before this group had mushroomed into a major operation "General Electric International Services" (GECIS), based in Gurgaon near Delhi, handling basic voice-based call center operations, claims processing, e-business, accounting, actuarial services and so on. Raman Roy was brought in as the chief executive of GECIS. From an employee base of eight at the beginning, they grew to 600 in 1998 and almost 12,000 in 2003. (See the case study on GECIS in chapter five of this book.) India and the world took note of this extraordinary development.

Some of the senior managers left GECIS to establish their own companies and work independently. Most notably of them all, Raman Roy, established his own company, "Spectramind," which he later sold. It is now a wholly owned unit of the software giant, WIPRO. The concept of subcontracting out ITES and BPO operations to an independent entity based in India, rapidly caught on, and an increasing amount of work was transferred to India.

In July 1999, four young Indians working with U.S. multinationals sensed an opportunity when apparently they read a report somewhere which seemed to show that well over 65 percent of all online transactions are abandoned due to a lack of any customer support. At the beginning of 2000, the four entrepreneurs established a company, Daksh, also in Gurgaon. One of the founders was related to Ashish Gupta who had set up Junglee in the United States, which was later acquired by Amazon. Ashish Gupta became the angel investor in Daksh and brought in Amazon as one of its first customers. In a short time, Daksh became a huge success story with many leading international organizations as customers and a turnover rising from zero to $60 million in four years. In early 2004, IBM bought out Daksh for $160 million.

Now all the world' s majors were scrambling to India to get a piece of the action. GECIS was followed quickly by Citigroup, HSBC, Accenture, Dell, Hewlett Packard, and many others streamed in. Today, India provides ITES and BPO services to nearly all the Fortune 500 companies and many others, covering every conceivable sector that can be outsourced.

Exports of ITES from India have risen from US$565 million in 1999–2000 to US$2.4 billion in 2002–2003. Analysts predict that by 2006 export revenues from ITES will rise to a staggering US$6 billion. But this will still be only a small portion of the global ITES/BPO business expected to be US$1.6 trillion by 2006.

India has the human resource, now being defined as "wetware." The infrastructure is now in place. The larger IT companies are getting into or expanding their ITES activities as also going in for high-end designing work. It, therefore, is entirely conceivable that by 2010, India could earn export revenues of US$100 billion. That, at least is the target the industry sector has set for itself.

Chapter Four

Cultural Portrait: Impact of Hinduism on Indian Managerial Behavior

The born traveler—the man who is without prejudices, who sets out wanting to learn rather than to criticize, who is stimulated by oddity, who recognizes that every man is his brother, however strange and ludicrous he may be in dress and appearance—has always been comparatively rare.

Hugh and Pauline Massingham, "The Englishman Abroad."
Cited in Craig Storti, *The Art of Crossing Cultures*

Introduction

> Many, perhaps most, people who go abroad to live and work genuinely want to adapt to the local culture. And most of them do not. It's not that they don't appreciate the reasons for adapting to the culture or know that it is all but essential to being successful in their work and at ease in their society, but rather that true cross cultural adjustment and effective cross cultural interaction are more elusive than we might imagine."[1]

Managers engaged in cross-border transactions are often faced with the need to bridge the cultural gap that exists between their cultural background and that of their foreign counterparts who possess a different cultural background. This is by no means an easy task. Although globalization has increased the interdependence among different societies, the growing interdependence has not necessarily brought about a convergence in managerial values, although without doubt, pockets of global homogenization may be found in all societies.[2]

"Culture is to a human collectivity what personality is to an individual."[3] Culture has a profound impact on the ethos of society. It influences the way in which it engages with the outside world as well as the way in which it deals with its own internal problems. Culture sets the parameters for what are considered acceptable as well as unacceptable forms of behavior in a society. It affects the way in which people think and resolve conflicts in their everyday life. As Adler points out "Our ways of thinking, feeling, and behaving, as human beings are neither fully random nor haphazard, but are profoundly influenced by our cultural heritage."[4]

The essence of culture is neatly captured in the definition by Hofstede who defines culture as "the collective programming of the mind that distinguishes the members of one group or category of people from another."[5] In this definition "culture" is likened to a software program that governs the manner in which people think, behave, and/or respond to any situation facing them. This does not imply by any means that every individual in a given culture will think and behave in the same fashion; all that it suggests is that every culture has its own unique way of relating with the world with different individuals differentially exhibiting the impact of culture, personality, and the situation in any concrete situation.

The "collective programming" encapsulates the "core assumptions," that govern the functioning of society. These core assumptions manifest themselves as *values*, which determine what a society considers valuable or desirable.[6] It is important to note that members of a society are generally not aware of their own cultural values and it is this unawareness that often causes unpleasant surprises/shocks when they interact with members of another cultural group. The human mind is comfortable with order and predictability, both of which are called into question in an alien cultural environment. It is the disconfirmation of one's unconsciously held expectations that often gives rise to what has commonly been described as *culture shock*.[7]

What aspects of the Indian value system are going to be troublesome for the Western expatriate manager? What are the origins of the dominant values in the Indian society? How do these values shape Indian managerial behavior? These are the issues that we address in this chapter. At the outset it is perhaps useful to state that the Indian culture exhibits a level of "complexity" that makes facile generalizations often difficult. The complexity of the Indian culture stems from the fact that the Indian social system as embodied in the basic tenets of Hinduism has over the years been subject to a myriad of influences stemming from Islamic rule, British colonialism, and more recently, the advent of globalization. The fundamental underpinning of Indian culture is still provided by the fundamental principles of *Hinduism* that continue to shape Indian thought and behavior. We will make an attempt in this chapter to distill the basic elements of Hinduism, and to sketch out their impact on the conduct of business practice in India.

The Nature of Hinduism

The term "Hinduism," was first used by the British in the nineteenth century to describe the beliefs/values of individuals who were neither Christian nor Muslims.[8] Scholars note that even the word *Hindu* was first used by the Persians to refer to the individuals who were living near the river Indus, around sixth century BC.[9] A unique feature of Hinduism has been its ability to incorporate a wide variety of different beliefs. As Wendy Doniger notes "It is axiomatic that no religious idea in India ever dies or is superseded—it is merely combined with the new ideas that arise in response to it."[10] This has a number of implications. First, given the "all encompassing" nature of the Indian thought, scholars note that it is often hard to define Hinduism precisely.[11] Second, the primary focus of Hindu thought has been on incorporating new developments instead of trying to refute them.[12]

This logic of assimilation was predicated on the worldview that the world is only one, although it may be called differently by different people. An emphasis on assimilation also reflected a spirit of tolerance in this way of thinking. As scholars note

"Hinduism's openness to new ideas, teachers, and practices, and its desire for universality rather than exclusivity, set it apart from religions that distinguish their followers by their belief in particular historical events, people, or revelations."[13] In the process of assimilation, Hinduism developed the capability of offering something to everyone, notwithstanding the fact that there is a vast gap between the culture of the priestly classes (the *Brahmins*) and that of the masses.[14]

The Vedas are a body of religious literature that provide the foundation for Hinduism. Although many Hindus may not be familiar with its contents, they have an unparalleled status in Hindu thought. Scholars have observed that "In the traditional Hindu understanding, Vedas are said to be non personal and without beginning or end. This means that the truths embodied in the Vedas are eternal and they are not creations of the human mind."[15] Some parts of the Vedas have furnished the basis for Indian rituals and continue to influence Hindu thought.[16] The philosophical basis of Indian thinking is expounded, above all, in the *Upanishads*, which constitute the last of the Vedas. The Vedas were transmitted verbally and not written down for many centuries after their composition.[17] Oral transmission reinforced the monopolistic status of the *Brahmins* in the Hindu society and as Lannoy points out "it was not numbers which became the key to both power and wisdom, as in Europe, but the Word."[18]

What are some of the key beliefs in Hinduism that have shaped, and continue, to shape Indian thinking and behavior? While there is a wide corpus of beliefs associated with Hinduism, just as there with any other social thought, we will focus on, what are widely considered to be, the key aspects of this philosophy. The key beliefs revolve around (a) the nature of the ultimate reality (*Brahman*); (b) the doctrine of *karma*; (c) the principle of *ahimsa* (non injury); and (d) the four stages of life (*ashramas*); (e) the concept of *dharma*; and (f) the principle of hierarchy.[19]

The Nature of Ultimate Reality

This, in many respects, is the core foundational principle of Hinduism that has attracted widespread attention both in India as well as throughout the world. Hindus believe in an ultimate transcendental reality that is called the *Brahman*. The transcendental reality is beyond reason and may be hard to even describe in words.[20] The ultimate reality stands in marked contrast to the illusion (*maya*) of the phenomenal world, which we have to navigate everyday.

The dominant school of thought in Indian philosophy (i.e., the Vedantic school) makes the argument that *Brahman* is both the creator as well as the preserver of the Universe and this vital life energy (*atman*) is present in all things, animate or otherwise.[21] The normative implication of this principle is that individuals should strive to unite their inner self with the ultimate reality. The attempt to realize this unity constitutes the heart of spiritualism in the Indian subcontinent.

The Doctrine of Karma

This is a core doctrine in the Hindu philosophical system. Simply put, the doctrine asserts that individuals will be rewarded for good deeds in a future life and penalized for actions that are morally inappropriate. Coupled with the doctrine of transmigration, the implication is that individuals with good *karma* will gain rebirth in a social setting that represents an improvement over their current situation. Over time, they are also more likely to attain *moksha*, that is, get united with the *Brahman* and in doing so will escape from the clutches of the illusory world.

Likewise, individuals with a bad *karma*, may be reborn in a social setting that represents a decline in their social status. It also makes it that much more difficult for them to attain liberation. Some have argued that this doctrine engenders pessimism and fatalism, but if present actions influence future outcomes, there is an active role for human agency, and there is less reason to be pessimistic.

Doctrine of Ahimsa

The ideal of *ahimsa* is another characteristic of Indian thought. Most fundamentally, the Hindu thought went against the inclination to inflict harm upon others. As Wendy Doniger points out, the concept of *ahimsa* was not related to vegetarianism, although over time the two did mutually influence each other.[22] This principle gained its most prominent exponent in Mohandas Gandhi, the Indian leader, who steadfastly employed the principle of "non violence" in exerting pressure on the British to leave India.

The Four Stages of Life

Many scholars have characterized the Hindu philosophical thought as being "other worldly in orientation."[23] Although elements of this are clearly present in Indian thought, it is not the only orientation that is dominant in Indian thinking. There is much in Indian thought that also values an individual leading a fulfilling life within the phenomenal or the illusory world. The idea of fulfillment is developed within the context of the life stages that an individual has to go through. Indian philosophers conceived of four different stages, namely, that of a *student, a married person, withdrawal from the world of the "maya,"* and the ultimate stage that involved *renouncing* the world. Indeed, when an individual was raising a family, issues of wealth were obviously of importance. Within this life cycle, individuals had specific responsibilities associated with each of these phases, and it was their duty to fulfill them.

The Concept of Dharma

"*Dharma*," refers to behavior that is considered to be morally appropriate. Scholars have pointed out that in Hinduism, there is not one *Dharma* but that there are many *Dharmas*. There is the *Universal Dharma*, which refers to behavior that is appropriate under all circumstances. This is complemented by *dharmas* that focus on (a) how women should behave; (b) how individuals should perform their vocational duties; (c) how individuals should act during their life cycle; and (d) how elders should act toward those who are younger to them.[24]

The existence of different *dharmas*, has the implication that the different *dharmas* may compel individuals facing conflicts with the unenviable task of making difficult choices. As Dhand points out "At all times, one has several possible duties to perform, given one's location on numerous interlocking matrices of relationships. One must determine which duty is the most pressing at any one time and act accordingly."[25] When deciding on the appropriate course of action in a given situation, the individual, as Dhand, points out perceptively "relies upon relational metaphors rather than an ideology of individualism."[26] The importance of relational metaphors is also stressed by White who notes "For the real order and harmony in society rests as much, if not more, upon the obligations within a social group as upon the shared virtues of all people in society."[27] The crucial implication of this being, that individual actions are governed by *relational logic* and for that reason may be particularistic even though they may be justified by universal ideals.

The Principle of Hierarchy

Although the hierarchical order is not unique to Hindu India, it is without question, a key aspect of this civilization. As Sinha writes "Hierarchical order signifies that the whole cosmos and everything within it—animate as well as inanimate—are arranged in a hierarchical order of being superior to some and inferior to others."[28] As argued earlier the social order of the society is hierarchical, resting as it does on the *caste system*. At the apex of this hierarchical order are the *Brahmins*, the knowledge/priestly class who maintain a monopoly of wisdom.

The Indian hierarchical system has often been characterized as a closed stratification system in which upward mobility is difficult, if not impossible. Although this has clearly been the dominant view more recent scholarship seems to suggest the caste system is not as monolithic as it has often assumed to be. As Dipankar Gupta points out "different and conflicting hierarchies exist at subjective levels. . . . Very often in practice we find more than one hierarchical order in effect."[29] The crucial implication of this line of reasoning is that while the Hindus may be preoccupied with the hierarchical order, there may well be dissent about the nature of the hierarchical ranking.

Cultural Implications of the Hindu Belief System

What are the key cultural implications of the Hindu belief system? In this section we outline some of the major cultural implications of the Hindu worldview. Scholars note that religion is often closely intertwined with culture in that it is likely to critically shape the beliefs and values that shape individual behavior.[30] A direct impact of this is evident in the goals that individuals seek to pursue. Emmons and Paloutzian note that religion shapes an individual's ultimate concerns.[31] Ultimate concerns refer to the goals that are likely to be the most meaningful for them in their lives and which they should seek to pursue. Religious beliefs are also likely to influence the inner psychological states of the individuals while also simultaneously shaping the way in which members of a given society interact with each other.[32]

In our view, the Hindu belief system (a) shapes the individual's orientation to the world; (b) embraces rationality and emotionality that play a simultaneous role in the thinking process; (c) induces individuals to behave both individualistically as well as "collectivistically" at the same time; (d) tolerates the paradox of spiritualism and this worldly orientation; and (e) induces context sensitive patterns of behavior.[33] While this categorization by no means captures all aspects of Indian behavior, it does, in our view highlight dominant tendencies, the origins and implications of which we will discuss in the next few paragraphs.

Orientation to the World

An important cultural belief deals with the way in which individuals conceive of their relationship with the external world. Scholars have drawn a distinction between cultures that seek to attain mastery over nature, those that wish to live in harmony with it, and still others that expect to be subjugated by nature.[34] Cultures in which attaining mastery is the dominant cultural imperative will leave no stone unturned in attaining their goals.

Individual accomplishments, as also societal accomplishments, are valued highly with an emphasis on attaining success both at the individual and the societal level institutionalized with huge rewards for success and large penalties for failure. The most suitable example undoubtedly is that of the United States of America, where the search for success begins at a very early age. By contrast, cultures where mastery over nature is not the preferred cultural imperative may display passivity and helplessness in dealing with the external world. Scholars maintain that in the Indian tradition the dominant cultural orientation is one of subjugation to nature.[35] This orientation stems from the Hindu belief that the phenomenal world is illusory. If, the world of day-to-day living is indeed an illusion then why should one make any effort to transform it?

This cultural value orientation may, without question, lower achievement motivation, may lessen the centrality of work in one's lives, and may also lower the motivation of the individuals to display initiative and creativity. There is evidence to suggest that this is still the case in India, although the impetus for enhancing competitiveness in light of the liberalization of the economy is causing some organizations to change directions.[36]

In their study of Indian managers Jones and Jackson found that the managers were "comparatively less motivated by autonomy, personal development, achievement, and managing uncertainty."[37] Similarly as Professor Srinivasan observes "The Indian approach of conservatism and conformism, of adjusting and satisfying, is a major drawback when it comes to making world leaders."[38] These observations have also been demonstrated in experimental simulations involving Indian students.[39] In a study of problem solving that involved comparing Indian and German students, Stroschneider and Gusch found that the Indian students were not proactive enough in dealing with the problems that they were faced with. Referring to the Indians the author/s note "they are more likely to ignore key aspects of a scenario, rely on a purely feedback controlled strategy, make decisions without having the necessary information available, fail to adapt their interventions to changing circumstances, and forget about effect control."[40]

But by contrast, Sinha points out that Tata Steel was very effective in responding to the challenges of a more demanding environment. As he notes "The managing director impressed upon the employees that the company was facing a crisis, it was not in a position to hold that many employees, some had to go, the company must invest money in upgrading technology, modernize plants and systems, and so on.

The employees accepted the reality. Over 35,000 accepted attractive separation packages and left without making any loud noise, and the remaining ones fell in line, although some of the older and senior ones did not change their minds."[41] The implication of this fact is that while there may well be cultural beliefs that may stand in opposition to proactive behavior, the impact of these beliefs may be mitigated by effective leadership that is able to create incentives for radical change.

Rationality and Emotionality as Complementary Modes of Thought

Intellect is a highly valued attribute in India and its importance was valued both in the past as well as the present. As Lannoy points out "Indians became great mathematicians, inventing the zero, the decimal system, and the sine function . . ."[42] In modern times, the growth of the software industry, and the large number of engineers and scientists that graduate annually from Indian higher education institutions provide an eloquent testimony to the computational and the mathematical ingenuity demonstrated by the Indians. These skills are reflective of a strong tendency to rely on logical principles in decision-making. It may also be a form of hyper rationality, in which the individuals seek to find the best possible solution to a given problem. Scholars have often described this as an "idealistic mode of thinking" in that it is a "thinking" process whose only restraint is the human imagination.[43]

It is due to this rationality that Indians often have high aspirations that are the outcome of pursuing perfection to its logical conclusion. Although high aspirations are an essential precondition for attaining high outcomes, high aspirations may not necessarily lead to high outcomes. Swami Bodhananda Sarasvati, a spiritual management guru in India suggests that an orientation toward perfection leads to inaction in the Indian managerial context.[44] One can deduce this mode of Indian thinking from the basics of Indian philosophy, which emphasizes the search for the *eternal universal* (*Brahman*). The *Brahman* is the ultimate reality that we need to discover if we are to attain the ultimate state of bliss.

The highly developed capacity to reason has a number of different implications. It suggests, first of all, that Indians are great debaters and that it may be difficult to win an argument with them. There are few arguments that are completely infallible, and the clever Indian, can easily find weak spots in them. If logic is the normative ideal that all of us should follow in making decisions, then it only stands to reason to make the related assertion that the logical argument is also the most *morally defensible* one. The key implication of this line of reasoning is that a *logical argument* is ipso facto superior to a *pragmatically expedient one*, and for that reason may not easily brook any compromise with an alternative mode of thinking. It may also be argued that this strong analytical capability may become an end itself, with the very process superseding the goal that it is supposed to achieve.[45]

Illustrating this is a study of Indo-German joint ventures conducted by the Indo-German Chamber of Commerce. Commenting upon the German perceptions of Indian managers, the authors note, "Because they are convinced of their own being right, they fail to see their weaknesses, are not ready to cooperate, and appear mentally inflexible."[46] A further implication of this is that spontaneous decision-making may be somewhat infrequent given the need to subject everything to a logical scrutiny.

While rationality characterizes the Indian decision maker at one end of the spectrum, emotionality captures the other end of the spectrum. By emotionality we mean the ability and the willingness of the manager to express emotions in social situations. Unlike East Asians, where emotionality is taboo no matter what the circumstances, there are few such restrictions in the Indian social context. As Langauni points out "In such a society, feelings and emotions are not easily repressed, and their expression in general is not frowned upon. Crying, dependence on others, excessive emotionality, volatility, and verbal hostility, both in men and women, are not in any way considered as signs of weakness or ill breeding."[47]

This is not to imply that the Indian managers will always display emotionality; the argument is only that there are no such taboos as in East Asia. The high degree of emotionality exhibited by the Indian decision maker is a product of several factors. First, the Indian decision makers take a *moral* approach to problem solving, and this in itself, is likely to make the decision maker exhibit emotionality.[48] Second, the Indian does possess a core individualistic self, and this certainly guarantees that the Indian decision maker will be comfortable in experiencing and expressing emotions.[49] Third, the Indians do possess a very high degree of pride based both on the past achievements of the Indian society as also on what India has accomplished most notably in the post liberalization era.

It therefore, stands to reason, that the Indians may react to situations emotionally. However, the emotionality that is displayed by the Indian decision maker is not necessarily in opposition to rational aims (although it could be), and in that sense is quite compatible with rationality. However, it is quite conceivable that the expression of it as such, may be misconstrued by the Western expatriate manager.

The fact that the Indian decision maker so closely intertwines rationality with emotionality in decision-making may have a number of alternative implications. The process of making decisions may not be that linear or that straightforward. Periods of progress may be followed by that of re-evaluation or re-adjustment, as the decision maker seeks to reconcile the imperatives of reason with that of emotion. While the need for attaining this balance/adjustment is probably universal, the time path is likely to be culturally variable.

Given that time is viewed in a cyclical fashion in India (as discussed in chapter five), we would surmise that the cultural imperatives for restoring this balance may lack a heightened sense of urgency. Alternatively, one may presume that, a heightened sense of emotionality may reaffirm the commitment of the Indian manager to search for the "ideal solution" and in doing so may make the fashioning of compromises somewhat difficult. A third possibility is that the manager may keep shifting from one end of the spectrum to the other, without defining a "clear cut" position.

Coexistence of Individualism and Collectivism

Scholars have drawn a distinction between the cultural dimensions of individualism and collectivism. In individualistic cultures people give priority to their personal goals over those of other important in groups whereas in collectivistic cultures individuals give the greatest priority to "in group" goals.[50] The individualist also tries to express his/her uniqueness and is often direct in communicating his/her preferences and expectations. By contrast, the collectivist seeks to fit in with the group and seeks to infer the intentions of the other group members in subtle ways.[51]

The individualist is also not afraid of conflict and believes that the truth can be found through rational argumentation. By contrast, the collectivistic self is primarily concerned with maintaining harmony, and an overt manifestation of conflict is most clearly unacceptable to him/her. The central goal of the collectivistic self is to manage conflict rather than to resolve it, which is the clear preference of the individualistic self.[52] The one key implication of this is that individualists are much more upfront and comfortable in dealing with their emotions (in so far as individuals could be) but collectivists are shy in even acknowledging, much less dealing with their emotions.[53]

The Indian culture has traditionally been characterized as a collectivistic one.[54] The nature of the self is well captured in the way the Indians conceive their identity. As Sinha observes "Their identity is devloped around 'We' rather than 'I.' Indian names often include parts of parental names (e.g., Mohandas Karamchand Gandhi), place of origin (e.g., Firak Gurakhpuri, Majrooh Sultanpuri), or mythological characters implying connectivity with ancestors, physical milieu, and even the world of gods and goddesses."[55] It has also been maintained that India is characterized by vertical as opposed to horizontal collectivism.[56]

The distinction between the two is that while horizontal collectivism emphasizes the sameness among individuals, vertical collectivism lays stress on maintaining the integrity of the hierarchical order. The hierarchical order is inviolate and the subordinates must maintain its integrity. As Sinha observes "They must not retort to seniors even when the latter is wrong, must not lose temper overtly, must not smoke or drink alcohol in front of him, must not behave that amounts to undermining his authority, must not call him by his first name or so on."[57] Consistent with this, a project manager of a British/Indian outsourcing team noticed that the Indians were willing to accept incorrect orders because they were unwilling to challenge their superiors.[58] In a similar vein, a manual prepared by the Canadian Development Agency for Canadians seeking to do business in India makes the observation that the "Sir Culture" is deeply ingrained in the Indian society.[59]

Although there is no question about the collective nature of the Indian self, the collective self goes hand in hand with the individualistic self as well. It is the individualistic self that strives for attaining unity with the *eternal reality* (*Brahman*), and it is the individualistic self that seeks to maximize benefits for one self.[60] Consistent with this, Roland has argued that Indians possess "a highly private self where all kinds of thoughts, feelings, and fantasies are kept to oneself but only revealed in a highly contextual way in certain relationships (personal communication, Nandita Chaudhri)."[61] Scholars also maintain that Indians behave in a collectivistic manner when they are interacting with members of the family, but that they behave in an individualistic manner when interacting with non-family members.[62]

Other interesting implications follow. One interesting insight is that the Indians may either use collectivistic behavior to attain individualistic goals, or conversely they may use individualistic behavior to pursue collectivistic goals. This is in addition to the more typical method of either using individualistic behavior to attain individualistic goals or conversely utilizing collectivistic behavior to attain collectivistic goals. The impact of conflicting psychological impulses on Indian behavior is well noted by Gupta who writes "Due to their more accessible private self Indians are more likely to engage in cribbing, blaming, gossiping and rumor mongering, frittering away their energies in non-productive form which may even have an anti-productivity ripple effect."[63]

The fact that Indians possess both an individualistic as well as a collectivistic self has a number of different implications. Perhaps the first point to make is that because of the existence of both of these selves Indians display a high degree of "*behavioral flexibility.*" This trait, although not without its drawbacks, is particularly useful in the global environment where the manager is confronted with a wide range of different situations and must adapt to them. The notion that Indian managers demonstrate this flexibility is well illustrated in a comment made by R. Gopalakrishnan, a manager at Hindustan Lever. As he points out "I find that in the US, 'Asian' means Far Eastern and Indians are not even considered Asian! Americans see the Far Eastern manager as polite, sensitive, and team oriented, whereas the Indian leader-manager is seen as direct, aggressive, and individualistic."[64] Interestingly enough, global companies are now actively seeking to recruit Indian managers for managing their international operations.

For example, at the time of writing, the Boston-based footwear company Reebok has hired Muktesh Pant to be its Chief Marketing Officer for Reebok worldwide while simultaneously transferring Reebok's Indian marketing manager, Harpreet Singh Thind as the Marketing Director for the company's regional offices in Hong Kong.[65]

Second, the existence of these different selves would also imply that while at first, the Indians may be reluctant to deal with conflict, the conflict in the Indian workplace context *cannot be indefinitely contained.* This, again, has both positive as well as negative connotations. On the upside, the willingness to deal with conflict may be viewed as positive because by dealing with conflict you *acknowledge a willingness to deal with problems.* The downside, of course is, that if the conflicts are not managed well the situation can become very destructive. A third and a related implication is that in the Indian work setting, *transparency* may be difficult to attain and maintain with a lack of transparency clearly impeding the development of an optimal organizational culture.

In an Indo-American joint venture in the telecommunications sector, a lack of transparency was perceived by the employees to be a problem, notwithstanding the fact that transparency was one of the core beliefs that the top management had sought to instill in the joint venture.[66] Some other interesting examples in this regard are provided by Sinha in his study of multinational joint ventures in India. One of his cases involved the subsidiary of a Swedish company operating in India. The firm had acquired a number of Indian companies to strengthen its position in the Indian market. The managing director of the company was an Indian who had been headhunted from an American company. As Sinha points out "Shekharan and his team had the reputation of enforcing American style of forceful and achievement oriented management."[67] Consistent with the professed value system Shekharan fired a branch manager whose performance was not acceptable and likewise got rid of a junior manager who went for hair cut during office hours! But at the very same time, as Sinha notes, "a branch manager, who was fired for indulging in unethical business practices, dubious money transactions, womanizing, and drinking during office hours was reinstalled only after three months."[68]

The Paradox of Spiritualism and This-Worldly Orientation

One of the major themes in Indian philosophical thought revolves around the illusory nature of the phenomenal or the material world. As Laungani points out "The ultimate purpose of human existence is to transcend one's illusory physical existence, renounce the world of material aspirations, and attain a heightened state of spiritual awareness" (Radhakrishnan, 1923/1989; Zimmer, 1951/1989).[69] This search for the ultimate bliss is without question likely to affect individuals' attitudes toward money, their dedication toward work, and/or their ability to withstand frustration stemming from material unfulfillment. As Gopalan and Rivera point out "Consequently, over the centuries, not much emphasis was placed on social, technological, and economic progress in India to satisfy human needs and wants, as the bulk of attention was focused on 'after life.' "[70]

How true is this statement in modern-day India, and especially after 1991 when economic reforms were initiated? (Indeed, there are some scholars who even dispute the notion that India was ever characterized by otherworldliness.) A casual observer of modern-day India might be forgiven if he/she were skeptical of the above statement. The rapid growth of the information technology industry in India; the desire among Indian companies to aspire to a world class status; the constant comparison being made by India's elite between India and China, are all suggestive of an alternative mind set, that while not indifferent to spiritual concerns, appears to be equally motivated to engage with the illusory world.

Not to forget the commonplace practice of haggling in the Indian marketplace, which Western expatriates often find it difficult to deal with, or the sometime sharp practices that the Indian trader has often been accused of. Interestingly enough, Shoba Narayan has made the argument that the Indians have a natural inclination to uncover good deals. As she notes "Whether it be telephone calls, or salwar-kameezes, chappals or chapathis, Silicon Valley companies or Bollywood, Indians have the uncanny ability to spot value for money."[71] All of this would seem to imply a mind set that is *cognitively flexible*, in that, the Indian seems to be able to shift from one mode of thinking to another without causing any serious internal dissonance.

What are the implications of cognitive flexibility in this realm? First of all, *cognitive flexibility* suggests that it is not difficult for Indians to pursue both the quest for money as well as spiritual concerns at the same time. A study of Indian business leaders in modern day Chennai came to the conclusion that the business leaders "are not much given either to philosophical abstraction (beyond the basic notions just outlined) or to extensive ritual observance."[72] Hariss describes them as "modern day ascetics" that is, as individuals who work hard but do not exhibit flamboyant behavior. But it is perhaps worth keeping in mind that the younger generation may be somewhat more brazen about acting in a flamboyant manner.

There is, however, no denying the fact that in contemporary India, money is acquiring increasing prominence. With the advent of multinationals in particular, salary levels have risen sharply, and individuals are constantly shopping for better offers. The advent of a consumer-based society, the dynamics of television advertising, and the increasing integration of India in the world economy have all sought to enhance the *quest for a good life*. *Cognitive flexibility* also allows the Indians to pursue each of these options with the maximal effort with none of these options interfering with the other. In other words if Indians are focused on maximizing money they will do so wholeheartedly. Likewise, if their primary focus is on the spiritual quest they will commit to it wholeheartedly. Finally, *cognitive flexibility*, also provides an inbuilt safety mechanism for the individual, in that if the needs at one level are not being fulfilled, the individual can compensate for it by shifting his/her goals. The fundamental point is that *appearances notwithstanding*, Indians are *fully engaged* in this world. If their actions, at times, may be seen to lack vigor or enthusiasm, it is not for any lack of engagement with the world; only that their *mode of engagement* may differ.

Context Sensitivity of Indian Behavior

"I feel that the most difficult thing is that the Indians will tell you one thing, think another, and do a third thing, which is not what a Dane would do."[73] This comment made by a Danish manager highlights the fact that the Indians behave differently in different situations. Although the link between thinking and behavior is imperfect in all cultures, there are differences in the degree to which there is a close association between thought and action.[74] The context-sensitive nature of Indian behavior is shaped by three aspects of the environment, namely, *desh* (place), *kal* (time), and *patra* (person).[75] As Sinha observes "Public places such as at work evoke different norms and values than the private settings such as a family. A crisis like situation allows people to deviate from the code of conduct or to put in extra ordinary performance. Personally related friends, family members, and relatives are trusted and favored while strangers (out group) members are distanced, mistrusted, and discriminated."[76]

A behavior that may be appropriate in one context may be considered inappropriate in another social context. A good example is the comment made by one of the managers in the Indo-American joint venture in the telecommunications sector. "The senior executives," Nagarjuna observed, "present different faces to the organization. They do not speak the same language with all the employees on the basis of what the company believes. They only present their personal views. As a result employees at lower levels get confused."[77]

The context-sensitive behavior of the Indians has a number of different implications. First of all, *context sensitivity* may foster the perception of unpredictability, and in doing so, it obviously makes it more difficult to develop trust among the actors. Second, *context sensitivity* may impede effective communication. The person may say one thing, but may mean the exact opposite. As Chellah notes, "Since we do not speak up and question things, we end up accepting something even when we are not sure or convinced about it. What is seen as supportive and cooperating behavior in the beginning could soon become an irritating problem for business partners."[78] Third, *context sensitivity*, may make the entire interaction very fluid with no clear cut beginning or ending. In other words, everything may be possible, but by the same token, nothing is possible. Finally, *context sensitivity*, may make the notion of finality irrelevant. It is the immediacy of the situation that counts, and since situations are always evolving, nothing can be set in stone.

The Hindu Belief System and Managerial Behavior

Organizational success is dependent both on how the organization copes with the demands of the external environment, as also on its ability to create a corporate culture that will enable it to function efficiently as well as effectively. In this section we will explore the impact of Hindu beliefs on organizational functioning in the Indian context.

The starting point of the analysis is the recognition that cultural beliefs/values shapes (a) how individuals perceive the world and their mode of engagement with it; (b) their preferred ways of relating or interacting with individuals; and (c) their orientation toward change that is, change desirable. These fundamental orientations in an organizational context are expressed in (a) attitude toward *work*; (b) preferred *leadership style*; (c) approaches to *problem solving*; and (d) and *intra and inter organizational cooperation*. Each of these aspects are elaborated in the following paragraphs.

Attitude toward Work

Scholars have noted that historically work was not valued very highly in the Indian sociocultural milieu.[79] Indeed, as Sinha points out "work is not intrinsically valued in India. There exists a culture of *aram* which roughly means rest and relaxation without [being] preceded by hard and exhausting work. Although there are large regional variations, it is not infrequent to find a large number of people sitting here and doing nothing."[80] The lack of centrality of work in an individual's life may be attributable to a number of different factors. Without doubt, the cultural orientation stressing subjugation to nature as opposed to attaining mastery over it has some role to play. It has also been maintained that in the Indian sociocultural context work was not viewed as an activity essential for individual's survival.[81] The idea that an Indian derives his/her sense of identity more from his/her family than from work has also been made by some.[82] The impact of these cultural influences was perhaps reinforced by the historical legacy of a regulated business environment till 1991, which lessened the need for innovative/creative behavior.

How is the work culture in post liberalization India? There is evidence to suggest that in the new competitive business environment, firms are trying to reinvent and/or reshape their culture to attain higher levels of performance. One good example of an Indian company attempting this rejuvenation is Tata Steel. The company undertook a number of initiatives to attain its goal of becoming a "world class company." It engaged in rightsizing, instituted a performance ethic program, initiated both a process of disinvestment as well as outsourcing, and instituted measures to enhance the overall quality of its products.[83]

The results have truly been impressive. Sinha and Mohanty point out that by 2003 Tata Steel was the least costly steel company in the world.[84] As they note "The most remarkable achievement was Tata Steel's more than 100 percent capacity utilization. Tata Steel imported the best technology from a variety of sources and made it work better."[85] Without a change in the underlying work ethic, it would have been difficult to imagine such a transformation. It is true that even before the restructuring, the company did enjoy a lot of goodwill among its employees due to its familial culture, but while that may be necessary in the Indian cultural context, it is by no means sufficient to either attain or sustain higher levels of performance.

Tata Steel is by no means a unique example. The successes of companies like Ranbaxy or the Reliance group would have been difficult to imagine without some attempt being made on their part to reshape the work milieu. Multinational firms operating in India in the new liberalized environment have also been successful in transforming the work ethic of their Indian employees. In a study of subsidiaries of an American, a Swedish, a Danish, Japanese, and a Korean multinational firm operating in India, Sinha noted that these firms were able to establish a high performance culture in their Indian operations.[86] "Pay for performance" was the motivational principle followed by the multinational firms with the Swedish, the Danish, and the Korean company employing this principle to the greatest degree. The impact of this was reinforced by constant top management attention to work-related issues and by an attempt to inculcate greater self-discipline and developing new management systems and procedures.

Consider, for example, the case of the South Korean subsidiary in India. Vikas Sharma, the Human Resources Vice President of Kimco notes, "Every individual in KIMCO gets a numerical target that he must achieve. There is no escape. Targets are often raised requiring people to stretch themselves a bit. . . . We take good care of our employees, but they must perform and keep improving their performance."[87] The overall implication of these findings seem to be that there is a shift in India from a *soft*-oriented work culture toward either a *technocratic*, or a *work-centric* nurturing culture.[88]

Soft oriented work culture gives precedence to familial obligations over work *technocratic oriented* work culture emphasizes output/performance without adequate concern for an employee's overall well-being while the *work centric* culture seems to encompass both of these concerns. Indeed, it has been maintained that in the Indian cultural context it may well be the *work centric* culture that is the most appropriate. This is because Indians fundamentally view the status of the family at the very least, on par with that of work.[89] The crucial implication of this is that a *work context*, which does not permit an individual to fulfill his/her familial obligations, will not be sufficiently motivating for the Indian employee.

Preferred Leadership Style

As outlined, the Indian culture is one that may be most accurately described as a *vertically collectivistic* one. This characterization has a number of different implications. The first is simply that Indians have a tolerance of, and respect *hierarchy*. As Gopalakrishnan points out "In the Indian milieu, leadership is by personality. It is the magnetism and personal charisma of the top man that is believed to make the difference."[90] This is as true of the family as it is of the work place setting. The acceptance of hierarchy engenders a particular style of interaction between the superior and the subordinate. Under no circumstances can a subordinate criticize or openly question the superior even if the subordinate feels that his/her superior is in the wrong.

Likewise, the superior will not tolerate any criticism that may emanate from his/her subordinate.

Indeed, it is argued, that the Indian not only conforms, but that at times he/she may overconform.[91] Over conformity may produce a "yes" culture in which the subordinate quietly accepts whatever the superior tells him to do. Never mind the implementation. Similarly, it is imperative that norms of protocol be rigidly followed. In a study of State Bank of India, Das points out that "the peculiar culture in the bank required that officers should wear neckties and even jackets, especially in the administrative offices and while in the presence of senior officials. The discomfort this sartorial norm entailed when the weather was warm, or when the air circulation was not satisfactory in the work place, was not particularly relevant when conforming to the behavioral standards expected by the senior officer."[92]

Hierarchical norms are also likely to encourage "dependency seeking" behavior among the subordinates.[93] The implications of dependency are many. First of all, dependency places premium on *vertical relationships* as opposed to *horizontal ones*. In other words, while hierarchical relationships are accepted and norms of behavior understood, such norms do not exist in *horizontal interactions*. The crucial implication of this is that communication/information flows occur in a *vertical structure* rather than in a *horizontal one*.

In other words, relationships with peers may be difficult to initiate, and even harder to maintain. A second observation is that the Indian subordinate may not undertake any action without the express approval of his/her superior. The subordinate may always seek the superior's attention. While some of the behavior may clearly have instrumental motivations, it may also be designed to attain *reassurance*, that is, that the subordinate is well thought of by his/her superior. As Sinha points out "They need continuous feedback and patting on the back to sustain their efforts what they want to achieve."[94]

Many Indians are in search of what is often described as a *sneh-shradha* relationship. In an idealized form of this relationship, the senior looks after the well-being of those who are dependent upon him, while the juniors demonstrate unconditional loyalty to their benefactors. If, for one reason or the other, the mutual reciprocity does not occur, the person who feels that he has been let down may come to harbor feelings of anger.[95]

An example is the relationship that had developed between Jahawarlal Nehru, the first prime minister of India, and Krishna Menon, the then defence minister under him. Vertzberger points out that Menon was extremely dependent on Nehru and had an "almost hysterical apprehension of losing Nehru's affection and esteem."[96] The idea of making oneself dependent on one's superiors has a long tradition in Indian history. Sinha notes that "The genesis of the behavioral strategy of making oneself totally helpless dependent on a more powerful person so that the latter will be morally obliged to take care of the former goes back to the Vedic period where the devotional approach was aimed to get the blessings of gods and goddesses."[97] Indeed, the idea of total dependence is well illustrated in the *guru–shishya* relationship that is so characteristic of the Indian culture. This is a relationship characterized by total dedication on part of the *shisya* (student) to the *guru* (teacher) and implies an unwavering faith in the teacher.[98]

While from a Western perspective, the idea of dependency is often viewed in negative terms, from an Indian perspective, the theme of dependency is not only *natural* but also *invigorating*, in that it can be used to redirect the energy of the subordinates in positive ways. A good example of a positive effect is found in the concept of "*nurturant leadership*" that has been developed by Sinha.[99] According to Sinha, the leader in India has to not only induce the subordinate to work hard to accomplish the stated goals, but must also be sensitive to the employee's familial needs. Indeed, if a leader is able to accomplish this, he will not only get the employee to commit himself to the task, but perhaps even more importantly, the employee will leave no stone unturned to fulfill the task.

What is important here is the recognition that the commitment shown by the Indian employee is *personal* rather than *organizational*. It is also more *affective* rather than *instrumental*. A good example of *nurturant leadership* style in action is provided by the case of Tata Steel. Russi Mody, who was the former Chairman and Managing Director of the company, gave the following advice "Given a choice being between results oriented, rules oriented, or people oriented, choose the last one; and the rest will fall in line automatically."[100]

The ability to cultivate *dependency relationships* with Indian subordinates, is therefore, one of the key challenges confronting a Western expatriate manager. This is not likely to be easy for the idea of *dependency* is very much at variance with the Western cultural tradition that values *autonomy, independence*, and *contractual relationships*. It would be fair to say that the cultivation of dependency relationships require frequent socialization with subordinates in both task and non-task related situations and this may not be very easy for the Western expatriate manager who may wish to draw a line between work and non-work activities.

Similarly, the cultivation of dependency relationships requires a high degree of *non verbal sensitivity*, in that, the Western manager must be able to discern the intentions underlying the communication of his Indian subordinates who may not express their feelings very openly. Insofar as a Western manager lack this competence, his ability to develop such a relationship will most certainly be impaired. While it would be fair to say that the Western expatriate manager may not be held to the same standard as the Indian manager by his subordinates, it would be fair to say that the Indian subordinates would certainly be *disappointed* if the Western expatriate makes little attempt to cultivate a dependency relationship. The study by Sinha about multinationals operations in India did note that while the Indians did perceive the Western expatriates in positive terms, they did feel that *personal touch* was missing.[101]

Approaches to Problem Solving

Gosling and Mintzberg have argued that there are five kinds of managerial mind-sets, namely, the *reflective*, the *analytical*, the *worldly*, the *collaborative*, and the *action mind* set.[102] Managers everywhere are faced with the fundamental imperative of finding the right balance between *action* and *reflection*, and as they point out "Every manager has to find a way to combine these two mind-sets—to function at a point where reflective thinking meets practical doing."[103]

The reflective mind-set highlights the importance of a thoughtful assessment of past experiences; the analytical mind-set encourages a comprehensive approach to decision-making, that is, an approach which seeks to analyze a decision from as many vantage points as possible; the worldly mind set encourages an approach drawing on insights from different cultures; the collaborative mind-set is concerned with building and maintaining relationships; while the action mind-set is focused on initiating change as and when necessary. As they point out, not all managers are likely to possess all of these mind-sets, with different managers having a predilection or preference for one over the others.

This distinction has been drawn because it provides a convenient way for discerning alternative ways by which managers deal with problems. The reflective manager will focus on learning; the analytical manager on making the best possible decision; the worldly manager will draw inspiration from goings on in the world to make decisions; the collaborative manager will focus on relationships, while the action-oriented manager will be preoccupied with constant change. Given the Indian cultural proclivities outlined earlier, what kind of mind set is *likely* to be most characteristic of the Indian manager?

The point has been made earlier that the Indians have an "idealistic mode of thinking" that is, they have a tendency to strive to attain a *mythical ideal.* The search for the *mythical ideal* is grounded in a very well-developed set of analytical abilities, which has led them to perfect the art of analyzing problems. Indians have a highly developed capacity for abstract and critical thinking, which in its most extreme form, may lead to fantasizing.[104] Information search is often extensive, and the information is often subject to critical scrutiny, with the goal of trying to control or minimize error variance to the maximum degree. Consider, for example, the remark made by a Danish manager in his interactions with the Indians:

> When you start negotiating they will never accept your proposal, and they will try to squeeze as much as possible. They will negotiate for weeks trying to get the best deal. And eventually you get so tired of negotiating for the last 5% that you eventually agree to their price. But then he will return to himself and ask himself what is wrong, as he has already accepted my proposal. So he starts squeezing again, so it's very difficult.[105]

This is a mind-set characterized by high ideals and it follows, naturally enough, that an idealistic mind does not easily admit compromise for the fundamental reason that the search for truth *is an absolute given.* In this cognitive orientation, an alternative perspective that focuses on *harmony* is unsustainable.[106] It is also worthwhile noting that it is easier to sustain this position when, *time* and/or *outcome* pressures are viewed as not constraining.

Indeed as Kumar notes "while Indians may be relatively quick in setting up excessively high imaginary ideals that they would like to realize, they are not troubled by their failure to realize them."[107] In intellectual pursuits, there is no question, that this mind-set is without doubt an invaluable asset. In the day-to-day world of commercial transactions this *mind-set* may either yield *exceptional results* or, at the other extreme, may yield *few successes.* In any event, we would surmise that the *analytical* and perhaps, to a lesser degree, the *reflective mind-set* may be most characteristic of the Indian manager. The one crucial implication of this is that while the Indian managers may be exceptionally good in *formulating strategy,* they may be somewhat weaker in *implementing strategy.*

Intra- and Inter-Organizational Cooperation

If there is one facet of Indian behavior on which there is near or near universal unanimity, it is the fact that Indians are not team players.[108] While this may be true of the individualistic Europeans as well as the Americans for whom cooperation is not necessarily easy, it is the presence of *anarchical individualism* that makes cooperative behavior so much of a rarity in India.[109] *Anarchical individualism* reflects a pattern of interaction among individuals in which cooperative behavior is either minimal or a rarity. Individuals may not share information, may discount the validity or reliability of information that is being given to them by others, and/or launch dysfunctional personal attacks against their colleagues with whom they share an adversarial relationship.

In a study of the Indo-American telecommunications joint venture, Panda and Gupta note that jealousy had led to "information hoarding" among employees.[110] This naturally had a detrimental impact on organizational functioning. Similarly a Danish business consultant, who had been living in India for eight years, noted "Teamwork in India is close to impossible. Cooperation between individuals is possible, but it is a real problem with teams, as Indians don't pull together as part of a team. . . . They are not able to agree so how can they work together towards some set target."[111] The study of multinationals operating in India that was conducted by Sinha also noted the difficulty of intra organizational cooperation, in at least some ventures. An example is the case of a Swedish subsidiary in India. Shekharan, the Managing Director of Swedish Home Care International in India, noted that "There are China walls between the groups of managers still carrying the hang over effects from their previous companies and there are power centers that prevent us from having synergy."[112]

One would surmise that the *context-sensitive* patterns of Indian behavior may make the resolution of this problem a little more challenging, in that, it is only by altering the *context* within which the Indians are interacting that a solution may be found. However, reshaping the *context* may require subtlety and nuances that are challenging not only for the Western expatriate but also for the Indian manager, as Panda and Gupta demonstrate in their study of the Indo-U.S. telecommunications joint venture.

We began this chapter by making the observation that bridging cultural differences is essential to create synergy, but that such *bridging*, is neither easy nor inevitable. Therefore it is absolutely vital for the Western expatriate to make a sincere attempt in understanding Indian *thinking* as well as *behavioral* patterns. The Indian mind, as noted in the introduction is closer to the Western mind than it is to the East Asian mind and the discussion in this chapter reinforces that message. The Indian mind also partakes of Asian sensibilities surrounding the concept of the *family*, although it is fair to say that even the Indian *family* is in many respects highly *individualized.*

It is, perhaps in this sense, that the Indian culture is a *complex mosaic* that is both *teasing* and *inviting*, in that it necessitates the Western expatriate to expand his/her horizons. This expansion is the essential first step in *navigating the cultural divide*. It is further discussed in our last chapter where the cross-cultural competencies that are essential for functioning in the Indian environment are examined.

Chapter Five
Understanding India

Anything you can say about India, the opposite is also true!

Interview with Shashi Tharoor, UN Under Secretary, *Tufts Magazine*

How do you try and explain India in a single chapter? Here is a country of more than a billion people, with 18 major languages, 1,600 minor languages and dialects, umpteen castes and sub castes, 50 or so recognized tribes, and 6 ethnic groups. India is the world's largest producer of milk, has the largest number of post offices, the world's largest railway network, the second largest pool of technically trained manpower, the largest number of students graduating from universities every year and not forgetting, the world's largest democracy, which can proudly boast of a fully electronic voting system developed totally indigenously.

India is the country of the Taj Mahal, the famous Mughal Gardens, and many other grand buildings, temples, and monuments and yet, there are clear signs of urban decay. Home to, or the origin of, some of the brightest and richest in the world, and yet there is, outside of main metropolitan areas, unmistakable poverty, lack of basic healthcare, and a creaking infrastructure. All this overseen by an over arching bureaucratic system now much refined and perfected from the archaic framework inherited from the British colonizers. How then does one provide a capsule of an explanation?

Pavan Varma, the famous Indian diplomat and author, in the preface to his recent best selling book, *Being Indian*,[1] writes, "India is a difficult country to characterize, and Indians not easy to define, especially today, when they are in transition, emerging from the shadows of history into the glare of a globalizing world. This book is an attempt to try and understand who we really are, in the context of the past, and the framework of the future. The task is fraught with dangers. India is too big and too diverse to allow for convenient cover all labels. To every generalization there is a notable exception. For every similarity there is a notable exception. For every similarity there is a significant difference."

Shashi Tharoor further anguishes,[2]

> What is the due to understanding a country rife with despair and disrepair, which nonetheless moved a Mughal Emperor to claim, "If on Earth there be paradise or bliss, it is this, it is this, it is this?" How does one gauge a culture, which elevated non violence to an effective moral principle, but whose freedom was born in blood and whose

> independence still soaks in it? How can one portray the present, let alone the future of an ageless civilization that is the birthplace of four major religions, a dozen different traditions of classical dance, eighty five political parties and three hundred ways of cooking the potato? The short answer is that it can't be done, at least to everyone's satisfaction.

In one of the halls of the very famous Indian academic institution, The Indian Institute of Science hangs a large black and white photograph of India's first successful space rocket being hauled to its launching pad by a bullock cart. Nothing fancy like NASA's facilities in Cape Canaveral or in Houston or even those of the Russians at Baikonur. This, more than anything else exemplifies the contradiction that is India. Here is a country with a space program budget of well under $500 million, a fraction of what the average large U.S. Corporation spends on normal R&D, yet India is able to design, develop, fabricate, and test its own space launch vehicles, including geostationary ones, as well as highly sophisticated payloads, and with a moon mission now on the cards. All this without the help of any other country or recourse to the organized "stealing" of scientific secrets as some other large countries have allegedly done. And yet, the first rocket gets transported to a launch pad on a bullock cart and it worked.

Given that India and Indians are so full of contradictions, this chapter can only make an attempt, howsoever feeble, at highlighting and explaining in as simplistic a manner as possible, just a few of the more interesting aspects of life in India, that managers and businessmen from overseas are likely to encounter. For a more detailed analysis of *Being Indian*, perhaps Pavan Varma's book[3] of that title would be recommended reading.

Chapter Two gave a background of the Indian caste system and its impact on the business sphere. Chapter four discussed some other cultural issues and their impact on Indian managerial behavior. A brief look at the nature of Hinduism, and the core doctrines of the Hindu philosophical system has been studied. The traditional hierarchical system that prevails in India as also the "collectivistic" and context sensitivity nature of Indian culture has been examined. This chapter looks at the more practical and day-to-day issues that Western managers operating in India, should be aware of.

Concept of Time

Ever so often in India, Western managers, and even Westernized Indian managers, to their great distress, are confronted with situations in which work or deliveries promised at specified times and dates just do not materialize. Common courtesies apart, in a modern world increasingly adapting to "just in time" delivery situations, this failure to adhere to time schedules can be quite traumatic. Indian Standard Time (IST) gets transformed into "Indian Stretchable Time!"

Well, blame it all on the hidebound Western concept of time as propounded by Augustine and, as explained by Stephen Hawking in his masterly *A Brief History of Time*. According to Augustine, there are two competing types of time—The Christian "Linear" and the Pagan "Cyclic." The Pagan cyclic time is deemed contrary to "free will" that is required for rewarding and punishing individuals. Hawking stipulates that free will is essential for the philosophy of science, which in turn justifies modern science.

Cyclic time, however, with reincarnation manifestations of "life after death" (the cycle of *Samsara*), and the possible ultimate attainment of *Nirvana* (exiting the rebirth cycle), based on human conduct in life before death, and involving a belief in "equity," was totally unacceptable to the ancient Christian Church. This was especially true of the Lutherans with their "time is money" philosophy developed at a time when their own life patterns were transforming from the ancient agricultural societies with traditional cyclic patterns. Further, the great scientist, Sir Isaac Newton, influenced by his own personal theological bent, was a great proponent of linear time and its implications on physics. This provided the Church with the scientific authority to regulate human behavior through time beliefs. Newton's thinking was for many years the foundation of the then "scientific" approach to time until these very concepts were so comprehensively shaken by Einstein's Theory of Relativity.

Hinduism, however, has little to do with the linear concept of time and the linear nature of life, where everything has a beginning, an interim, and an end. Hinduism as a philosophy views time in a cosmic perspective. According to Hindu belief, the process of creation moves in cycles and each cycle has four epochs of time (each ranging from 2,500 to 10,000 or so human years, depending on different philosophical schools), which follows an earlier era, and so the cycles continue. Thus for Hindus, time, space, and causation are only mental processes in which time is an illusion created by the human mind, while in reality both past and future are both simultaneously present in a cosmic void. Such a concept of time "cyclicity" thus provides for a social organization with an emphasis on equity, spontaneity, and harmony.

While this philosophical basis of cyclical time may provide some explanation of the commonly perceived Indian disregard for "Secular time," it is very difficult to provide satisfactory explanations to the paradox of Indians being extremely punctual and very precise about "Religious time." Religious times are those related to specific rituals and other actions or avoidance of actions, based upon highly precise time calculations based on calendars, planetary configurations, phases of the sun and the moon, and other factors stipulated in religious tracts.

Dates and timings of weddings and other important events are fixed with great precision on the basis of "religious time." Important events, meetings, functions, shopping and other activities must be avoided during specific times of each day termed *Rahukala*. Leading newspapers daily publish these times calculated with great precision. Almanacs provide these calculations for longer periods of time. A former prime minister of India refused to file his electoral nomination papers at the designated time because of *Rahukala*. Recently, a noted Hindu Seer, allegedly involved in criminal cases, requested the judge not to pass an order on his bail petition during the *Rahukala* period of the day. Unfortunately for the Seer, the judge did pronounce a negative order during that period.

Rahukala is associated with the mythical planet "Rahu" (the seizer) and is believed to be the cause of eclipses. Mythology has it that Rahu was a mischievous demon who was decapitated by the God Vishnu at the behest of the sun and the moon. It is further believed that the decapitated Rahu roams the heavens trying to devour the sun and the moon (and hence the eclipses), and to spread mayhem and evil all around. The negative effects of Rahu are said to be at a peak during certain periods of the day termed as *Rahukala*. Those unfortunately born during these periods, are perceived to be doomed to live without peace, money, and general well-being.

Just as there are inappropriate times for activities, including a whole fortnight in a year, which is deemed inauspicious for any shopping (on account of remembrance of ancestors), there are highly auspicious dates and times to perform ceremonies and celebrations. These dates and times calculated with great precision by priests, using convoluted astrological methodology, determine, for example, the peak wedding season. On the most auspicious dates during this season, literally hundreds of thousands of marriages take place countrywide.

Admittedly, such precise calculations of auspicious or inauspicious times are not based on Judeo-Christian linear time concepts, as they do vary from day to day and year to year. Yet, the paradox of conformity to precise religious times as against a disdain of a nebulous cosmic secular time needs to be explained. The answer, perhaps, lies in the fear of retribution for non-conformance to religious norms and requirements, and hence the danger of being stuck in *Samsara*, the cycle of rebirth, possibly as a lower life form, next time around.

"Jugaad"—The Indian Penchant for Improvising

"Jugaad" is a colloquial word in the Hindi language that means a resource, connections, special applications, or a "trick" to use them in an unconventional way. Essentially therefore, implying that the "ends" *must* be achieved, and, that the "ends" justify the "means."

The story, possibly apocryphal, is told that when a Japanese automobile major was planning to establish India's first modern car manufacturing unit, they sent to India a team of specialists to find out the skill levels and facilities to repair and service cars around the country. Now this was a time when India only manufactured a small number of the old model Ambassador (derived from the old British Morris Oxford Car) and Fiat cars, and some old, vintage, imported cars. Waiting lists for locally manufactured cars ran into years. Proper supply chains for spare parts were almost nonexistent.

Yet, every repair and service organization, irrespective of size, the Japanese team spoke with, said that notwithstanding shortages of parts, lack of proper service equipment, deficiencies in infrastructure, they had no problem in repairing not only locally made cars but also the aging imported cars for which no spare parts were available. On being questioned by the incredulous but impressed Japanese about how this was possible, the inevitable response was, "by the use of 'Jugaad.' " Glowing tales of this "new technology" that the Indians had developed were sent back to Japan.

Indian car mechanics, mostly without formal training, were able to contrive or locally fabricate parts or make adaptations and in some cases, even use handmade bits and pieces, glues and epoxies, to ensure that the vehicles were back on the road. This is what Pavan Varma[4] calls "creative improvisation" in a resource starved situation. Further, it is "a tool to somehow find a solution, ingenuity, a refusal to accept defeat, initiative, quick thinking, cunning, resolve, and all of the above."

Jugaad, is therefore the Indian penchant for seeking solutions "outside of the book," implying a very high degree of thinking out of the box and a disdain of what the developed and resource rich countries would say, established norms, methods, and conventions. This "quick fix" inventive and innovative approach, uniquely and at times irritatingly Indian, finds manifestations in activities across the board, be it manufacturing, construction, the service industry, defense, and even electronics and the IT sector. A few examples are listed below.

In the 1980s, the United States turned down India's request for purchase of Cray Supercomputers desperately required for weather and monsoon studies, on the grounds that these supercomputers could find applications in the defense and space sectors. Indian engineers and scientists responded to this challenge by stringing together massively parallel processing computing modules and writing appropriate software to create "PARAM," a locally made supercomputer. And this within three years and a miniscule budget of $10 million!

In an article in the *Times of India*[5] Sudip Talukdar writes that during the 1971 war with Pakistan, "negligible foreign exchange reserves foreclosed buying replacements for defective firing pins, in practically half of the Russian made tanks deployed on the western border. Senior military commanders took a calculated risk in assigning the operations branch of an army division to scout for a local alternative. A nondescript 'rickety old Sikh,' located in the Punjab interiors, agreed to fabricate one. Over months of trials at his lathe workshop, the Sikh perfected a firing pin almost as good as the original. He duplicated hundreds of them at a cost of only 10 percent of the original."

In the rural areas of the some northern states of India, visitors may chance upon the most unusual of all automotive contraptions called the "Maruta" possibly a take off on India's leading automobile company, "Maruti." This vehicle, if it may be called that at all, is sort of manually strung together as part tractor, part trolley, and part bullock cart, with one single gear and operating at only one speed. It works! No vehicle registration or insurance are needed nor are available, yet the contraption does the work of satisfactorily carrying passenger and agricultural produce over bumpy unpaved village tracks.

A few years ago a leading Indian manufacturer of washing machines was shocked beyond belief when their records showed massive sales of their products in the hinterland of the state of Punjab, and in small towns and villages along the main national highways in the north (dotted with small eateries for truckers and motorists). These were not clearly their traditional market targets for sophisticated washing machines, so an investigative team was promptly dispatched to ascertain the cause for this great boom in washing machine sales in places known to be short of running water. To their profound shock, the investigators found that their prized machines were not being used for laundry purposes at all but had been very successfully adapted to produce huge quantities of "Lassi" or buttermilk, the staple drink of the region.

Possibly the best example of Indian Jugaad is the home cooked office lunch (termed "tiffin") delivery or supply chain system in Mumbai, undertaken by a group of some 5,000 individual entrepreneurs, called "Dabbawallas" (meaning, the tiffin carrier delivery men). This operation involves the collection of some 150,000 to 175,000 containers of cooked lunches from individual homes and the subsequent delivery of these to the correct individual recipients at various offices and schools, at precise designated times, all over the city, every single working day. What is so unique about this system is that it is a Six Sigma quality operation implying an efficiency rating of an incredible 99.999999 percent, better than that of any courier or logistics company, and all this by a unique locally developed, innovative system. An achievement hailed by international management experts, chambers of commerce, international media, and also honored by a personal visit by Prince Charles of the United Kingdom.

The containers are picked up from homes between 9 A.M. to 9.30 A.M. by a dabbawalla who is an independent entrepreneur. Each container carries an indelible ink alphanumeric coding (not bar coding) of some ten characters signifying the various transfer and delivery stages, as well as the individuals who are to be involved in the process. The first carrier brings his load of containers up to the nearest suburban commuter train station where a sorting and consolidation of loads brought by other dabbawallas takes place on the basis of stations nearest to delivery points. The sorted loads are then carried forward by a different set of dabbawallas to the designated points at train stations nearest to points of delivery. A further step of sorting and consolidation takes place, this time on the basis of geographical sub areas and clusters of buildings and another set of dabbawallas gets involved in the final delivery. After lunch, the reverse process kicks in and the lunch boxes are returned home for cleaning well before the lunch recipient is back from work. The cost to individual clients works out to between $3 and $6 per month and even after paying off costs, tickets, and association dues, each dabbawalla is reported to be making a decent profit, a feat well beyond that of the modern day logistics companies.

Corruption

"Corruption is not unique to India, it is a global phenomena," so said the former prime minister of India, the late Mrs. Indira Gandhi, in an attempt to mitigate the political fall out arising out of charges of corruption brought against persons close to her in her government. True, there is corruption in many parts of the world, not just in India. True, corruption is not a recent development, but has existed through history, and not just in India. True, the levels and scale of corruption in some parts of the world, including the developed world, have been staggering in comparison to known and proven cases in India. Yet, there is something quite different about corruption in India, that it only very sporadically raises public angst and ire despite the fact that India is consistently placed at the bottom half of the Global Transparency Index.

According to Pavan Varma,[6] "Corruption of course is not unique to India. What is unique is its acceptance, and the 'creative' ways in which it is sustained. Indians do not subscribe to antiseptic definitions of rectitude, as are common in the Scandinavian countries. Their understanding of right and wrong is far more related to efficacy than to absolutist notions of morality." Further, he writes, "Corruption has grown endemically because it is not considered wrong, so long as it yields the desired result."

There are well-known cases of prominent businessmen and industrialists in India who, while being strictly religious and diligently observing all known rituals with regular visits to temples and priests, have had no qualms in indulging in corrupt practices to derive favors and advantages from politicians and bureaucrats, or in short changing the nation of income taxes, sales taxes, and customs duties. There is, of course, the famous case of a former Minister of Telecommunications of the Government of India whose house when searched by the investigative agencies, revealed a stash of staggering numbers of currency notes stuffed in mattresses, garbage bags, pillow cases, and steel trunks. On being proceeded against, humiliated, and dismissed from the Government, this former minister promptly set up a political party of his own and incredibly was re-elected with a thumping majority in the next elections. Clearly, the electors were more impressed by the improvement in the telecommunications infrastructure and other benefits that he had brought about in his constituency and the state than about the probity related to his misdeeds.

What then explains this indulgence in, as well as the permissive attitude of Indians toward hydra headed corruption? Reading ancient Hindu literature confirms that corruption in ancient India was already well-recognized as a major problem. Many references are available, not only in the ancient Hindu texts such as the Vedas but also in India's two great mythological epics, the *Ramayana* and the *Mahabharata.* Many scholars believe that the Hindu attitude to corruption owes its origin to the teachings of the *Brahmanas* which are the scriptures detailing the ritualistic and ceremonial parts of the Vedas. When segregated from the metaphysics of the Vedas, the teachings of the *Brahmanas* with their highly materialistic interpretations, bring about major aberrations particularly with regard to worship for ostentation, social recognition, and even a form of "proxy worship" by giving money and riches to priests.

The *Brahmanas* have many hymns extolling material "well-being," in the form of gold, silver, produce and other riches. Followed in isolation, away from the underlying metaphysics of the teachings of the Vedas, one can very easily interpret that the aim of life is "material prosperity and the pleasures of the body and senses." Little doubt then, with the active connivance and support of many self-seeking and rapacious priests as well as "Godmen" of dubious credentials, a whole culture has built up over generations that has found it highly convenient to accept and follow the easier material path of the Brahmanas while maintaining the dichotomy, and façade, of being pure and religious as required by the underlying Vedic Hindu philosophy.

Mr. N. Vittal, a former Chief Vigilance Commissioner of India, responsible for overseeing the country's anti corruption activities, in a speech[7] to a Rotary District Conference observes that classical Hinduism preaches the concept of tolerance whereby a sinner although having led a life of sin can indeed find redemption by chanting the name of the Lord and seeking appropriate forgiveness. Society at large has also come to accept this. At another level, according to Vittal, "Hinduism with its belief in rebirth, provides individuals with innumerable opportunities to improve. There may be set backs for sins committed but then virtue is also earned." Vittal further states that "as we trace the social roots of corruption in our country, we can identify that this eternal message of tolerance, the sense of forgiveness, the hope held for sinners to come on the right path, probably have also led to the tolerance of a sin like corruption."

The interesting thing about corruption in India is that it flourished in the times of all those who came to rule India. History is full of tales and anecdotes about the corruption of rapacious rulers, bureaucrats, officers, and minions during the Mughal as well as, surprisingly so, British rule. History is unfortunately silent whether this happened due to the tolerant attitude to corruption of the Hindus or was it just plain greed given the somewhat transient probability of the rule of these conquerors and colonizers?

Recently, the British auction firm Christies, auctioned Indian treasures worth some $10 million. These had been spirited away or illegally acquired as gifts by Lord Clive, the hero of the British East India Company. (Please also see chapter one, "India—A Commercial History Perspective"). Clive's corruption became so famous that he had to face a Parliamentary disciplinary probe in London and committed suicide at the age of 49. Lord Warren Hastings, the first British governor general of India was, if anything, worse than Clive. He openly indulged in large-scale corruption, took favors from princes and rich Indians and took away anything that he fancied. Finally, the British government had to order his impeachment. Over the years of British rule, many Indian treasures were systematically spirited away to London not only for personal gain but also as presents for the Monarch. The tale of the famous "Kohinoor" diamond is only too well known to bear repetition here.

By the time India became independent in 1947, corruption in daily life and particularly so in the common person's interaction with the government and bureaucracy. It became significantly worse in the socialistic heydays of the "license-permit" Raj where money and other inducements were asked for and provided, to obtain tightly controlled and hard to get licenses, import permits, foreign exchange, tax concessions, and other permission or favors required to conduct even normal business and trade.

With the growth of Indian politics and the reduction in the overall influence of the ruling Congress party, after the debacle of the war with China in 1962, and Nehru' s failing health, politicians of all parties needed to collect large sums of unaccounted money to be spent on fighting elections, which by then were beginning to become expensive propositions. Bureaucrats at all levels, taking an example from their political masters joined in the act and hence an unholy nexus was created. Corrupt and greedy businessmen and industrialists, happy to obtain political favors for the smooth and unfettered running of their companies were only too happy to oblige. It was only the liberalization of the economy in 1991, which dispensed with a substantial part of the license-permit regime that a substantial reduction in the levels of corruption could be achieved.

However, the rapid transformation and growth of the Indian economy in the post-liberalization period has brought about a new angle to corruption in India. With increased levels of consumerism and the powerful effects of a rapidly growing media, especially cable television, the desire to have the latest, the best, the most expensive of things transcends all aspects of daily life, especially in the metropolitan cities. Wealth and its overt display, has now become an expression of available power and influence. The gratification of the senses is considered of paramount importance. As Vittal[8] states, "Power is never demonstrated in a society unless it is misused. In certain communities, I understand, being as much corrupt as possible and amassing wealth is seen as a 'macho' demonstration of competence."

Cricket—India's Obsession

No chapter on understanding India could ever be complete without a write up on cricket, one of the great legacies bequeathed to the country by the British colonial masters. In many ways, to understand India, somehow one must try and understand cricket and more so, the great Indian obsession with this game in all its manifestations and versions. Any foreigner who can talk cricket with Indians is automatically accorded a different status, as businessmen from the United Kingdom, Australia, New Zealand, and South Africa will readily vouch for.

Anywhere you go in India, from the dry dusty plains of the north, to the greener pastures in the south, the coastal regions of the east and west, you will find people of all ages playing cricket with improvised and make shift kits and accessories, no real playing fields, and with attire of all kinds, including rolled up loin cloths, pajamas, shorts, and what have you. Not quite the classical game played wearing immaculate white shirts and trousers.

Kids play cricket with a little rubber ball, a bunch of lines on a neighbor's wall and any reasonable piece of wood, which can be used to hit the ball. There is even a version of cricket played using hexagonal shaped pencils with appropriate marks on the sides, which can be easily and surreptitiously rolled over during boring school and college classes. In some of the average football sized playing fields of Mumbai, it is not uncommon to see multiple cricket matches being played at the same time, with the players and balls merrily crossing over other games in progress. The story is told about one of India's greatest ever cricket batsmen whose great prowess in playing dead straight was developed in the narrow alleyways where he was brought up in Mumbai. Any error in hitting across would have resulted in serious damage to windows of neighboring houses and flats with clear and contingent consequences.

When the national side is playing even a not so important match, work and classes tend to come to a near standstill. Every television and radio set would usually be tuned on to a live commentary. Even FM radio stations normally playing constant streams of pop music regularly interrupt programs to provide updates. It is pretty common to have television sets in offices showing live matches. In important official meetings, secretaries bring in slips of paper with regular updates of the score. On flights on airlines in India, flight deck crews regularly monitor an ongoing match commentary and provide their passengers with regular updates.

Prior to important cricket matches especially those involving the national side, special prayers are organized and appropriate offerings made at temples and other places of worship around the country. Some die-hard fans undertake fasts and other penance in an effort to ensure the victory of their team. There are also some dedicated cricket temples where sets of cricket gear and the photographs of the team are placed during prayer offerings.

No other activity is as important as the matches played against England or Pakistan or any of the matches in the World Cup of cricket, anywhere in the cricketing world (all of a dozen or so countries). During matches, especially when the one-day version of the game is being played by the home side, the country comes to a virtual standstill. Roads are deserted, there are very few students attending classes, and even India's parliament has been known to have been adjourned for critical cricket matches. Live television broadcasts of scheduled parliamentary proceedings are replaced by cricket commentaries. During a recent extremely crucial match between India and Pakistan, with the Indian side close to a historic first-ever series win over their arch rivals on Pakistani turf, all the security guards, immigration and customs officers at Delhi's Indira Gandhi International Airport were seen huddled around TV sets showing the game live without a thought about opportunities for terrorists, smugglers, or illegal immigrants.

India even conducts diplomacy using cricket. When the recent peace initiative with Pakistan was started, the Indian cricket team was, after many years, allowed to go to Pakistan to play matches. The schedules were very carefully planned with an eye on the ensuing elections to the national parliament. The then prime minister is reported to have then remarked that the captain of the Indian cricket team had the most difficult job in India and not the prime minister. Consequently, the captain and the team were duly briefed on various political and other aspects prior to undertaking the tour. In past tours of Pakistan, a losing Indian cricket captain invariably lost his job and in some cases, silently receded into oblivion, unhonored and unsung.

India is fundamentally not a sports-playing nation and has very little to show for all the money that is spent by the Government of India as well as the private sector on sporting activities. In the recently concluded Athens Olympic games, India bagged a solitary medal (silver) for shooting. The international accounting firm, Price Waterhouse, comes out with a projected medal tally prior to the Olympic games, based on the population and the economic wealth of countries. The only major country that does not conform to this projection is India, in marked contrast to say, China. Price Waterhouse ascribes this anomaly to India's passionate love for cricket to the exclusion of all other sports.

A study on sports in India conducted by "Synovate," a leading global market research firm, found that cricket, cutting across all genders and social classes, is the favorite game to watch on television (93 percent), also the favorite game to watch live on television (74 percent), in addition to being the favorite game to play. The sport viewed next was soccer with a measly 5 percent of viewers. The study further goes on to state that celebrity brand recognition of major Bollywood movie stars and leading cricket players was the same as was the media endorsement fees of top Indian movie stars and cricketers. Even companies from non-cricket playing countries seem to have cottoned on to this. Among the largest advertisers during live television cricket matches are the major Korean white goods companies and most of the successful international automobile manufacturers operating in India. Surely there is a lesson to be learnt here.

It is said that Indians are basically passionate about three things—food, movies, and cricket. While food and movies are easily explainable, the love of a foreigner's game, which has now almost become a religion in the country, needs some understanding and explaining. Food, movies, and even more so, cricket are in fact the major unifying factors in India. The Indian cricket team along with the Indian Armed Forces is possibly the most inclusive "institution" in the country. The cricket side comprises of players from various states, languages, religions as well as different social strata of society.

No scientific explanations have so far been proffered for this obsession and passion for cricket. Perhaps this seeming irrationality is beyond authentic scientific study.

When the British (actually the English) first introduced cricket into India sometime in the eighteenth century, local Indians were principally included in games as sort of ball boys, who would run around, retrieve and return balls hit to various parts of the ground, saving the Colonial masters the effort of doing so in the tropical heat of India.

By the nineteenth century, Indians (usually as teams composed on religious or community affiliation) were allowed to play against the British as well as against each other. The fact that Indians being quick learners were, at times, able to beat their colonial masters at their own game, must have been a major reason for the growth of popularity of the game in the early days. There is even an Oscar-nominated Indian movie based on a supposedly true story set in 1893. In this movie a rural youth with no prior cricketing knowledge, and in reaction to the onerous tax regime imposed by an obnoxious colonial bureaucrat, bets the future of his village on a cricket match against a team comprising of the local British. A rag tag village team cobbled together and coached by a young sympathetic English lass, with dollops of prayers to the local deity, do manage to narrowly beat the bureaucrats.

Many cricketing tales have also been written about a couple of Indians from princely backgrounds, who studied at England's top educational institutions, excelled at the game, played in England's cricket team, and ended up famous, and received great accolades for their delightful performances.

Early in the twentieth century, tales of cricketing prowess of young Indians from very modest backgrounds, one actually starting as a groundsman's helper in the city of Pune, and performing with great distinction against the English in the cities of western India, also spread around the country. The word had gone out. Not only could Indian's beat the English, but were also good enough to play for England itself! The natives could match their colonial masters, another non-violent victory.

Another explanation is also possible. As noted, Indians love local movies with all their intricate and convoluted plots with twists and turns, heroes, villains, heroics, action, and drama, the underdog versus the superior, the noise, both on and off screen. A good Indian movie also has a cast of actors but with opportunities for individuals to stand out as being special. A good cricket match, with the inherently arcane and convoluted set of rules, has all of these attributes barring the on screen music, which can and tends to get provided by those witnessing a match.

Movies and cricket matches, also provide ample opportunities for spectators to loudly exercise their vocal chords either in support of or disparaging the action on offer. Couple all this with the fact that a cricket match, unlike the shorter duration soccer or hockey matches, provides Indians with an opportunity to indulge in their other passion, eating and drinking, while a match is in progress. The geometrical rise in popularity of the game, after the underdog Indian team beat the mighty champions from the West Indies at the World Cup in England in 1983, with a whole lot of dramatic twists and turns, with the heroics of a team with an all "inclusive" representation from across the country, appears to confirm that Indians see cricket as a surrogate, sporting extension and variation of their favorite Indian movies.

Chapter Six
Strategizing Success in India

Not by the templates of globalization, nor by the principle of one-world-one-market can transnationals triumph in India. To win over the country's 1 billion customers, transnationals must understand just how global, and how Indian they must be.

"Business Today," July 7, 1999

With a population of more than a billion people, a large, steady, and rapidly expanding market, abundant natural resources, excellent skilled manpower, science and technology expertise, a thriving private sector, existence of a proper legal framework, a liberalized economic environment, knowledge of the English language, a large English language media presence, India should be, in theory, an easy market to crack. The reputed international management consultants A.T. Kearney in an October 2004 report ranked India as the third most attractive foreign direct investment destination. Yet, while some foreign companies have done extremely well, others have floundered.

Companies like GE, Samsung, LG of Korea, Piaggio, Cadbury, Siemens, ABB, and so on may be cited as examples of successes in India. Yet, comparisons with failures are inevitable. Kentucky Fried Chicken (KFC) in its first coming was a flop in India, but McDonald's and Pizza Hut are successful. Hyundai with its cars has been successful but Daewoo, also from Korea, could not make a go of it. The Korean white goods manufacturers are today the leaders in every segment of their products, yet Sony, although perceived as a good brand with superior products, has recently shut its manufacturing facilities in India. There are many such examples.

An article in the *Business World* of June 1999 had a headline that read, "*Think India to win India*—Why some MNC's have done better than others in the Indian market." Very appropriately put. It is obvious to any analyst of the Indian business scene that companies that could "think Indian" and got their localization strategy right have emerged as clear winners. Companies that possessed powerful brands, technology, and resources, that stuck to the old globalization formula of "One world, One strategy," floundered. India just does not conform to a standard globalized template.

For example, KFC, a powerful international brand backed by huge resources, introduced a standard international formula of fried chicken in India. They unfortunately forgot that India is the home of the extremely delicious battered and spiced

"Tandoori Chicken!" No prior taste trials were done. The product was not localized to Indian tastes and the pricing was considerably higher than that of a good piece of tandoori chicken. No amount of advertising or promotion helped, as Indians just did not like the taste of the product. Worse, KFC forgot that a large majority of Indians are vegetarians and did not provide adequate vegetarian options on their menu. The result was that, shortly after the initial euphoria of a newly introduced international brand died down, there were very few takers for KFC in India. It was only in 2005, many years later, that KFC introduced a 'non chicken' vegetarian platter to its menu.

Contrast the KFC experience with that of McDonald's. In addition to spending considerable time and resource in getting their supply chain right (just as KFC had done), McDonald's put in considerable effort in getting an "Indianized" menu in place with Indian names prefixed with "Mc" or "Mac," prior to launch. The menu, substantially different from their standard international offerings (and not just because of the requirement of substituting the taboo beef with mutton), had the right taste for Indian palates, with adequate options for vegetarians too, and all this at highly competitive prices even when compared with non-branded competing Indian products. Most importantly, responding to local sensitivities, the nonvegetarian, cooking and serving streams were clearly segregated. The results in terms of rapid expansion of outlets around the country speaks for itself.

Similar to this experience was the success of Lee jeans when compared with Levi's. Although Levi's was clearly the better known brand and with Lee's having relatively insignificant brand recognition in India, the latter managed to perform substantially better in the initial years. Levi's launched their products in India at the premium end of the pricing pyramid. The average Indian teenager, the target market, just did not have that kind of money and was reluctant to ask his parents to spend a hefty amount in Indian Rupees to acquire a Levi's # 501 pair of jeans.

Lee on the other hand, entered into a strategic partnership with the Arvind Group, one of the world's largest producers of denim cloth as well as jeans in the economy segment in India. With this partnership, Lee was able to introduce into the Indian market, international standard branded products at price levels that the target customers were willing to pay for a premium product. In a very short period, Lee was able to capture about 49 percent of the market share, leaving Levi's to rethink and rework their India strategy.

It goes without saying that multinational firms must be responsive to the local political, cultural, economic, and social realities if they wish to prosper in that environment. The idea that local responsiveness is important for a multinational firm's effectiveness in the host country environment has now become the conventional wisdom.[1] Often, this gets expressed in the widely quoted phrase "Think globally, but act locally." In common parlance, local responsiveness means adaptability, and as we look at it, adaptability has several dimensions, namely strategic, organizational, and cultural.

Strategic adaptability deals with the effectiveness of the multinational firms in positioning themselves in the Indian market. Organizational adaptability deals with the issue of the structure and processes that the multinational firms have developed to manage their Indian operations, while behavioral adaptability, pertains to how effectively have the expatriate managers adjusted to the local cultural realities. Our starting point is the recognition that a multinational firm must demonstrate adaptability on all of these levels, if it wishes to prosper in the Indian sociocultural milieu. It goes without saying that if the multinational firm has not positioned itself appropriately in the Indian market environment it may not perform very well. That said, even if the firm's strategic adaptability is good, it may be unable to translate a good strategy into good results if it fails to demonstrate organizational and/or behavioral adaptability.

This chapter looks at the level of adaptability exhibited by the multinational firms in the Indian business environment. The impediments to such adaptability are explored and the importance of developing cross-cultural competencies if one is to succeed in the Indian business environment are stressed. In particular, some of the cross-cultural competencies that are vital for succeeding in India and the ways they could be developed are highlighted.

Strategic Adaptability

Lured by the prospects of a large market, many multinational firms, when they first entered India following the economic reforms of 1991, sought to cater to the high end of the market, as we have seen in the case of Levi's. In doing so, they accepted low volumes, for, at times, dubious high margins. As the Economist Intelligence Unit points out, this strategy was replicated by companies in just about every industry.[2] A good example of this strategy was visible in the automotive sector in which multinational firms sought to ignore the small car market, which ironically, accounts for 85 percent of the market.[3] It was, therefore, not surprising that many of these firms failed to sell a large volume of cars. It was not till Hyundai attained success in the small car market that other firms were forced to rethink their strategies.

If an exclusive focus on the high end of the market was unwise, so was a policy of relying on a multi-brand strategy.[4] A good example of this is the experience of the Swedish company, Electrolux in India. The company entered India in 1995 and in the first few years following its entry the company decided to pursue a multi-brand strategy. Although this strategy had succeeded in other markets, it did not survive the test of time in India. The company's repeated attempt at altering its multi-brand strategy reportedly made things worse. As one of Electrolux's competitor has noted "In the durables market, you need good value and a trusted name—that's all. You may be a global giant, but in India, you need to have more than just sophistication."[5]

Other examples are illustrative of this theory. When Daimler, the German auto maker entered India in 1994 in a joint venture with the Indian company Telco, it assumed that it would be able to sell about 10,000 cars per year. In reality, the company was selling only about 1,000 cars per year. This discrepancy in assessment led to huge losses and by 1999 the company had lost about US$73.31 million, which was nearly half its equity base![6] One of the reasons for the inaccurate assessment was a lack of good understanding about customer motivation. As noted "Once a car in the price range of Mercedes-Benz is sold to a family, which is always to the top most of the family, no further cars can usually be sold to that family because the hierarchy will not allow that. The same car cannot be bought by people at different levels in the hierarchy, more so when Mercedes is considered as a symbol of power and status."[7]

Another notable example is that of Nike, a leader in sportswear. Although the company has a 40 percent share in the U.S. market, it has not been successful in translating its strengths in the United States to the Indian market.[8] Analysts note that there are several reasons for this failure. First, the company was not sufficiently aggressive in penetrating the Indian market. Its marketing budget was not that high, it utilized standardized promotions using the likes of Michael Jordan who was not that well known in India, and moreover, the company was relatively slow in introducing the Indian market to the latest designs.[9]

Although there are some stories highlighting the difficulties faced by multinational firms in India, there are many success stories too. One of the most notable success stories, as noted earlier, is that of the Korean "chaebols" who have come to dominate the market for consumer durable goods such as color TVs, washing machines, and refrigerators in India.[10] They entered India in the mid-1990s and it was expected that companies such as Samsung, Hyundai, and LG would have combined sales of US$3 billion with these sales being accompanied by handsome profits.[11] What did the Koreans do to be so successful? Analysts note that a number of factors have worked in favor of the Korean companies. First, unlike many Western companies, they did not rely excessively on their preexisting brand reputation in formulating a strategy for the Indian market.[12] Through customer surveys they were quick to realize that Korean products were not considered top quality by the Indian customer and the only way to change this perception was to do something dramatic. The introduction of their latest products in the Indian market was one notable way of changing this perception. This was supplemented by a very aggressive advertising campaign, which led the Koreans to outspend their competitors.[13] A policy of indigenization, coupled with aggressive attempts to expand the distribution chain, is the other factor that has led LG, in particular, to acquire a commanding presence in the country. As the managing director of LG in India notes, "Which other company has this kind of commitment in India. We are there in the remotest corners of the country. We have warehouses all over so that there is quick movement of goods."[14]

One American company that is doing well in India is the Michigan-based Amway Corporation. Amway is a US$6.2 billion company whose competitive strength lies in multilevel marketing. The underlying philosophy of the company is to create a network of independent business owners who will sell Amway's products. The company entered India in 1995 but it was not until 1998 that the company began operating in India in any meaningful way. The company has entered into contract manufacturing deals and has also increased the number of offices from five at inception to twenty-six currently.[15] The total revenue of the company has doubled within a year, rising to about 2,000 million rupees from 1,000 million rupees, the previous year.[16] What factors have allowed Amway to prosper from inception unlike its other compatriots from North America and Europe? Perhaps the most compelling explanation for the divergent performance of Amway vis-à-vis its competitors comes from a quote by William Pinckney, the Managing Director of the company. As he notes, "A lot of companies that were bigger than Amway did not do well here simply because they came in with a lot of assumptions. They did not take time out to personally go out into the market and learn. You can't learn about India by reading up stuff. You can't spend money alone. You have to interact, learn, and adapt to the market. We did that."[17] In a similar vein, Dinesh Keskar, President of Aircraft Trading at Boeing notes, "But every MNC has to remember that *India* is a place for long term investment, not an initiative that you do for a year and expect instant returns. . . . This logic extends to all industries, not just airlines. In every case you have to invest and be patient. Patience is a great requirement for *doing business in India*."[18]

If the accuracy of assumptions is an important factor in shaping success in India, why is it the case that many global players have been found wanting in their approach to the Indian market? First, in a rush to gain the first mover advantage, many companies got carried away by the pressures of the situation, and probably did not do a systematic examination of the Indian environment as was warranted. Second, their past successes elsewhere led them to be overconfident and while lip service may have been paid to the idea "Think global, but act locally," they probably never acted on this in a culturally informed way. Many companies were also probably looking for immediate or short-term returns and within this calculus, local adaptation did not play a central role. Adaptation is without question costly and the time frame for returns is medium to long term. Many companies also probably got mesmerized by the vastness of the Indian middle class and assumed that the Indian middle class was very much like the middle class in Western countries, both in terms of tastes as well as income.

What steps can multinational firms undertake to ensure a more accurate assessment of the market characteristics in India? The following initiatives will help the multinationals get a more realistic/accurate assessment of the Indian market conditions.

(a) Double-Check Your Market Data

Analysts point out that in the Indian environment accurate statistics are often hard to come by.[19] This makes an accurate assessment of the market size somewhat difficult and may indeed be the reason why some global companies have failed to attain the expected level of success in India. Indeed, as Ramachander points out, "The Indian market place is just getting too complex and confusing for any one manufacturer to unravel it all. It seems that India is a federation of regional markets which are homogenized only in the managers mind."[20] The implication of this is that the growing complexity of the Indian market requires the multinationals to develop "well nuanced" strategies for coping with this complexity. They need to have a good understanding of the target segment that they are catering to and the underlying motivations of the consumers within that target segment. As Harmeet S. Pental, Managing Director, Avon Beauty Products noted, "It takes time to understand the Indian market."[21]

(b) Recognize that Personal Interactions with Customers and Distributors are Absolutely Vital in Gaining Relevant Information

As the Korean company LG's Kim noted, "US company do office marketing, we do feet marketing."[22] The implications of this statement are profound. Essentially, what the Koreans have been doing is to engage in extensive personal interactions with their distributors throughout the country. The Korean company is not alone in this regard. Hindustan Lever requires its executives to spend a minimum of eight weeks in the Indian villages to get a better understanding of the mind-set of the Indian consumer.[23]

Personal interactions are useful in the Indian market environment for a number of different reasons. First, given the emphasis on relationships in the Indian sociocultural environment, an attempt to foster relationships will most certainly elicit the commitment of the Indian party. Further, if these relationships are nurtured, a more enduring loyalty may also be created and that is surely advantageous for the multinationals. It is also worth noting that the Indian respondents often do not give the most accurate responses to paper and pencil measures.[24] The major implication is that that relationships are vital for getting the most accurate information. Clearly, these relationships do not develop overnight. Furthermore, given the vastness of the country, the development of relationships will require a significant investment of time and money. That said, the benefits of such relationships are likely to be enduring.

(c) Be Open to Information that may Contradict Your Preconceived Assumptions

It is important that multinational managers recognize that while they, individually, and their companies collectively, may have been successful in other markets, success in one market does not necessarily guarantee success in another market. Success, and repeated success, often makes managers overconfident and they may be reluctant to listen to information that contradicts their deeply held beliefs. It is therefore essential that multinational managers value information that may not be in conformity with their preconceived notions. In the hierarchical culture of India an avoidance of this bias may be further complicated by the fact that your Indian subordinates may not be willing to contradict you, even if they do not agree with your stance on a particular issue. If anything, this makes it even more imperative, that as a manager you are more attuned to the environment in which you are operating.

There is the famous case of an international brand leader in shaving razor blades, which set up operations in India for the compact twin-bladed razor, which was such a success worldwide. Now, this razor works fine internationally and gives a very high quality performance. But the simple fact that constant running water at reasonable pressures to clean the interstitial space between the blades after shaving was not available at that time, to a large segment of potential users in India seemed to have escaped the attention of this multinational, with disastrous effect.

Organizational Adaptability

If strategic adaptability is essential for ensuring that the multinational firm is well aligned with its external environment, organizational adaptability ensures that the firm is able to effectively execute its desired strategy. Organizational adaptation is primarily dependent on three sets of factors namely (a) the composition of the top management team in the Indian organizational unit; (b) the emergent corporate culture in the local organization; and (c) the degree to which there is effective coordination between the parent firm and the Indian subsidiary or joint venture, as the case may be. It must also be emphasized that the dimension of adaptability is not a static dimension; as the environment changes so must the different levers essential for ensuring adaptability.

(a) Composition of the Top Management Team

Examples of flawed strategies relating to senior management personnel also abound. Several of the transnational companies that failed in India, especially those from Continental Europe that did not usually have the luxury (unlike many U.S. and U.K.

companies) of the availability of expatriate Indians among their own management cadres, brought into the Indian entity extremely expensive managers from their existing units. In most cases these managers had no experience of international management and worse, were quite devoid of the requisite cross-cultural skills.

Management of Indian enterprises requires some exceptional skills including being able to develop relationships with and tackle prickly unionized labor, petty bureaucrats and people in the supply and distribution chains. Not forgetting, of course, the need for extraordinary crisis management skills given the somewhat underdeveloped nature of infrastructure available in most Indian towns. With a background of operating at management levels of a "well and smooth running ship" many of the foreign expatriate managers have been found severely wanting.

There is the story of an expatriate manager in a Scandinavian controlled entity in India who could not handle a situation where several of his Indian colleagues were technically and managerially far superior to him although being paid a fraction of his own salary. In his home base he had never attended a board meeting let alone saddled with fiduciary responsibilities and ensuring compliance under the company and labor laws of the country. In a short period this manager decided that a substantial part of his working day was better spent in the bar of a leading city hotel.

There are of course great success stories of foreign expatriate managers in India, but one theme runs through all these tales. The success of these managers can inevitably be linked to their having been able to imbibe India and its culture in all its manifestations, and most important of all, they were able to "Think Indian!"

Should then the top management team in the Indian subsidiary consist primarily or exclusively of Western expatriates or should they utilize local nationals to the maximum possible extent? This is a recurring dilemma confronting multinationals in whichever country they operate and India is no exception in this regard. One of the major advantages of using expatriates is that they possess credibility with their colleagues back home and this may make it easier for them to convince the parent company about making local adaptations.[25] Expatriates may also help to create a more transparent corporate culture as well as facilitating knowledge transfer between the parent unit and the subsidiary. All of this, no doubt, is conducive to effective strategic implementation. As noted, countries such as the United States, United Kingdom, Canada, and so on, do have an advantage in this regard as several of them can send out persons of Indian origin, as expatriates.

The tremendous success and rapidity that has been enjoyed by the Korean "chaebols" in the Indian market place would have been inconceivable had expatriates not been at the helm of operations in India and with a clear operating link with the top management in Korea. But a further analysis would reveal that these Korean expatriate managers put in place a highly competent second level of Indian managers, which provided the downstream interface with great success. The mere fact of having an expatriate is clearly no guarantee of success, but in circumstances where bold and aggressive action needs to be undertaken fast, with full backing of the head office, expatriates can provide that extra edge. Coupled with the fact that the Indian employees have more positive perceptions of competent Western expatriates as managers vis-à-vis their Indian counterparts, the advantages of employing expatriates in some instances is somewhat strenghtened.[26]

This is not to say that expatriates should always be used or that the use of locals will inevitably lead to problems or indeed vice versa. In many ways the use of expatriates is risky, as seen above, because the expatriate may or may not be able to adapt to the cultural requirements of the host country. They may also be less aware of the challenges posed by the local environment and may demonstrate a lower level of commitment.[27] Although the Indian environment is now clearly much more hospitable to the expatriates than was the case previously, challenges remain. Given that expatriates are also expensive, it is understandable why firms may be somewhat reluctant to employ them.

In the Indian business environment, Western multinationals have by and large sought to utilize either Indian locals for managing their operations or have transferred back to India, employees of Indian origin. The strategy of sending back employees of Indian origin to manage their operations has met with mixed success.[28] Apart from the fact that these employees may not fully appreciate the new found complexities of their homeland, they may also not be easily accepted by their Indian counterparts. There is, therefore, clearly no one best answer to this issue. Much will depend on the strategic imperatives facing the multinationals, their level of international experience and understanding of India as a market, and a scarcity or abundance of potential expatriate managers at their disposal.

(b) Corporate Culture

Corporate culture plays an important role in shaping a company's success.[29] Every organization is faced with the necessity to manage the marketplace demands and to act in an internally coherent way to execute organizational actions in an efficient and a timely way. This is to a large extent dependent on the ethos or the spirit that develops within the company. The ethos or the spirit captures the values or beliefs that guide organizational action. When a Western organization acquires an Indian company, establishes a joint venture, or sets up its own subsidiary it has to interact with employees that may be subscribing to an alternative value/belief system, and it is this incongruence that may be a source of culture clash and could necessitate the Western company to seriously think of marking its imprint on the corporate culture.

Consider the case of "Worldwide Telecommunications Company," a U.S.-based telecommunications company that had entered into a joint venture with an Indian company, "Subcontinental Software Solutions." The company experienced two major problems. First, one of the employees of the U.S.-based company who had traveled to India for a trouble shooting assignment claimed that she had been sexually harassed in India. The senior VP of operations, claimed, on the other hand, that the employee in question was not culturally sensitive. Another dramatic incident occurred later when the American company learnt that one of the employees had stolen the technology that had been developed by the joint venture, and was planning to start his own company![30]

Alternatively, consider the case of the Swiss-based Schindler, a company that held a dominant position in the world market for escalators.[31] Silvio Napoli was put in charge of managing the Indian subsidiary. Initially, Napoli had difficulty in ensuring that the targets were met, despite the fact that he was a hard taskmaster. The problems were multiple, ranging all the way from a questioning of the company's strategy by other managers to the issue of noncompliance when the Indian management team acted in contravention of the agreed upon strategy.

Nevertheless, Napoli was not a person to give up easily, and toward the end of 2000 the company had managed to sell more than 500 elevators, which was just short of the 1997 business plan.[32] He was able to accomplish this by reshaping the culture of the company. As Napoli notes,

> We've hired a bunch of bright, action-driven individuals who will want to feel fulfilled in their career with Schindler. At the moment, not only are they performing extremely well, but they're also feeling a sense of belonging, but this is of course something which needs to be constantly nurtured. So career development path incentives, recognition, these aspects need to be given incredible attention, and I think action plans to tackle each of them must be devised and implemented as soon as possible.[33]

In any case, the Western company initially experienced some degree of difficulty in executing its strategy effectively. Although the nature of the problem is clearly different in each of the two illustrative examples, they both highlight the importance of developing an appropriate culture in each of the two parent organizations. The critical question therefore is: What kind of a corporate culture is appropriate in the Indian business environment and how can this culture be created in the first place?

First of all, it is no doubt imperative, that the multinationals strive to create a culture that both, *values as well as rewards performance*. Many multinational firms are indeed doing just that and as Sinha's studies reveals, many of them have been fairly successful.[34] What is most important in accomplishing this is the transparency and consistency with which the parent multinational enforces the *norm of excellence*. Given the fact that the Indians often view expatriates more positively than their compatriots, it could be surmised that an expatriate may be more effective at the entry point of the multinational firm in institutionalizing these norms. If performance norms are important, then so are the norms for *cooperative behavior*, which, as pointed out earlier, may be somewhat difficult in the Indian organizational context.

Given a variety of factors that work against cooperation, this may not be easy, but overcoming this barrier is nonetheless essential if a more cohesive culture is to emerge. A combination of mechanisms ranging from increased incentives, to training/workshops in which managers may actively learn how to cooperate, to exemplary leadership at different levels of the organization may all play a part in instituting new forms of behavior. Finally, there needs to be a better appreciation of learning to behave *ethically*. Although differences in culture undoubtedly affect perceptions of ethicality, multinational managers must still strive for some common frame of reference, as this commonality may well be in the interests of everyone in the long run. These may help to mitigate potential problems of corrupt payments, sexual harassment, environmental neglect, and the like and may help the multinational firm avoid unwarranted attention unlike Bofors, Union Carbide, or more recently Enron.

(c) Effective Coordination between the Parent Company and the Subsidiary

It is vital that the parent company and the subsidiary have a shared vision concerning the activities of the subsidiary. What contribution will the subsidiary make to the overall goals of the multinational firm? What kind of objectives must a subsidiary seek to realize and what might be the most effective means of doing so? What degree of autonomy will be allowed to the subsidiary and what kind of control mechanisms will be put in place to monitor the performance of the subsidiary? Will the subsidiary be managed by an expatriate or will local managers be given the discretion to operate the subsidiary?

Our fundamental proposition is that when there is a unified vision, it makes it that much easier for the subsidiary to formulate and execute strategies that may be beneficial both for the subsidiary as well as for the multinational firm concerned. That said, there is by definition, an inbuilt tension in the relationship between the multinational firm and the subsidiary, stemming in large part from differences in the strategic objectives of the multinational and the subsidiary. The impact of these differences is further heightened by the fact that most often both the subsidiary manager as well as executives at the parent company feel that they possess the monopoly over truth. An inability to see an alternative perspective makes finding common ground difficult. Conflicts may involve strategic issues and/or more mundane issues of implementation. If these tensions are not reconciled, they can lead to sub optimal decisions, and/or ineffective execution/implementation. Over time it may sap the morale of the employees leading to high levels of attrition.

How can "divide" be minimized and/or overcome? There is, to be sure, no one best or clear cut answer to this situation, but based on the case studies at the end of this book we can make a few recommendations. First, it would be helpful, if the Indian employees were brought to the corporate headquarters for training. Ideally, this ought not to be confined only to the top management team. This would be conducive to creating, a "common vision," and there may well be a better understanding on either side about the ground reality. A good example is the case of ST Microelectronics, which transferred 40 engineers from India to Italy for a period of two years. The idea was to not only become intimately familiar with the companys technologies, but perhaps more importantly understand the corporate viewpoint. In the process one would suspect that even the top-level managers at ST Microelectronics's headquarters in Italy would have become more familiar with the ground reality in India. At the same time, on their return to India, these engineers provided training to other local employees and in doing so strengthened the basis of Indian operations.

We believe that it also important that the top managers in the parent company understand the Indian environment and demonstrate a high level of commitment to their Indian operations even though they may not be directly involved in directing day-to-day operations. While such a commitment may not necessarily guarantee an absence of conflict, we can confidently say that it will create the motivation to manage conflicts positively, and that is surely a big step. Although this recommendation may sound commonplace, it is often ignored, perhaps for understandable reasons, but with negative consequences nevertheless.

It is hard to understand GE's success in India without noting that the former CEO of General Electric, Jack Welch, was extremely committed to the Indian market. A good instance of this is GE's establishment of GE Capital International Services, one of India's largest business processing outsourcing firms. Initially, there was resistance in GE's corporate headquarters to initiate this venture but Jack Welch's strong backing allowed this venture to develop in India. Indeed, it became a very successful unit within GE.

Finally, we believe that it is vitally important that top managers in the parent company be perceived as being responsive to the concerns of the subsidiary. If anything, the subsidiaries should be encouraged to become sources of innovation. The story of Wartsila Diesel, the Finnish company, is once again instructive in this regard. As the case study indicates, the Indian subsidiary of the company was strongly encouraged to transfer its success in an innovative project with one customer to other customers overseas. Indeed, the Indian unit now spearheads the operation and maintenance services for Wartsila globally.

Cultural Adaptability

> To succeed in India you have to be one-half monk and one half warrior. I've learned to develop my monk part. (Silvio Napoli, Vice President for South Asia)[35]

> You have to have the heart and mind of Columbus if you wish to succeed in India. (Comment of a Finnish manager)[36]

Cultural adaptation is an important ingredient for being successful globally and India is no exception to this rule. Any Western manager operating in the Indian sociocultural environment will need to develop cross-cultural competencies to operate successfully. This is not to imply that such adaptation is easy or that a Western manager needs to adapt to every aspect of the Indian sociocultural environment. We would like to stress the importance of, *thoughtful adaptation*, that is, adaptation in which the Western manager undertakes actions that demonstrate respect for his Indian colleagues in particular, and with the Indians in general.

We should mention that while adjustment at work is no doubt most critical, there is also the broader issue of adjusting to the Indian socioinstitutional environment, as well as the related issue of being able to interact effectively with the locals. All of these aspects are often classified by analysts as work, general, and interaction adjustment respectively.[37] We should also mention that not only must the expatriate adapt effectively to the Indian cultural environment; it is equally critical that the spouse of the expatriate adjust well too. Often enough, it is the spouse's inability to adjust that has had a negative impact on the expatriate's ability to function effectively in the host country.[38]

What are the consequences of successful adaptation and what kind of cross-cultural competencies must a Western manager possess to navigate within the Indian sociocultural environment? When a Western manager adapts successfully to the Indian sociocultural environment, he or she is likely to (a) be able to develop good relationship with his/her Indian colleagues; (b) be able to communicate in a desired manner; and (c) is able to secure the cooperation of his/her Indian colleagues. These dimensions are identified as being the key aspects of intercultural competence.[39] As is fairly apparent, each of these aspects of intercultural competence are important in enabling a firm achieve its business objectives. Without a good relationship with his Indian colleagues, the Western manager may not be fully aware of all that is happening in the subsidiary or the joint venture. Effective communication is important to send the right signals and to ensure that the requisite tasks are carried out efficiently and effectively. Finally, cooperation is essential if the firm is to execute its strategy effectively and not get bogged down in dysfunctional conflicts. In addition to a positive impact at work, intercultural adjustment will also lead to a positive perception of the host country, and will allow the expatriates to reframe their expectations in a manner that facilitates smooth interaction.

Arguably, there is no better example of expatriate adjustment than that of Scott Bayman, President and CEO of GE India. Arriving in India in 1993 as country head of GE, much against the initial objections of his wife, Scott Bayman has now completed 11 years in India and is possibly the longest lasting CEO of a multinational entity's Indian operations. In his tenure, GE in India has grown into a group of 36 companies, wholly or partially owned, with investments of over $1 billion, combined annual sales in India as well as exports well exceeding $2 billion and employing 23,000 people (at the time of writing). Media reports indicate that the Bayman's have totally integrated themselves into Indian society, eat Indian food regularly, have learnt Hindi, the national language and shopping where the Indians would. The February 16, 2004 issue of *Business India* quotes Mrs. Bayman as saying, "I'm nowhere ready to leave. We've lived here longer than any other place. This really is home!"

If intercultural competence is essential for succeeding in the Indian business environment, what kind of skills does a manager need to possess to operate in the Indian environment and how might these skills be developed? These issues are explored in the following sections.

The Nature of Intercultural Competencies

Scholars have noted that intercultural competencies have three essential components, namely (a) cognitive competencies; (b) affective competencies; and (c) behavioral competencies.[40] Cognitive competencies refer to the ability of an expatriate manager to accurately assess the nature of the underlying situation he is faced with. If, for example, he finds that the assigned task has not been completed on time it is perhaps due to the fact that his instructions were unclear, or it is simply reflective of the fact that the employee is lazy or he is operating under different constraints. An accurate diagnosis of the situation is essential for undertaking appropriate actions.

Affective competencies refer to the ability of the expatriate manager to maintain a calm demeanor even when his/her expectations have not been met and he/she is feeling very angry. Bureaucratic obstacles, corruption, or misdirected effort by his/her employees may all have the potential of generating such emotions. It is important under these circumstances that the manager not act in haste, for a violent outburst of temper may be unproductive. Behavioral competencies refer to the expatriate's ability to utilize a variety of alternative behavioral strategies for attaining his/her goal. If, for example, a bureaucrat is being unresponsive or difficult, the manager must try another tack to convince him of his/her case.

It also needs to be stressed that these competencies have both a stable as well as a dynamic component.[41] Openness, emotional stability and extrovertedness represents the stable component, whereas cultural knowledge, the ability to manage stress and conflict may represent the more dynamic aspect of these competencies. The implication of this is that while there are certain competencies that can most clearly be learnt, there are others that vary from person to person, meaning that some individuals are likely to better adapt than others.

More recently, scholars have sought to synthesize the different intercultural competencies within the rubric of "cultural intelligence."[42] A high level of cultural intelligence implies that the manager is able to discern an underlying pattern in the different cultural situations that he/she encounters, maintains motivation even when efforts to attain certain goals are unsuccessful, and is successfully able to execute behaviors in the new culture. As some scholars have noted, "You will not disarm your foreign hosts simply by showing that you understand their culture; your actions must prove that you have entered their world."[43] As these scholars note, different managers have different ways of dealing with the unexpected or the unfamiliar. There are some who will never be comfortable in an alien environment; there are others who seek to understand the expectations of that culture and, adjust their behavior accordingly. Still others rely on their intuitive abilities or project an air of confidence while others seek to mimic their hosts, and there may well be very few who possess all three of the necessary abilities.

Development of Intercultural Competencies

If intercultural competencies are so critical to succeeding in the Indian business environment, how can such competencies be fostered? At the outset we must understand that intercultural competencies do not develop overnight. While there are, to be sure, individual differences in learning capability, and while some may surely find the cultural barrier representing a high hurdle, many, if not most, managers can without doubt, develop this capability.[44]

That said, the development of intercultural competencies requires a multifaceted approach that necessitates (a) intercultural training that specifically targets the individual's weaknesses in relation to Indian culture; (b) a prolonged exposure to the Indian culture; and (c) appropriate support from the parent company that motivates the individual and his family to endure the challenges of the Indian culture, which may be rather distinct from their own.

Intercultural training has many advantages. It can help (a) lower the expatriate's stress; (b) enable them to enjoy more congenial relations with the host country nationals; (c) facilitate goal accomplishment; and (d) facilitate self-development.[45] As discussed earlier, the cultural distance between the Indians and the Western expatriates is not inconsiderable. This no doubt has an impact on all facets of cross-cultural managerial interaction ranging from issues of communication, decision making, negotiation, to managing strategic partnerships.

Even though these cultural differences are fairly apparent, Western companies appear to have not paid sufficient attention to this dimension. As one observer notes "Western senior management does not have a particularly good track record in planning for cultural difference, and more often than not, does not factor in the significantly different management styles of their Indian colleagues and how this inevitably influences intended outcomes."[46] Whatever be the reasons for this neglect, it is clearly not helpful in facilitating expatriate adjustment.

Most often cross-cultural consultants are brought in when a major crisis has erupted.[47] It would be reasonable to presume that cross-cultural training may reduce the frequency of crisis intervention, although to be sure, it is not a panacea to all problems. Most fundamentally, cross-cultural training may help to recalibrate the expectations of the Western expatriate manager and in doing so facilitate adjustment. Thus, the Western manager may learn how to cope with the Indian hierarchical structure or how to better negotiate with the Indians. For a Western expatriate who is expected to spend several years in India, it would be helpful to provide pre-departure training, as well as training on arrival in the host country. A combination of both types of training is useful because it alleviates pre-departure anxiety as also allows the expatriate and his family to reinforce their learning in the Indian environment.[48]

In addition to the issue of training, it is important that the multinationals allow their expatriates to spend sufficient time in India to develop individual cross-cultural skills. Although this may not always be possible, either due to strategic considerations, or the desire of the expatriate to leave for family reasons, it is a fair assumption to make that the greater the exposure of the expatriate to the Indian environment, the greater the likelihood that he will succeed. As time goes by, the expatriates will move away from the stage of culture shock to a new state, where they may become more accepting of the host culture.[49] It is fair to say that not everyone will make the successful transition and the time duration for successful adaptation may also vary from one individual to another. That said, the greater the length of stay the greater the probability of developing cross-cultural competencies to operate in India.

Third, the development of intercultural competencies is likely to be further facilitated by parent company support. Their support is critical if the motivation of the expatriate to further his/her intercultural competencies is to be sustained. The support may take many forms, ranging from the provision of adequate training to a deeper appreciation of the cultural challenges that the expatriate may be facing. It may be further reinforced by providing clear signals that the assignment in India will ensure that the expatriate's career possibilities are enhanced.

This chapter analyzes how multinational firms may adapt to the Indian environment. There are three dimensions of adaptability—strategic, organizational, and cultural, and the ways by which a multinational firm's adaptability can be enhanced are outlined. Adaptability will not be achieved overnight and nor will the gains from adaptability be evident immediately. That said, adaptability is a prerequisite for succeeding in the Indian market and its importance cannot be overestimated.

Although India has now begun to embrace liberalization, as well as globalization, there remain pockets of tension that continue to erupt from time to time. How effectively the multinationals manage those pockets of tension is dependent on their level of adaptability. This will certainly tease and test the multinationals, but on the other hand, good adaptability may make them more resilient, and more inseparable from India. Many companies have already done so and many others are on the way.

To conclude it would be extremely pertinent to summarize the following ten key success factors for multinationals operating in India, contained in a report[50] prepared by the Boston Consulting Group for the Confederation of Indian Industries, after an analysis of the operations of successful leading European companies in India. These points indicate that to successfully operate in India, perhaps a whole different management paradigm needs to be considered. This involves "Indianizing" (a) the value proposition, (b) pricing, (c) marketing and distribution, (d) product specifications and features, (e) product branding, (f) maximizing the empowerment of local management team comprising of as many competent local managers as possible, and (g) providing local management with full backing at the global level.

(a) Commitment at the Global Level

1. View India as a key focus area—"Directs appropriate resources towards India and ensure speedy and favorable decisions."
2. Formulate bold, long term, targets that drive decision-making—"Aligns the organization behind exhibited market potential and helps circumvent short term hurdles."
3. Create processes that accelerate the integration as well as localization of the organization—"Helps find the right balance of autonomy allotted to the local team and aligns organizational objectives in India."
4. "Change the rules" regarding global metrics, standards to meet market challenges—"Allows fine-tuning of metrics to fit with Indian market realities and sets the organization to take full advantage of the India opportunity."

(b) Empowered Local Management

1. Build for the long term in India regarding people, HR practices and relationship with external stakeholders—"More cost effective, enhances continuity, and leverages understanding of local environment."
2. Define a value-added role for the country management—"Motivates local team to perform and facilitates transfer of responsibility."
3. Establish local team management and credibility—"Provides the local team the required business flexibility and smoothens the strategic decision making process."
4. Leverage Indian opportunities beyond the product market—"Draws attention to the Indian organization, derives value for global organization, and gains competitive advantage."

(c) Localized Product—Marketing Business Models

1. Localize parts of the value chain to obtain Indian cost and capability benefits—"Builds competitive advantage by achieving effective cost structure, maintaining quality standards, and leveraging the effects of scale."
2. Formulate India—specific business model strategies (product, value, pricing)—"Delivers the right product at the right price with right positioning, *for India.*"

Case Study One: Wartsila India Ltd.

Wartsila, a Finnish company with over $3 billion global turnover, is the world's leading ship power supplier and also a leading provider of decentralized power generating solutions.

Wartsila entered the Indian market in 1983 to tap the potential power generation market in the country, which at that time desperately needed good quality, cost effective, decentralized power solutions. The company had developed very efficient heavy fuel technology by which the engines made by Wartsila could burn residual fuel oils that emerged from the oil refining process. As this fuel was of a very poor quality, the cost of generating power from this fuel was considerably lower than that of generating power from other liquid fuels such as high speed diesel and kerosene.

Wartsila started off by supplying only basic imported equipment but in a very short time, responding to the needs of the market, developed its Indian operations into providing complete power solutions, including long-term operations and maintenance contracts. Wartsila, effectively became a reliable and efficient power utility.

In a further short period of time, recognizing the need to optimize the cost of its power solutions and to also provide international quality service and support locally, for power as well as for marine propulsion equipment, Wartsila set up an Indian subsidiary in April 1986, with a manufacturing facility near Mumbai.

Wartsila currently has about 3,000 MW of installed capacity in India, which is supported by a local organization of over 800 people, with offices in seven cities across the country. The Indian entity enjoys a market share of more than 70 percent in the heavy fuel oil and gas based power generation, based on Internal Combustion Engines.

With the recent discovery of very large natural gas sources in India, Wartsila, once again quickly grasped the market potential and rapidly launched an impressive range of power generating solutions based on this fuel and already set up several power plants around the country.

The key factors in the success of Wartsila in India may be summarized as under:

(a) *Excellent and reliable products*—The company has now been in India for over 20 years and almost 70 percent of its business in the country is from repeat customers. The product is truly the best in its class in the world, not only in terms of technology but also in reliability.

(b) *Building long-term relationships*—The company lays great stress in the building of business relationships on the basis of trust and performance and actively pursues long-term commitments rather than short-term gains. The company culture very much reflects the culture of Finland, its country of origin. Performance must speak for itself and actions should speak more than words.

(c) *Belief in its people*—Wartsila in India has one of the largest staff complements among its worldwide operations, yet it is manned completely by Indians. The company believes in empowering its staff and providing them with a great deal of operational freedom with the only proviso being that of delivering more and better than promised.

A report prepared by the Boston Consulting Group for the Confederation of Indian Industry lists the following as the "success factors" for Wartsila in India:

1) *Global management processes*: A deep rooted trust based relationship between global management and country leadership enables due flexibility for local management to

make strategic and operational recommendations. Targets are then aligned with local plans, alleviating short-term bottom line pressures to enable growth in market share.

2) *Local management processes*: Local management had driven a highly successful personnel transfer program and has also leveraged India's advantage to position it as a key contributor to the global organization in IT based services, engineering and O&M services.
3) *Customized business models*: O&M services were originally developed in India in response to a request by a large industrial client and have caught on with Wartsila globally. As a result, the Indian operation has become the global expert in designing and implementing these services.

Case Study Two: ST Microelectronics

ST Microelectronics is a more than $7 billion turnover global leader in the designing and delivery of Semiconductor/Integrated Circuit solutions for a large variety of electronics applications. The Indian entity was established in 1988 and has now become possibly the most important design center of ST Microelectronics' worldwide operations, with the NOIDA (near Delhi) center being the largest outside its home base, Europe.

The Indian entity started IC design activities in NOIDA in 1990 and its success led to the establishment of the second major IC chip designing center in 1995, also in NOIDA. This unit has now become the core of the company's Indian operations and incorporates functions like sales, marketing, customer service, and technical support in addition to the chip and system design activities.

ST Microelectronics now has about 2,000 employees in its Indian operations including its third newly, opened design center in Bangalore. The Indian entity provides a wide spectrum of "Intellectual Property" designed products including system-on-chip designs. Designing activities at NOIDA include IP/IC designs, system application designs, and management information systems designs.

ST Microelectronics is the world leader in circuits and systems used in consumer digital electronics including DVDs, high definition TVs, web cameras, PDAs, and so on. A very large portion of the software needed for these products is also carried out in the Indian operations. The Indian entity is also involved in designs for wired and wireless telecommunications, and in Telecommunication Peripheral Automation involving the designing of embedded software for telecommunication companies.

The NOIDA design center has already some 70 global patents to its credit with a large number of these in the "Field programmable gate arrays" sector. Further, the Indian operation has already started work developing a design platform in the very advanced 65 nanometer technology framework and developing a processor chip family called "Nomadik" for mobile multimedia terminals. "Nomadik" enables real time, two-way audiovisual communications and supports downloading and streaming of multimedia such as MP3 music, MPEG4 video, and JPEG still images.

According to Mr. Pasquale Pistorio, President of ST Microelectronics, "ST India's talents in design and development helped us in no small measure to shape our world leading portfolio of products and technologies." By 2007, the company hopes to hire another 5,000 highly qualified professionals for its Indian operations.

In a report prepared by the Boston Consulting Group for the Confederation of Indian Industry, the following are described as the success factors for ST Microelectronics in India:

1) *Global management processes*: ST Micro's global CEO's personal vision has been a key driving force behind the success of the Indian operation. Global management has provided the overall cultural and support framework for the India operation to grow and succeed. At the outset, 40 engineers were sent to company headquarters for an extensive 2 year training program—these later returned to India to spearhead the operation and initiated training other employees, establishing the base for the Indian operation to develop.
2) *Local management processes*: Local management has boosted India's position from a project *execution* to a high value-add project *ownership* destination, gaining full project responsibility and performing cutting edge work e.g. system-on-chip (SOC) design. This was done by developing, and proving, India's cost competitiveness and strong technical capabilities. Beyond objective performance measures, management found it important to invite as many executives from the company to come to India and witness the operation first hand. The confidence eventually spurred the representation of all corporate divisions in India—establishing India as a critical link in the worldwide system.
3) *Customized business models*: ST Micro recognizes the importance of developing and retaining high quality talent, and as such has customized Human Relations policies to the needs of its India employees. Global benchmarks for employee development and benefits are tailored to Indian priorities e.g. supporting family values, and a preference for accelerated development. This has earned the Indian subsidiary its reputation as one of the best employers in India.

Case Study Three: GE Capital International Services (GECIS)

GECIS is India's largest and one of the oldest Business Process Outsourcing (BPO) companies and can safely claim to be the pioneer that triggered off the global BPO boom in India which now has every international company of significance establishing similar activities in the country.

When the Indian economy started to grow after the liberalization process was initiated in 1991, GE Capital started operations with its commercial and consumer finance services, the latter as a joint venture with an Indian partner, HDFC. Both these businesses helped GE Capital establish itself in India and set up the base to enter into a major credit card operation as a joint venture with the State Bank of India. With a firm base now in the country, GE Capital was ready to look at other businesses in India.

GECIS actually had an unintended start in 1998. Promod Bhandari, an Indian expatriate chartered accountant working in GE's corporate finance division in Connecticut, was sent out to India to support its appliances business. By then British Airways and American Express had positioned a small portion of their global "backroom" operations to India. Bhandari sensed an opportunity here for GE. With the help of an ex-American Express employee and the full support of the then vice president of GE Capital, an eight-person team was set up to handle simple address changes. The idea of remote processing services grew out of a company brain storming session which identified BPO as a possible business, leveraging India's ample supply of well-educated, English-speaking manpower available at highly competitive rates.

With the initial success of this trial activity, the BPO operation, now titled GECIS, was expanded to undertake more work for other divisions of GE. The local workforce was rapidly expanded. Because of the non-availability of adequate number of people with BPO experience, bright youngsters from the call center business, hotels, airlines, and courier services were hired at the rate of 50 managers and 500 operators every month.

A group of managers was put together to visit GE operations in many other countries and pitch for new business highlighting the skill sets and capabilities available with the Indian operations especially in that of remotely handling back office operations. Senior mangers were imparted thorough voice and skill training, etiquette skills, as well as process orientation. They were also sent overseas for rigorous advanced training. The team was now ready to deliver the highest possible international standard of business process outsourcing. It was also time to move up the value chain.

Overcoming the initial resistance within GE to outsourcing, and given the firm backing of Jack Welch himself, as many as 700 processes were sent out to India to take advantage of the pool of talent available at GECIS at cost advantages of over 50 percent. GECIS was now doing advanced analytics, network security, accounting, processing of claims, customer technical support in addition to basic voice-based call centre operations. The workforce at Gurgaon, Hyderabad, Jaipur, and Bangalore operations combined, was now a staggering 12,000 employees with a further 4,000 at back-up centers in China, Hungary, and Mexico (but reporting to the Gurgaon Headquarters). The annual turnover of GECIS leaped to US$420 million, which now included revenues from services provided to third parties.

With Jeffrey Immelt replacing Jack Welch at the helm of GE, there was however a rethink at headquarters about the positioning of GECIS in the larger framework of GE's global operations, however useful and profitable the company proved to be. As Scott Bayman himself has stated, "GECIS was funny money. We are a technology company and wanted to unleash the capability of GECIS, which is not a strategic fit." On November 9, 2004, GE sold a 60 percent stake in GECIS to two global private equity firms (General Atlantic Partners and Oak Hill Capital Partners) in a whopping $500 million deal.

Chapter Seven
Communicating with Indians

Human beings draw close to one another by their common nature, but habits and customs keep them apart.

Confucian saying

Now it is not good for the Christians health to hustle the Asian brown for the Christian riles and the Aryan smiles and he weareth the Christian down. At the end of the fight is a tombstone white with the name of the late deceased, And the epitaph drear "A fool lies here who tried to hustle the East."

Rudyard Kipling

"What kind of a bird are you, if you can't sing?" chirped the bird "What kind of a bird are you, if you can't swim?" quacked the duck

Prokofiev in "Peter and the Wolf"

The great common door through which most forms of negativity enter is premature expectation. . . . All expectations are a judgment.

Communication is a fundamental aspect of human interaction in that individuals cannot but not communicate.[1] One may be effective or ineffective in accurately conveying what one wishes to say to the other party, but without question whenever we interact with another individual one does convey some message, whether or not we intended to convey that message to the other party. Above all, communication is a goal-driven activity in which one is either conveying some information to the other party to get them to do something or are trying to extract information from another person to further one's own objectives. Whether it is setting up a business meeting, or making an offer to buy or sell a particular commodity, communication serves as the medium to help accomplish these goals.

Even within the confines of a particular culture communication is not necessarily problem free. Individual differences in personality, age, gender, social skills, and socioeconomic background are all likely contributors to communicative difficulties.[2] That said, communicative difficulties increase when one crosses cultural boundaries. As the cultural distance increases, so do the *assumptions* on the basis of which individuals communicate. Individuals socializing in different cultures communicate on the basis of *radically different assumptions* without necessarily being acutely aware of the assumptions that are shaping their behavior.[3]

The aim here is to assess the causes and the consequences of the communicative difficulties between the Indians and the Western expatriate manager. We will also outline ways by which the Western expatriate manager might handle these challenges both efficiently as well as effectively. However, prior to discussing the specific problems that the Western expatriate manager might be faced with when interacting with his/her Indian colleagues, we will briefly discuss the general nature of the cross-cultural communicative challenge. In other words, what makes cross-cultural communication so difficult? What are the consequences of conflicting communicative styles? What contextual factors may aggravate the difficulties of cross-cultural communication?

The Role of Assumptions in Shaping Intercultural Communication

The argument has been made that managers socialized in different cultures operate on the basis of different *assumptions* in any specific situation. The *assumptions* reflect the knowledge structures on the basis of which, managers or for that matter individuals, relate with other individuals as well as with the broader external environment. These structures are often referred to as *schemata* that is, an organized body of knowledge that (a) shapes the way that managers perceive events/people; (b) influences the judgments/interpretations made by managers; and (c) conditions the way that they are likely to respond to situations.[4]

This organized body of knowledge exists at varying levels of consciousness, corresponding to what scholars have characterized as the difference between the *surface* and the *deep culture*.[5] The surface culture consists of visible symbols and artifacts whereas the deep culture consists of deeply ingrained values that are neither explicitly visible, nor accessible. In the Indian cultural context, one example of this surface culture might be the fact that the Indian women wear a distinctive dress called the *saree* and one example of a more deeply embedded cultural trait might be their perception of time (see chapter five, "Understanding India") or the belief in the principle of "moksha" or reincarnation.

The assumptions on the basis of which managers interact with their counterparts from other cultures influence the communicative process in a number of different ways. First of all, the assumptions have a direct bearing on how we perceive our counterparts: are they trustworthy or are they not trustworthy? If the inference that one's counterparts are not to be trusted is drawn, it will undoubtedly have a negative impact on future interaction. The manager who considers that one's counterpart is not trustworthy may be less inclined to share information or believe what his/her counterpart has to say.

Consider, for example, the tendency of the Indian employee to adopt a deferential posture when dealing with a person in an authoritative position. This cultural proclivity is interpreted by North American, as well as European managers, as indicative of distrust.[6] Alternatively, when the North American or the western European manager, tries to expedite the pace of discussions it is often counterproductive. Consider, for example, the comment made by an expatriate about the challenges of doing business in India: "Joel, in his frustration, tried to speed up matters, as a lot more issues had to be addressed, but the Indians felt that he was only interested in finalizing and implementing the deal. They also began to question his intelligence, abilities, and sincerity. His informal way of addressing them also made them feel uncomfortable and not respected. All in all, they didn't really trust him or the deal he was proposing."[7]

The assumptions also have a bearing as to what we perceive during the interaction with the manager from another culture. Perception is, by definition, selective because there is only so much information that we can deal with at any particular point in time.[8] This has the implication that managers from a particular cultural group are likely to be more sensitive to some events/situations vis-à-vis other situations. In the previous example, the Americans were very sensitive to the issue of time because for the Americans time is money. This is the reason why they tried to expedite the business transaction. In being sensitive to the issue of time, Americans overlooked the fact that there were other issues that were more important to the Indians and their inability to understand that fact led to the breakdown of the interaction.

Finally, assumptions are also likely to influence the way in which managers respond to situations/events confronting them. Consider the case of Raman Matthews, a software engineer who was recruited by Dream USA to work for them in the United States. As Dr. Araoz points out, Raman experienced communicative difficulties that negatively affected his confidence. As she notes "He was not sure if, as a foreigner, he would be able to really rise in this country. His ideas were often ignored, but the same ideas were accepted if someone else voiced it differently."[9] He almost considered quitting the company.

Consequences of Conflicting Assumptions

Conflicting assumptions have the potential of creating a wide range of intercultural problems. Some have suggested that conflicting assumptions lead to *disconfirmed expectancies, a sense of being an outsider, an intensification of ambiguity, and a sense of anxiety.*[10] When individuals find that their deeply held and cherished values/beliefs are no longer valid in an alternative cultural setting, they are likely to feel helpless and unsure as to what to do next. It is this helplessness and uncertainty that may produce both ambiguity as well as a sense of anxiety. Under these circumstances, it is unclear what will follow next. While some managers may no doubt deal with the cultural challenge well, others may not be very adept in confronting an alternative reality. Scholars maintain that most often, the natural impulse under these conditions is for the manager to *withdraw or exit the country.*[11]

A related problem is that when managers find that their expectancies are disconfirmed, whether in dealing with the local staff, or negotiating with the top management, for example, they may experience frustration, anger, and/or fear and anxiety.[12] These emotions arise because managers find that they have been unable to realize their goals, whether the goal is one of eliciting a direct response from the Indian employee, or the goal is one of completing the project on time. Although emotions are not a problem per se, it is how managers deal with their emotions that may well determine the success of the cross-cultural communicative endeavor. The problem is that when one gets frustrated, the natural impulse is to behave aggressively, and yet this aggressive behavior may only aggravate the problems.[13] In a similar vein, when one gets anxious, the natural impulse is to withdraw from the situation and this is equally counterproductive in that it will prevent the completion of a project.

Conflicting assumptions may also lead managers to make erroneous judgments as to why their counterpart behaved in a particular way or why a given event occurred. For example, if an Indian employee does not complete the assigned task, the typical North American or European manager may attribute it to the fact that the employee is lazy or not committed to the task. This may, however, not be the correct interpretation in the Indian cultural context, because the Indian employee may be relying on directives from the senior manager to complete the task. As Craig Storti points out, "In India, the manager calls all the shots. People don't take initiative until they get directions from the manager. They want to be closely supervised so that they don't make mistakes. American workers typically are hands-on."[14]

Most fundamentally, conflicting assumptions lead individuals from different cultures to evaluate the same behavior differently. There is the additional problem, that individuals from all cultures are prone to the self-serving bias, although the degree of such a bias clearly varies across cultures.[15] This bias has the implication that individuals attribute positive outcomes to their own actions and negative outcomes to situational factors. Scholars have noted that the self-serving bias is more prevalent in North America than it is in India.[16] We would suppose that the presence of the self-serving bias could make the resolution of conflicts more difficult, inasmuch as each individual tries to shift the blame to the other for a negative outcome. The fact that managers may not even be consciously aware that they are making these judgments or that their judgments are biased by their culture specific knowledge only aggravates the problem of developing shared understanding. In sum, incorrect judgments may prevent a relationship from achieving its potential and/or may slow down task efficiency.

Conflicting assumptions are also likely to accentuate the cultural distance between the Indian and North American/European expatriate managers. Even prior to the development of any misunderstanding, there is a natural tendency among members of different cultural groups to draw a distinction between "us" and "them." This preexisting barrier is associated with a natural inclination to hold more positive views of members of one's own group and more negative views of "out"-group members.[17] Individuals also have the natural inclination to gloss over the errors committed by their in-group members while rating members of the out-group on a higher standard.[18]

Often, individuals are likely to entertain stereotypes of the other culture, and while there is some kernel of truth associated with stereotypes, there is the real danger that it may lead to a "self fulfilling prophecy."[19] This is a situation where an individual from one of the cultural groups acts in a manner that confirms his/her suppositions about the characteristics of the individual from the other cultural group. Reliance on stereotypes also has the implication that individuals are likely to overestimate the link between the attributes of any given individual in a particular group with the overall group characteristics. This may make the individuals less open-minded and may increase the perceived gap between in-group and out-group members.[20]

The one direct and immediate consequence of conflicting assumptions is that individuals from different cultures may neither be able to accurately convey their message to the other party, nor for that matter, are they likely to accurately understand the message that is being conveyed to them by a person from the other culture. Incorrect inferences/interpretations may further poison the relationship and may make it harder for the parties to develop any confidence in each other. Ineffective communication often negatively affects employee motivation, enhances distrust among negotiators, is detrimental to effective leadership, and makes conflict resolution more difficult. In other words, an inability to communicate effectively is likely to have a negative impact on all facets of business operations, and for that reason managers need to pay particular attention to their communication.

The Indian Communicative Style

The communicative style of a particular cultural group can be analyzed on the basis of different dimensions.[21] The four dimensions that have garnered a lot of attention in the literature are: (a) high context versus low context; (b) ideologism versus pragmatism; (c) associative versus abstractive communication; and (d) verbal versus nonverbal communication.[22] We outline the salient characteristics of each of them and then indicate how the Indian culture maps on to them.

(a) High Context versus Low Context Communicative Patterns

This is one of the most influential characterizations of different types of communicative styles and it draws attention to the fact that members of different cultural groups are more or less sensitive to the context of the message.[23] As Hall and Hall note "*Context* is the information that surrounds an event; it is inextricably bound up with the meaning of that event. The elements that combine to produce a given meaning—events and contexts—are in different proportions depending on the culture."[24] *Context* has a powerful impact on how people choose to convey information, and in particular, it influences the communication mode that people choose to employ. Scholars have drawn a distinction between indirect versus direct, succinct versus elaborate, contextual versus personal, and affective versus instrumental modes of communicating.[25] In an indirect communicative mode, messages are conveyed implicitly rather than directly whereas in a direct communicative mode people state their intentions as clearly as they possibly can.

The distinction between a succinct and an elaborate communicative mode rests on the fact that in the former, people rely less on words and more on nonverbal nuances whereas in the elaborative mode, verbal expression is clearly prized. A contextual style is accommodative of the relationship among the parties whereas in a personal style people try to lessen the barriers among themselves. The affective mode of communicating is more concerned with the "how" of communication whereas the instrumental mode of communication is intimately related to the issue of goal attainment. In high context cultures, communication is more often than not likely to be indirect, often elaborate, contextual, and affective rather than instrumental.[26]

In practical terms what this means is that in these cultures people will not overtly express their wishes and/or express rejection of any terms/conditions regarding a proposal. It also has the implication that in these cultures individuals may state the same thing in so many different ways. Likewise the communicative tone and the content of the message will be heavily dependent on the hierarchical quality of the relationship among the parties. Finally, the communicative patterns in this context are not likely to be intimately related to the issue of goal attainment.

Many have pointed out that the Indian communicative style is indirect in nature.[27] The Indians often do not like to say "no" directly for fear of offending to the other party. As Girish Paranjpe, President (Finance) of Wipro Technologies states, "Indians do not speak up in meetings and do not like confronting the client, which sometimes leads to awkward situations like project delays and cost overruns."[28] Similar comments have been made by others as well.

Wendell Jones, Vice President Worldwide Service Delivery at DEC, who managed the outsourcing relationship between NASDAQ and Tata Consultancy Services, noted that communicative difficulties stemming from differences in cultures was one of the major problems that he had to deal with.[29] Commenting on the interactions between the Germans and the Indians, Sujata Banerjee notes, "Well, it is difficult for Germans when an Indian says 'no problem' as the German *suspects* that the real *challenges* are not being admitted. For the Indian, 'no problem' simply means, 'I know there will be problems, but I am doing the best I can *at my end*.' "[30]

The Indian communicative style is also characterized by elaborateness rather than succinctness. The Indians like to talk and express their viewpoint in multiple ways. This behavioral tendency is most likely reinforced by the fact that Indians are context sensitive. Context sensitivity has the implication that all possible contingencies must be outlined and their implications clearly delineated. As Araoz points out, "The Indian engineer is often unaware that verbosity is very hard on Americans, who generally like co-workers to be succinct and logical in their business communication."[31]

The Indian communicative style is also very contextual, in that what individuals communicate, and how they communicate is shaped by the nature of the relationship between the individuals. For example, the Indian culture is hierarchical and this affects the pattern of communication between employees at different organizational levels. The Indian employee may adopt a very deferential attitude toward his superior and for this reason may be reluctant to initiate communication, much less convey information that may not be palatable to his/her superior.

As an Indian manager, working in the subsidiary of a Danish company, noted, "We Indians cannot say 'no' to our boss. The boss will get angry."[32] The director of British American Corporation, a company studied by Sinha, noted, "Indians wasted their time talking too much. They rarely stick to the agenda in a meeting. There is a wide gap between what Indians professed and what they actually did. They were more concerned about what other people would say than what was the 'right' thing to do."[33]

Finally, it would be fair to say that the Indian communicative style is more affective rather than instrumental. This is a style that "requires the listener to carefully note what is being said and to observe how the sender is presenting the message. . . . The part of the message that is being left out may be just as important as the part that is being included."[34] A good example of this may be gleaned in the interactions between the U.S. Ambassador Allen and India's first prime minister, Jawaharlal Nehru. When the United States decided to give military aid to Pakistan in 1954, President Eisenhower instructed the American ambassador in India to meet Nehru and convey the message that this action was not directed against India. During the meeting Nehru was calm and restrained, leading the American ambassador, Allen, to conclude that Nehru was not offended by this action. However, as Cohen points out, this represented complete misjudgment by the American ambassador. He failed to understand the real meaning behind Nehru's reaction.[35]

(b) Ideological versus Pragmatic Communicative Style

An ideological communicative style utilizes the dominant ideology extant in that culture at a particular point in time to structure communication, and as Triandis has pointed out this "assumes that the other person has the same view."[36] By contrast, a pragmatic communicative style utilizes a mode of communication that achieves the intended goal. The Indian communicative style is often ideological, shaped as it is both by an idealistic mode of thinking, and more recently by a resurgence in Indian nationalism. Indeed as Perry points out, "Washington D.C. based Pew Research Center's 2003 Global attitude survey found India was the most nationalistic place on earth with 74% of the respondents 'completely agreeing' that Indian culture is superior."[37] An ideological mode of communication uses one particular point of view to look at all types of problems. This has the implication that "When the universalistic person communicates with a particularistic, pragmatic opponent, the universalistic is likely to see the pragmatist as dealing with trivialities and as not having great thoughts, while the pragmatist is likely to see the 'universalists' as theoretical, fuzzy thinking, and dealing with generalities."[38] A related problem is that it may be hard to find common ground between the ideologist and the pragmatist, given that they are operating on the basis of radically different philosophies.

Historically, the ideological mode of thinking was dominant in India, and especially insofar as multinational firms were concerned. Even with the onset of liberalization in 1991, foreign investors, at least initially, were greeted with some degree of skepticism. The high profile disputes involving many independent power producers and the likes of Cargill are a testimony to this fact. However, with the rapid rise of India's software industry, and the recognition that international firms have played a positive role in its development, is, to be sure, altering the way in which foreign investors are being viewed in India. That said, there is without question an upsurge in Indian nationalism, with a strong desire for India to be recognized and accorded its due status in the world as a major power. This of course, has the implication, that all communication has to be viewed from the prism of Indian pride and greatness.

(c) Associative versus Abstractive Communication Style

Scholars have also drawn a distinction between an associative and an abstractive communication style.[39] An associative style of communication does not engage in sharp differentiations between who the person is and what the person does. By contrast, an abstractive communication style makes such differentiations. This difference has important implications for the way messages are transmitted and how they are decoded in different cultures. If, for example, there is no sharp differentiation between who the person is and what the person does, it may be difficult to give negative feedback to the other person without offending him/her.

It may also make it difficult to discuss the merits or demerits of any policy action in the abstract without assessing its implications for the individual or individuals concerned. It would be fair to say that while the Indian culture comprises both the associative as well as an abstract mode of communication, the associative style may be somewhat more dominant. This follows from the fact that the Indians are highly sensitive to criticism and may find it hard to follow the well-known precept of Fisher and Ury to "separate the people from the problem."[40] Although the issue of saving face may be less important in India compared to the Confucian cultures of China, Korea, Taiwan, and Japan, there is no question that face related concerns are important. When one considers the fact that status, caste, age, and hierarchy are important, it is inevitable that issues of face become important. Communication designed to give feedback, elicit task related compliance, motivate employees, must therefore be sensitive to these concerns.

A good example is that of Tata Steel, a company that was actively trying to reshape its corporate culture. As Sinha points out, many senior managers resisted the change to an alternative system that was more egalitarian. He cites the comments of a young officer who noted, "There are senior managers who are power hungry; I mean those who are brought up in the old culture. For them this change is erroneous and obnoxious. They feel they should be informed, their consent should be solicited, and all the files must be routed through them."[41] The interpretation of their behavior is that the senior Indian managers would have lost face as a consequence of the alternative system, even though the system may have increased the efficiency of the organization.

(d) Nonverbal Communication

Scholars are often at pains to point out that while individuals often pay attention to words, much of the most important communication often occurs nonverbally.[42] As Copeland and Griggs note, "On a very unconscious level many of us abroad can turn people off even when we are on good behavior."[43] This may occur for a number of different reasons such as making inappropriate gestures, or maintaining an inappropriate personal distance with the other party. Likewise, eye contact may make individuals in some cultures uncomfortable just as touching or informality may make others unhappy. Nonverbal behavior has four main components to which managers must pay attention. These are the issues of (a) distance; (b) touching; (c) eye contact; and (d) body movement.[44]

The North American/western European expatriate manager may find that the typical Indian manager/employee may have a very different style of nonverbal communication than what he might be used to do. One such example is provided by Gesteland who, when working in India, was taken out for lunch by his Indian business partner. As they went for lunch the Indian held the hand of Gesteland, and at least initially, it made him a trifle uncomfortable. In the European/American environment handholding is clearly indicative of sexual interest, but in the Indian environment, it only signifies friendship. Fortunately, Gesteland was able to recognize this aspect of the Indian culture soon enough, and this prevented any behavior on his part that may have been considered to be a cultural faux pas.[45]

The personal space or distance among individuals is dependent on the status of the individual one is interacting with. In general, this distance increases when one is talking with one's superior or when one is relating to someone who comes from a lower rung of the hierarchy. It has also been pointed out that while in the past Indians preferred to maintain eye contact only with a person of equal status, it is no longer true in contemporary India. As a manual prepared by the Canadian International Development Agency notes, "As middle to high ranking women employees in the public and private sectors look directly at a person while addressing them, they expect the same from their male colleagues."[46] Practitioners have also pointed out differences in the use of gestures, with the reference often being made to the fact that Indians often say "yes" by shaking their heads sideways, a gesture that would signify a "no" in the Western cultural tradition.

It is important to point out that nonverbal communication is unconscious and for that reason not very easy to control. That said, it makes it even more important that European/American managers pay attention to it, for otherwise they will end up communicating a message, which they never intended to. This can lead to an unsuccessful negotiation, demotivation of an employee, or an overall climate in which people fail to communicate effectively and in a timely way.

Communicating with Indians: Implications for Western Managers

What can Western managers do to enhance their effectiveness in communicating with the Indians? At the outset, it should be stated that there is no magical solution that will help Western managers improve the effectiveness of their communication with Indians overnight. It is also important to point out that Indian companies have now increasingly become cognizant of the cultural gap and are instituting training programs to enhance the cross-cultural skills of their employees in interacting with their European and North American counterparts.[47]

For example, the Bangalore-based Wipro Technologies is training their Indian employees to interact more effectively with the Americans. They have brought in American trainers and have hired consultants from companies such as McKinsey to provide training both in India as well as overseas. Infosys is also reportedly developing a program of change management for its employees.[48] One can reasonably surmise that one of its likely consequences would be a decrease in communication barriers over time. It is also important to point out that Indian professionals find it easier to communicate and work in the North American context vis-à-vis the European context for a wide variety of reasons, ranging from country-specific differences in language/culture in Europe, to a greater sense of conservatism in the European environment.[49]

That said, what concrete steps can the Western expatriate undertake to enhance his effectiveness in communication with the Indians? The Western expatriate needs to (a) have a better awareness about Indian communicative patterns; (b) be able to deal with his/her emotions more effectively; (c) avoid ideological debates; (d) be able to create the perception of an individual who enjoys working in the Indian subcultural milieu. The following paragraphs elaborate these steps.

(a) Better Awareness about Indian Communicative Style

This is a truism but that does not lessen its importance. If Western managers lack an appreciation of how Indians communicate, they may find themselves in all sorts of difficulties and may lose their motivation to effectively conclude their assignment. Although this recommendation has a commonsensical quality to it, it is extremely important for a number of different reasons. First, and foremost, heightened awareness has the implication that the Western manager is likely to have more realistic or accurate expectations about his interactions with the Indian counterpart.

When expectations are realistic/accurate, the manager may learn to recognize, for example, that the unwillingness on part of the Indians to say "no" does not imply that the Indian is in perfect agreement on the specific issue or subject under discussion. He may have to probe further to get the answer he/she is looking for. In other words, a heightened sense of awareness will minimize misunderstandings and/or miscommunication. Similarly, when expectations are accurate, the manager is unlikely to experience negative emotions like frustration, anger, or anxiety, and this is surely beneficial for the interaction at hand. Not only are the manager's attentions not diverted away from the task at hand; he is also unlikely to act in ways that may jeopardize future interaction. Accurate expectations may also convey to the Indian counterpart that the Western manager is truly interested in India, in that he/she has taken the time to learn about the local culture. This can only have positive effects on the interaction among the parties.

(b) Better Equipped to Deal with Negative Emotions

Negative emotions are often inevitable in intercultural interactions. As mentioned earlier, these emotions are a product of conflicting expectations. Although heightened awareness of another culture does limit the emergence and the intensity of these emotions, it cannot prevent them entirely for a variety of reasons. First, the expectations of Western managers doing business in India are not going to change overnight. It takes a while before managers can both fully appreciate an alternative way by which people live, and most importantly, internalize these new expectations in their daily interactions with the Indian colleagues. Second, even with the best of preparation, no Western manager can hope to fully or completely grasp the Indian cultural nuances, with the implication that sometimes they may experience these emotions notwithstanding their prior preparation or understanding about the Indian culture.

How then, can the Western manager hope to deal with these emotions effectively? It must be said at the outset that in managing emotions there are important personality differences, which some individuals, being either more able or capable of handling these emotions well. That said, the Western manager, can clearly take steps that will minimize their occurrence. One of the things that may help the manager deal with these emotions in a positive way may come from the recognition that *he/she is not alone*. In other words, he/she must consider the possibility that there may be other Western expatriates who may be experiencing the same emotions. This recognition may not only bolster his/her self-confidence but may also induce him to network with other expatriates in the area. Most importantly, this will lead him/her to the invaluable insight that he/she has not been dealt with in a unique way by the Indians. This, in turn, is likely to prevent him/her from developing a negative attitude about the Indians and that can surely be considered to be a positive development.

Second, even if the expatriate experiences negative emotions, he must resist the urge to express them. As Ambrose Bierce once remarked, "Speak when you are angry and you will make the best speech you will ever regret."[50] Emotions like anger, if expressed openly, will damage the relationship and make it that much harder to put the relationship back on track. This does not imply that the expatriate should not express his concern about any issue or issues over which he/she has reservation; the argument is only that these concerns should be expressed in a culturally sensitive way. The Western manager may express his concerns calmly, may seek to revisit the issue later, or use the services of a key informant who may serve as a culturally adept mediator.

Third, the Western expatriate manager could seek to reframe the situation. He/she may want to look for the positive in an admittedly negative situation. This is not easy, but that is not to say, that one should not attempt it. Maybe, just may be, there is something in what the Indians have said, that at the very least, may be worth thinking about. This does not by any means exhaust all that the Western manager could do, but it does provide a broad overview of the strategies that the expatriate managers may use in bridging the cultural divide with their Indian counterpart.

(c) Avoid Ideological Debates

It is very easy to fall in this trap, and exiting from it is likely to be difficult. The Indian mind-set is both nationalistic and idealistic, and while the latter may be changing as India integrates itself in the world economy, nationalism is unlikely to disappear any time soon. The Western mind-set is for the most part pragmatic (although there may well be differences across countries) and this sets the stage for a clash of conflicting ideologies. In a business related context, ideological debates on the rapidity of the economic reform process in India and how open India should be for the transnational corporation have emerged.

These debates have also carried over to the issue or issues of protecting intellectual property, privatization, and the role of the government in the economy. Ideological debates brook no room for compromise, and if anything, may harden the position of the parties further. They may also detract from effective problem solving and may be counterproductive in the extreme. What is interesting about India is that ideological conflicts notwithstanding, transnational corporations can function effectively and profitably in the Indian context (though the energy sector may be an exception).

(d) Creating the Perception of a Positive Attitude toward India

It is important that Western expatriates demonstrate a positive attitude toward India. This is a proposition that would be equally true for any culture one wishes to operate in, but this is likely to have a particular resonance in the Indian cultural context. The Indian mind-set has, fortunately or unfortunately, been deeply shaped by the colonial experience (see chapter one), and this has the implication that there is, at least initially, a certain degree of suspicion toward the foreign investor.

Clearly this suspicion may not be equally targeted toward all foreign investors, but it does mean that the foreign investor has to create a certain sense of reassurance in the Indian mind. This reassurance is best demonstrated by creating the perception that the expatriate has a positive view of, and toward, India. A good example is provided in a study of the BAC Corporation in India, conducted by Sinha. Mr. Wilson, a British national, who was the Managing Director of the Company, had adapted and felt comfortable with the Indian mores. As Sinha notes, "He freely mixed with employees, often took lunch with them, attended their marriage ceremonies, spoke broken Hindi and Punjabi, and seemed to love the Indian curry. Employees found in him a great listener."[51] This may indeed be one of the reasons as to why the Indian employees, by and large, had positive views of British expatriates.

Communicating cross-culturally is often never easy, nor entirely predictable. Each party seeks to communicate on the basis of its own sets of assumptions and this is without doubt, the starting point of any conflict. This chapter has attempted to outline the cultural divide separating the Western manager from his/her Indian counterpart. In years to come, this divide may be lessened, but in the interim some suggestions as to how best this divide can be mediated have been provided.

Chapter Eight

Managing Relationships with the Indian Government: The Critical Challenges for Multinational Firms

Introduction

Historically, the relationship between multinational firms and developing countries has been that of conflict.[1] This "conflict" view found its expression in the "obsolescence bargaining model" developed by Raymond Vernon.[2] This model conceptualized the relationship between multinational firms and host countries in terms of the key construct of bargaining power. When a multinational firm first enters a host country, it has the bargaining advantage at the point of entry but this advantage is lost once the multinational firm invests in the country. The fixed assets of the firm now become a hostage to the policies of the host country and the government can potentially alter the terms of the new bargain in its favor. This framework was originally applied to explain the expropriation of assets of multinational firms active in the natural resources sector. Subsequently, the framework was utilized for explaining investment of multinational firms in the manufacturing sector but with much less convincing results.[3]

Since the early 1980s, and continuing to date, there has been a shift in the tenor of the relationship between the multinational firms and the developing countries.[4] Many commentators now acknowledge that the relationship is much more cooperative rather than contentious, as was the case previously.[5] This shift in the tenor of the relationship, has been attributed by scholars to a number of different factors. Some have argued that there is now the recognition among the managers of multinational firms and host country governments that they are mutually interdependent, and to maximize the benefits of this interdependence, they must learn to cooperate.[6]

Others have suggested that this may be a consequence of a lack of other sources of capital for stimulating development and greater confidence among host country officials that they can deal more effectively with multinational enterprises.[7] It has also been suggested that globalization and market liberalization have altered the goals of host countries, in that they are now making a concerted effort to enhance their competitiveness in the world economy.[8] Finally, scholars have also argued that multilateral institutions have also begun to constrain what host countries can and cannot do in their interactions with the multinational firms.[9] One can gain a sense of the magnitude of this shift when one realizes that in 1985 multinational firms invested US$15 billion in the developing world whereas in 2002 they had invested up to US$162 billion.[10]

The increasing prevalence of cooperative tenor in the relationship between multinational firms and host country governments does not imply that the relationship is free of conflict. Both actors have their own goals and will seek to maximize their potential benefits from the relationship. The potential tensions that exist in the relationship between multinational firms and host countries revolve around both economic as well as noneconomic issues. From an economic perspective the critical issue is: Does the activity of the multinational firm enhance the overall economic welfare of the country? This is largely dependent on whether the activity of the multinational firm in the host country leads to positive or negative spillovers.[11]

Positive spillovers occur when the activities of multinational firms induce local entrepreneurs to adopt the new techniques that the multinational firms bring with them. An additional channel of influence is through the upgrading of human capital in the host country as the multinational firm trains its employees. Other mechanisms are through the provision of technical assistance to local suppliers, an upgradation of product quality standards, and the provision of higher quality intermediate inputs to local customers.[12]

If multinational firms were to transfer higher value-added activities to developing countries, positive spillovers are likely to be enhanced. Indeed, critics of multinational firms often argued that these firms were reluctant to share their technology, had a preference for using imported rather than local inputs, and often kept high value-added activities such as research and development centralized at corporate headquarters.[13] Additional criticisms centered around the fact that multinational firms introduced undesirable consumption patterns in the local economy, used transfer prices to transfer profits from host to home countries, and generated maximal profits using their monopoly power.[14]

Noneconomic issues are of no less importance to the host country in appraising the beneficial or harmful effects of foreign direct investment. One of the major concerns revolves around the potential power of these firms and their willingness to be complicit in actions that involve the overthrow of a government that may be hostile to them. Although these actions may not be commonplace, they nevertheless do cast a shadow on the integrity of the multinational firm.[15] The role played by ITT against Salvador Allende's government in Chile and the involvement of the United Fruit Company in the coup in Guatemala in 1954 are two such examples.

The involvement of multinational corporations in paying bribes to government officials is also an issue that generates antipathy against these firms. Although the U.S. Foreign Corrupt Practices Act explicitly prohibits the payment of bribes, many other developed countries such as France and Germany had much more lax standards. In countries such as France, Germany, and Japan, firms were allowed to deduct bribes as business cost.[16] More recently, the OECD has adopted a "Corruption Convention on the Bribery of Foreign Officials (CCBFO)."[17] Under the terms of the convention, which includes the world's ten leading exporters, governments were to enact legislation that would specifically make it illegal to pay bribes to foreign officials. Other potential negative effects of multinational firms on host country economies revolve around the fact that multinational firms may relocate to developing countries to take advantage of the lower and often lax enforcement of environmental standards. Similarly, it has been argued to some effect that multinational firms may produce a "race to the bottom," as they relocate/transfer their production to countries characterized by lower/lax labor standards and lowered wages.[18] A recent study conducted by analysts at the McKinsey Business Institute comes to the conclusion that on balance, foreign investment plays a positive role in emerging market economies.[19] The authors point out that in 13 of the 14 industries that they examined foreign direct investment was most certainly beneficial. The benefits of foreign direct investment were many.

First of all, foreign investment either provided consumers with a greater variety of products to choose from and/or led to lowered prices. They note, for example, that in India the prices of air conditioners, televisions, and washing machines declined by 10 percent after foreign firms entered the sector. Or consider the case of the automobile industry in India. In the early 1980s the Indian automotive sector was dominated by two companies that produced two models using 1960s technology and sold them for a price of US$20,000. In contemporary India there are a minimum of 30 car models, which are marketed in India with their prices reducing by about 8–10 percent every year.

Second, analysts note that the jobs created by multinational firms are often high paying ones, and not low paying ones as the critics charge. For example, in India's business process outsourcing sector wages are 50–100 percent higher vis-à-vis other white collar jobs requiring similar skills.[20] Other studies are also supportive of the fact that foreign investors have made important contributions to the Indian economy. Analysts note that the development of the software industry in India was greatly aided by multinational firms. Multinational firms such as Hewlett Packard, Motorola, and Texas Instruments developed strong links with local educational institutions and in doing so helped to upgrade the human capital in the industry. Other firms such as Nortel transferred leading edge technologies to their Indian collaborators, as well as management and marketing know-how, and in that sense increased the overall sophistication of the industry.[21]

Similarly in the automotive industry, the Swedish truck maker Volvo, had established a truck assembly plant in India in 1998. To facilitate the production of quality products, the company helped its Indian suppliers upgrade their technical and managerial capability. Interestingly, the greatest assistance was given to suppliers who were the weakest.[22]

While these studies are clearly supportive of the view that foreign direct investment is beneficial, it would be fair to say that no study can be fully or definitely conclusive in this matter. As Wells points out, "Some FDI is good; almost certainly some is harmful. But exactly what kind of investment falls into each category is frightfully difficult to determine even if the effects are measured only against economic criteria."[23] This means, that there will always be some investments that will be controversial and may lead to bitter wrangling between the multinational and the host country. An example is the foreign investment in the energy sector in countries as diverse as Pakistan, India, and the Dominican Republic. Many of these projects have attracted considerable criticism, and in the case of Enron in India, have led to a bitter dispute with the Indian government. Overall, it would be fair to say that multinationals are now viewed more positively than has been the case previously, although such a perception is likely to continue only if the interactions between the multinationals and the host country are viewed as being mutually beneficial.

India and the Multinationals: A Contested Relationship?

The relationship between the multinationals and the Indian government has passed through several phases. In the first decade after independence in 1947, there were few multinationals operating in India as the government was split about the desirability of attracting multinational firms.[24] The government was forced to adopt a more positive attitude toward multinational firms following the foreign exchange crisis of 1957. This crisis was putting a severe brake on the desire of the Indian government's decision to import foreign technology, which was essential for enhancing India's industrial development. The government then struck a bargain with multinational firms whereby the latter would be allowed to gain majority equity in exchange for their technological as well as financial contributions. This about-turn in Indian policy led to an increase in foreign investment. As Encarnation points out, "Just ten years after the 1957 crisis, multinationals controlled one-fifth of India's corporate assets, up from one-tenth at the time of the crisis. By bundling foreign equity with foreign technology, multinationals during the 1960s enjoyed a degree of bargaining power unrivaled in the history of independent India."[25]

This positive attitude toward the multinationals was not to last for ever. Beginning in the mid-1960s, the government decided to once again reevaluate its policy toward foreign investment.[26] This ultimately culminated in the enactment of the draconian "Foreign Exchange Regulation Act" in 1973. Under the new provisions, multinational firms were required to dilute their equity holdings to 40 percent. Companies that wished to attain higher levels of equity were either required to provide leading edge technology and/or export a significant proportion of their output from India. This was the period during which IBM and Coca Cola decided to exit from India, as they preferred not to follow the dictates of the new legislation.

As was to be expected, the number of foreign firms entering the Indian market annually declined from 101 in the early 1960s to 37 during the period 1968–1979.[27] Interestingly enough, even as the number of new foreign entrants declined, most multinationals that were already active in the Indian market preferred to stay rather than exit India.[28] Their decision to stay, notwithstanding the apparent unattractiveness of the new investment regime in India can be explained by a number of factors. First, given India's strict restrictions on imports, an exit would have meant a total withdrawal from the Indian market. Second, it appears that many of these multinationals were able to negotiate favorable agreements, even in an illiberal investment regime.[29]

Beginning in the 1980s the government decided to take a fresh look at the foreign investment regime. As Sinha points out, "They developed complacency about maintaining quality and range of products. The public sector undertakings accumulated losses in the name of building industrial base and indulging in welfare measures irrespective of their financial health. Employees bled many companies white by making personal or sectoral gains. There was too much of bureaucratization in granting licenses. Technology was getting obsolescent."[30]

The first beginnings toward a more liberal regime were initiated during this period. The government now sought to liberalize import of capital and technology and sought to attract the involvement of more multinational firms. Sinha points out that many of these new measures had a positive impact. As he observes, "The average number of foreign corporations that were approved during the period 1980–89 increased to 171.90 per year compared to 37.08 during the restrictive phase."[31]

Although the first steps toward liberalizing the foreign investment regime had taken place in the 1980s, it was the newly elected Congress government led by Mr. Narasimha Rao that gave a significant boost to foreign investors. Facing a grave balance of payments crisis, the government sought loans from the International Monetary Fund. The Fund did give India the loan but on the condition that it take steps to liberalize the economy. One of the major changes in the foreign investment regime involved the elimination of 40 percent cap on foreign equity. But for a few restricted sectors, the Reserve Bank of India now gave automatic approval for foreign investors to acquire 51 percent equity.

In 1998, the government also allowed foreign investors to increase their stakes in Indian banks to 40 percent. The insurance sector was also opened up to the foreign investors although a maximum cap of 26 percent was placed on foreign equity participation. More recently, the government has further relaxed norms concerning foreign direct investment with 100 percent equity ownership now allowed in the advertising sector.[32]

All the policy initiatives now undertaken by the Indian government are, without doubt, easing the path for multinationals to operate in the country. That said, tensions do continue to exist in the relationship between the multinational firms and the Indian government. These tensions can be traced to (a) a sentiment of nationalism that pervades the country and to which any democratically elected government must be accountable; (b) bureaucratic inertia/infighting that often slows down the approval process; (c) the prevalence of corruption; and (d) defensive strategies employed by local firms to ward off multinational competitors. These issues are elaborated below.

(a) Nationalism

Although the attitudes toward multinational firms are changing in India, there is still a certain degree of ambivalence about them. The Washington based Pew Research Center's 2003 global attitude survey revealed that India was the most nationalistic country.[33] Ambivalence has many sources, but perhaps one of the most important is the fear that multinational firms may pose a threat to a country's sovereignty.[34] If multinational firms come to dominate the Indian environment, decision-making may be transferred to outsiders and they may act in ways that may not be conducive to maximizing Indian economic, political, and/or social welfare. Indeed, this was the rationale underlying the Foreign Exchange Regulation Act of 1973, which required multinationals to dilute their equity holdings. Although this act is no longer in force and while attitudes, without doubt have changed, there is still this residual impact of nationalism that is ever present. This has, and continues, to affect government policy in a number of ways.

For example, in many of the privatizations initiated by the Indian government, most of the buyers were domestic rather than foreign companies. Although this was not by any conscious design on part of the Indian government, this outcome was welcomed by the then Minister of Disinvestment, Arun Shourie. As he noted, "Foreign companies never thought that this process would go through, so they aren't always willing to fully commit. It is not such a bad thing. If foreign companies were buying everything, there would be immediate backlash throughout the country. It is better that most of it comes from green-field investments."[35]

Perhaps one of the most dramatic examples of nationalistic backlash was in the investment undertaken by the now bankrupt U.S. energy firm Enron. Although this case is in many ways unusual, it does highlight how badly things can go wrong if a multinational firm is insensitive to the perceptions of its actions in an environment that harbors some degree of ambivalence toward foreign investment/investors.

Enron was one of the first foreign power producers to set up a power project, when this sector was opened up to foreign investment, following the reforms initiated in 1991. The company proposed to build a 2000 MW power project (US$2.8 billion) in the state of Maharashtra to overcome the state's deficiency in power supply. The initial negotiations were difficult and were not helped by the fact that the project did not receive the support of the World Bank. Nevertheless, an agreement was reached, but much to the chagrin of the company, when a new government came to power in the state they challenged the legality of the agreement and sought to cancel it "on grounds of fraud, corruption, and misrepresentation."[36] Although Enron contested these allegations, it did arrive at a new agreement with the regulatory authorities.

However, this was not to be the end of a long saga involving both the regulatory authorities and the wider public. Phase I of the project became operational in 1999 while phase II was not expected to be operational till 2002. The state government became concerned about the project along with other stakeholders, as they felt that the price charged by Enron was nearly four times that of domestic power producers.[37] Enron expressed a willingness to discuss the issue but was not willing to substantially change the terms of the contract. This negotiating impasse continued to deepen with Enron indicating that it will withdraw from the Dabhol project and the State Electricity Board stating that it will not buy any more power from the Dabhol Power Company. With Enron declaring bankruptcy in 2001, the other investors in this project (General Electric and Bechtel) sought to recover their investment by initiating arbitration proceedings against the Indian Government in 2003. There have been protracted attempts to resolve this dispute.

While Enron may have been an exceptional case in many ways, foreign power producers have faced some difficult times. As Rangan and McCaffrey note, "In late 2003, more than ten years after Enron began its ill-fated power project, foreign investors had not forgotten, how in the early 1990s, Enron was one of the seven international companies who accepted the Government's offer of 'fast track' approval to build power generation plants. All had since withdrawn from the sector and were tied up in litigation over the Government's alleged failure to honor guarantees on the original terms and conditions."[38] While foreign investors were understandably concerned about the fact that the contractual terms were not being met, it would also be fair to say that the contractual terms in these agreements were rather one sided with the buyer (usually a state-owned electricity board) bearing all the risk and the seller (energy producer) bearing very little of it.[39] Given the one sided nature of these agreements, it is easily understandable why these agreements provided a fertile ground for nationalist sentiment to gain expression.

More recently, Coke and Pepsi were involved in a difficult situation caused by the Center for Science and Environment, a nongovernmental organization based in India. This center made the allegation that the soft drinks sold by these companies contained pesticides that exceeded the European Union (EU) norms. Coke was alleged to have pesticides 45 times greater than the EU limit while Pepsi exceeded that limit 37 times.[40] As soon as these allegations were made, there was an uproar in the country. Many state governments decided to institute their own testing of the soft drinks of these companies while the Indian parliament prohibited the sale of these products on their premises. The impact of these allegations were consequential. Analysts point that within a week of the publication of the report by the Center for Science and Environment, the sales of colas had declined by 30–40 percent.[41]

Given the potential negative ramifications of this incident, Coke and Pepsi decided to work together to combat the negative publicity, notwithstanding the fact that the companies were "arch rivals." Fortunately for all concerned, the independent testing carried out by the central government revealed that, by and large, the pesticide content in the soft drinks was within the prescribed norms. Even in those cases where the pesticide levels exceeded the EU norms, they were only 1.6 to 5.2 times higher vis-à-vis the range of 11–70 reported by the nongovernmental organization.[42] The independent testing carried out by the government helped diffuse the crisis a bit, but once again, the incident reveals how easy it might be to raise nationalist sentiments in the country. It may be noted that at the time of writing, the Indian Supreme Court has directed all cola companies to print the limits of pesticides on the labels of the bottles and cans.

Many senior executives of multinational firms operating in India feel that they are highly salient targets for the political activists. Commenting on their feelings, Bhatia notes, "In private, they say they are the victims, convenient whipping boys in the name of 'Swadeshi', but it's a feeling that dares not speak its name."[43]

(b) Bureaucratic Inertia/Infighting

"In terms of bureaucracy, Canadian firms thought that uncertainty in business transactions, the length of time, and the paper work it took to set up operations in India were quite onerous. Once a contract was signed, there was still no guarantee of market access. One firm cited a change in state government that led to a project's cancellation. It took this firm over a year to find out the status of its project."[44] This observation highlights one of the major challenges facing multinational corporations seeking to do business in India. The idea that Indian bureaucratic behavior leaves much to be desired is a theme that is echoed by many.[45] As Gurcharan Das, a retired senior manager and distinguished author in India recounts, "In my thirty years in active business, I did not meet a single bureaucrat who really understood my business, yet he had the power to ruin it."[46] Mr. Das is not alone in making these observations. In a review of Mr. Shourie's book on governance, Luce notes, "Yet its senior civil servants, who include some of the world's most educated people, often seem to inhabit a parallel universe in which 'action' is defined by an internal code that bears little relation to the society it serves."[47]

The Indian bureaucrats have traditionally had a "smugness" about them, that is, a sense that they know the best. When this is coupled with their lack of specialist training, and frequent job rotations, it is unlikely to create a bureaucracy that is genuinely motivated and capable of minimizing problems rather than amplifying them.[48] This bureaucratic inertia is often compounded by interagency conflicts both at the central level as well as between the center and the state. If we add to this, the absence of a strong motivating factor to engage in innovative behavior, the problem only gets compounded. As Rufin, Rangan, and Kumar note, "The decision making process is slow. Bureaucrats are penalized for errors but not appreciated for performance."[49]

That bureaucratic behavior may well be a major impediment is dramatically illustrated by the A.T. Kearney's FDI confidence audit of India in 2001. This study revealed that bureaucratic hurdles were stifling the flow of foreign direct investment into India.[50]

(c) Corruption

The problem of corruption is as old as human history. As Kennedy and Di Tella note, "More than 2000 years ago, an Indian prime minister wrote extensively about the topic and Chinese officials were given an extra allowance to 'nourish incorruptibility.' Corruption played a prominent role in many of Shakespeare's plays. And the US constitution named bribery as one of the two explicitly mentioned crimes for which a president would be impeached."[51] As trade and investment has begun to flourish in an era of globalization, issues of corruption are once again rising to the forefront in the debate on the ethics of doing business overseas.

At the outset it may be useful to note that the term corruption embraces a wide range of potentially negative behavior. Elliot, for example, draws a distinction between petty corruption, grand corruption, and influence peddling that may vary in its legitimacy.[52] Petty corruption, as she suggests, involves low-level bureaucrats and is most commonly associated with circumventing bureaucratic regulations concerning industrial activity. Grand corruption entails the involvement of high-level officials and is often used to influence their decisions on major policy initiatives and/or procurement decisions on major contracts. Finally, influence peddling involves lobbying by private actors vis-à-vis politicians with the goal of influencing their decision-making.

There is a near unanimous consensus that corruption is ethically unacceptable and that it has negative economic, political, and social impact on the society.[53] One of the most outspoken critics of corruption is Peter Eigen, Chairman of Transparency International, a nongovernmental organization that is dedicated to combating corruption. As he notes, "Corruption distorts decision making, as kickbacks prevail over quality, particularly in tenders and privatizations. The effects linger for years, not only because a culture of corruption becomes the norm among public officials, but also because wasteful mismanagement diverts resources needed for education, housing and healthcare into the pockets of corrupt elites. In short, corruption costs lives."[54]

More broadly, analysts note that corruption has both direct as well as indirect costs.[55] The direct costs of corruption are most evident in the use of bribes while indirect costs may take the form of lowered investment levels, distortion in public expenditures, and lowered rates of economic growth among others.[56] A recent study came to the conclusion that corruption has a negative impact on foreign investment.[57]

Scholars have characterized corruption on two dimensions, namely its pervasiveness and its arbitrariness.[58] The pervasiveness of corruption refers to how frequently illicit transactions are the norm in conducting business in a given country. The arbitrariness of corruption refers to the unpredictability with which corruption is organized in a given country. As some scholars note, "In such a setting, firms are uncertain of whom to pay, what to pay, and whether the payments will result in the delivery of the promised goods or services."[59] The arbitrariness of corruption is likely to make corruption less predictable and this in turn will increase the transaction costs for a company seeking to do business in a country. We would suppose that the pervasiveness of corruption may also increase transaction costs, but if the corruption is well structured, its effects may be less damaging for the firm in question.

In chapter five, an explanation of some aspects of corruption was discussed in detail. As noted, corruption is widespread in India. This is demonstrated both in the rankings of Transparency International as well as popular perceptions in the country. In the 2003 survey, India was ranked 83 out of 133 countries.[60]

Similarly, an analyst notes, "Even among the Indians themselves, the picture has been bleak as may be seen from a 1995 poll which showed that corruption was pervasive among many professions, with 98% of the respondents believing that politicians were corrupt on the one hand, and 38% of them believing that ordinary people were corrupt on the other hand."[61] India's ranking on this index has fallen from 35 in 1991 to 71 in 2002.[62] Indeed, some scholars have maintained that corruption in India is both pervasive and arbitrary.[63] Scholars maintain that pervasiveness and arbitrariness of corruption have a negative impact on foreign direct investment.[64] It most certainly increases the costs of doing business and through that mechanism it may deter potential foreign investors.

(d) Defensive Strategies Employed by Indian Firms

The liberalization of the Indian economy in the 1990s exposed the Indian firms to international competition either via the entry of new multinational firms in the Indian market or through imports, which were now liberalized. Many Indian firms felt overwhelmed by the new competitive pressures, and especially so, because previously they had led a rather cushy existence. In the previous regime, there were few incentives to create a "world class" company.

The incentive problems were compounded by the fact that the Indian firms lacked the capability to exploit scale economies, often lacked access to state of the art technology, felt powerless in competing with multinational firms that possessed the advantage of a well-known brand, had limited access to capital, and did not possess management expertise for confronting the realities of global competition.[65] The insecurities of the Indian firms were fully exposed when the Indian market was opened up to both foreign investment as well as imports from abroad.

One of the consequences of liberalization was the fact that many multinational firms that already had joint ventures with Indian partners, either sought to buy their Indian partners out, or alternatively, wanted to set up 100 percent owned subsidiaries. This somewhat aggressive inclination of the foreign investor was viewed with great alarm by the Indian partner. As Amit Mitra, Secretary General of the Federation of Indian Chamber of Commerce and Industry noted "if a foreign direct investor or technology collaborator had formed a joint venture with an Indian partner under whose leadership a great brand name was created, shareholders garnered, and financial institutional loans generated, can the multinational simply walk away and form a 100 per cent equity company of its own through the new policy of the 'automatic FDI route', leaving the Indian company in the lurch?"[66]

Faced with this threat, the Indian industrialists lobbied the Indian government to announce a new rule (covered by the now infamous "Press Note 18"), under which if a foreign company in an already existing joint venture wanted to create a new 100 percent subsidiary, it would first have to get the approval from the Foreign Investment Promotion Board, and subsequent to that, an approval or a certificate of no-objection from the Indian partner before it could initiate the new venture. Although this was clearly designed to safeguard the interests of the Indian partner, it is also the case that the Indian partner could use this rule opportunistically. The Indian partner could use this as a bargaining tool to get the foreign partner to pay more for its share than might have been the case otherwise, or alternatively by challenging the investors' decision, it could delay matters considerably. In either case, the foreign investors' ability to undertake new 100 percent owned ventures is constrained by this new requirement.

This defensive maneuvering obviously did not please the foreign investors, and while there are now moves afoot to scrap "Press Note 18" or substantially dilute it, it is still a contested issue. (Authors note—since the time of writing Press Note 18 is substantially diluted.)[67] The recent decision by Suzuki to establish a 100 percent owned diesel assembly plant in Haryana caused the Minister of Heavy Industry Santosh Mohan Dev to question Suzuki's wisdom in doing so.[68] As analysts note, after the announcement made by Suzuki, the Indian government accused the company of breaching the joint venture agreement. Shortly thereafter, the parties did conclude a deal in which Maruti would receive a minority equity position in the diesel engine joint venture.[69]

As stated in the beginning of this section, the relationship between the multinational firms and the Indian government has been a contested one. This is now changing, especially with the new Congress-led Government in power. To be sure, these challenges can and are successfully overcome by some of the multinationals operating in India, but then these firms have proven adept in navigating the institutional divide. It is to this issue that we turn now, namely, what can and should the multinational firms do in managing their relationships with the Indian government?

Managing the Interface with the Indian Government: What should the Multinational Firm do?

To be sure, there is no simple or easy answer to this issue. The multinational firm will have to be politically, culturally, as well as strategically astute in dealing with the challenges in the Indian environment. Astuteness does not mean that the firm has to be manipulative; only that it has to demonstrate good common sense in operating in the Indian environment. Fundamentally, the multinational firm has to (a) act in ways that help it attain, maintain, and defend its legitimacy in the Indian environment; (b) learn to cope with the Indian bureaucracy; and (c) maintain a low profile in the Indian environment. These aspects are elaborated below.

Attaining and Maintaining Legitimacy

Legitimacy means that the multinational firm is viewed in a positive way by the vast majority of the stakeholders in the environment. It is widely accepted that a multinational firm, which is not viewed as having attained legitimacy, will have difficulties in either entering the market or maintaining its success over a period of time.[70] A firm that is not able to garner legitimacy may invite greater critical scrutiny from the bureaucracy as well as from nongovernmental organizations. Consider the case of companies like Enron or Union Carbide, both of whom faced substantial opposition in the country for either what they did or did not do in the country. Union Carbide exited the country following the environmental disaster in Bhopal in 1984, while Enron was confronted with a continuous series of negotiations and renegotiations concerning its power plant in the state of Maharashtra. While these are, to be sure, highly salient and politically charged examples, they do not detract from the fundamental point that a firm must behave in a manner that will allow it to garner legitimacy. So the fundamental question is: What can and should a multinational firm do?

(a) Be Sincere. Sincerity refers to the level of commitment that the foreign investor shows to the environment within which it is operating. This can be gauged on a number of different dimensions. First, is the multinational firm in the country only interested in being there for a short term or does it intend to be there for a longer period? Is the multinational firm willing to undertake actions that might benefit the wider community or is it solely interested in maximizing profits? Is it really interested in understanding the viewpoints of the local stakeholders and engage in a meaningful dialogue with them as opposed to thrusting its own views? Is it committed to behaving in an ethical way by not resorting to corrupt business practices and maintaining the same standards as they do in their home countries? This is not an exhaustive list of actions that might test a firm's sincerity, but it is clearly illustrative of them. Scholars note that sincerity is essential for attaining legitimacy.[71] Sincerity allows a firm to gain credibility and trust among stakeholders and this is surely beneficial both for the host country as well as the firm in question.

A couple of examples illustrate firms that were able to garner legitimacy. Consider the case of Hindustan Lever, a subsidiary of the Anglo-Dutch giant, Unilever. This company has been operating in India even before the country gained independence and continues to enjoy an excellent reputation in the country.[72] How has the company been able to do it? First of all, the company made a conscious effort to indigenize its Indian operations. It designed products that suited Indian requirements, used Indian citizens to fill in managerial and technical positions, and established a large number of research centers in India. The company also had the foresight to help promote the social and economic objectives of the Indian government and state. The company established factories in the high poverty regions in the state of Uttar Pradesh and was an active participant in sustainable development projects like energy conservation, soil conservation, and the like.[73] It is therefore not surprising that this is a company that is much admired by the Indian public.

In a similar vein, Hewlett Packard has chosen to participate in a community development project in India. The goal is to use technology as a catalyst for facilitating economic development in a depressed area of the country. Dubbed as the Kuppam "i-community" project, the company is working with partners in the public and the private sectors to rejuvenate this region.[74] This is an area in which "One in three citizens is illiterate, more than 50% of the households have no electricity, and in Andhra Pradesh, the Indian state where Kuppam is located, more than 4 million children do not attend school."[75] There are many specific initiatives that the company has undertaken under its rubric, but all of them are fundamentally designed to help the local populace utilize technology to help them access information or services offered by the government.

(b) Demonstrate Flexibility. The multinational firm should ideally demonstrate flexibility at all phases of project execution, ranging from project evaluation, to negotiation, to project execution. When Western firms have entered emerging markets, such as India, they have approached them with what Prahalad and Lieberthal describe as an imperialistic mind-set.[76] This way of thinking tends to assume that what might be true in western Europe or the United States may be equally true of a country like India (see chapter six). As they point out, in many respects this assumption is false.

Assuming that the Indian middle class may be very similar to the Western middle class, many companies have introduced products that will just not sell in India. Ford introduced the Escort with a price tag greater than US$21,000—clearly a luxury car by Indian standards.[77] If multinational investors have erred in overestimating market demand for luxury products, they have also overlooked the fact that developing products for the poor can be equally attractive.[78] For example, Hindustan Lever, the subsidiary of Unilever introduced a candy for people at the very bottom of the social strata. Within six months, this product was to become the fastest growing product in the company's product portfolio! Such actions are also likely to confer upon the company an aura of legitimacy, which may make it difficult for the others to attack the company.

At the negotiating phase, it is important that the foreign investor understand the cultural proclivities of the Indians and adjusts his/her negotiating style to the demands of the situation. This is not to say that the foreign investor give in to unreasonable demands, only that the investor must not unreasonably insist on rigidly following a particular pattern of negotiation. The benefits of flexibility may not be immediately evident, but it is likely to create a tremendous amount of goodwill, which will stand the investor in good stead in the long term.

Flexibility implies that you care about the other person as well as understand his/her needs and this can surely be beneficial. Indeed, one of the problems that plagued Enron's ill fated venture was their lack of flexibility, in the absence of coercion, and surely that did them harm. They substantially modified their position only when the contract was cancelled but by that time they had already accumulated a lot of animosity. Given the infrastructural weaknesses, and the constraints of a coalitional democracy, it is also more than likely that at the implementation stage the project may experience problems, as many independent power producers were soon to recognize. But again here, it is important that the foreign investor not overreact to the situation. Flexibility will be at a premium in coping with an often rapidly changing environment. If the foreign investor is able to adapt to it, it may come out with its reputation enhanced. The case study of Wartsila Diesel, a Finnish company that is quite successfully active in India and discussed in this book, is a perfect illustration of the importance of flexibility.

(c) Communicate with Stakeholders. In a vibrant democracy such as India, there are many stakeholders groups, each of whom may have their own particular agenda in dealing with the multinational. That said, it is important that the multinational seek to communicate effectively with its stakeholders. Stakeholders can pressure the government to alter its policy vis-à-vis the multinationals if the latter appears to be unresponsive to their concerns. For this reason it is important that the multinational firm seek to initiate and maintain a dialogue with the stakeholders.

The communication must be timely, accurate, and meaningfully address the concerns of the stakeholders, if the firm is to garner the support of their stakeholders rather than their hostility.[79] Indeed, some commentators have argued that it might be more advantageous for companies to forge alliances with some stakeholders, such as the nongovernmental organizations, rather than actively clash with them.[80] Nongovernmental organizations bring in legitimacy and are a powerful mechanism for highlighting the saliency of social concerns and often possess unique technical expertise.

Although effective communication with stakeholders is clearly no guarantee of a project's success, it would be fair to say that poor communication will surely make the project more difficult. Again, it is instructive to examine how Enron sought to communicate with its stakeholders in the development of the Dabhol project. It has been pointed out that Enron did not communicate with the different stakeholders effectively.[81] As has been pointed out, Enron's communications were characterized by a lack of consistency and a lack of clarity.

On the one hand, Enron undertook several positive initiatives when it agreed to provide good drinking water to the villages surrounding the project. The company also committed itself to opening a hospital and schools in the surrounding area. The positive impact of these actions was, however, counteracted by Enron's reluctance to discuss issues concerning the project with stakeholders other than the government, and the policy initiative they undertook to educate Indians about the benefits of this project. The latter, in particular, was viewed as an attempt to pressurize the Indians into accepting the project. Similarly, in a letter written to the chairman of the Maharashtra State Electricity Board on June 28, 1993, Joseph Sutton stated, "I feel that the World Bank opinion can be changed. We will engage a PR firm during the next trip and hopefully manage the media from here on."[82] This statement may also be viewed as an attempt to engage in "arm twisting" of the World Bank. Enron's inept communication strategy had the consequence of solidifying opposition to its project when a group of leftist and secular parties joined forces in Maharashtra to oppose the project.[83] Eventually, it led to a strong polarization in the position of either side, making the viable resolution of conflict more difficult.

(d) Learning to Cope with the Indian Bureaucracy. As articulated earlier, the Indian bureaucracy is not necessarily the easiest to deal with. Apart from the "know it all" attitude of the bureaucrats, the inter-agency conflicts, and a reluctance to give up power, there is the added problem of multiple layers of bureaucracy. All this leads to delays, uncertainty, and a tremendous sense of frustration among the foreign investor who wishes to gain approval for a project or seeks the implementation of a negotiated agreement. It would be fair to say that for the foreign investor seeking to enter India for the first time, this may represent a hurdle that only time can overcome.

This has, first of all, the implication that any foreign investor seeking to enter India must have a *medium to a long-term horizon* to make it worthwhile for him/her to learn and master the intricacies of the Indian bureaucratic functioning. If the foreign investor has a joint venture partner, there is of course the possibility that bureaucratic interaction will fall in the lap of the Indian partner. In the short run, that is clearly the most viable alternative, although over a longer period, it may be useful for the foreign investor to build up his own links with the bureaucracy. This may open up a new channel of communication and may also serve as a potential restraint on the possibility of opportunism by the Indian partner. The foreign investor must factor the almost inevitability of bureaucratic delays while developing a viable project. It is also important to note that given the potent mix of ideology, idealism, and nationalism in the Indian mind-set, it is advisable to avoid any polemical arguments for they will lead no where.

Finally, and perhaps most importantly, the foreign investor must not be fazed by bureaucratic obstinacy and must not necessarily conclude that bureaucratic actions are necessarily targeted at him/her. Indeed, even the Indians face a similar set of bureaucratic obstacles in their day-to-day life.

(e) Maintain a Low Profile. Although the Indians are aggressive by inclination, it does not naturally follow that they will accept aggressiveness from others, especially from foreign investors. Aggressive persuasion, if attempted by the foreign investor, and especially by companies from the United States or United Kingdom will be viewed rather negatively. Enron is a perfect example. The company touted the benefits of its project and used highly placed government officials in the United States to press its case. This is not to say that the investor must not be persuasive in convincing the community of the benefits that it brings; the point is that this persuasion

must be managed collaboratively in relationships with other local constituents than in an imperial top-down fashion. Further, the rhetoric adopted by the foreign investor at any phase in project development must not aggravate the sensitivities of the different stakeholders. Clearly, this is not easy, and in a nationalistically charged environment it is definitely not possible to please everyone. What is crucial here is the recognition that any critical sentiment against the foreign investor does not cross a critical threshold beyond which the crisis cannot be managed.

Dealing with governments and bureaucracies, is for sure, a challenge everywhere. India is no exception in this regard, although given the unique developmental trajectory of the country, the Indian environment poses some unique challenges. The challenges and the ways in which multinational firms can deal with them have been highlighted in this chapter. At first glance, the Indian environment may prove rather daunting to the foreign investor. This is perhaps true, but the point is that these challenges can be effectively addressed if the multinational investor approaches the Indian market with the *right frame of mind.* This means being humble, being proactive but collaboratively, and being willing to engage in a two-way interaction rather than imposing a one way imperialistic mind-set.

Chapter Nine
Negotiating and Resolving Conflicts in India

If there is any one secret of success, it lies in the ability to get the other person's point of view and to see things from that person's angle as well as from your own.

Henry Ford in G.R. Shell, *Bargaining for Advantage*

The negotiator must appear as an agreeable, enlightened, and far seeing person; he must beware of trying to pass himself off too conspicuously as a crafty or an adroit manipulator. The essence of skill lies in concealing it, and the negotiator must ever strive to leave an impression upon his fellow diplomat of his sincerity and good faith.

Callieres, 1716/1963, 124, cited in W. Masterbroek, *Negotiating as Emotion Management*

As we know, the ability to negotiate is an important managerial skill. Whether dealing with employees, external stakeholders, or other business partners, managers must possess the skill to negotiate effectively. Managerial effectiveness in negotiating will determine whether a joint venture deal is signed, or a valuable employee is retained by a company, even though he/she may have other more lucrative offers. Negotiation is most fundamentally a tool for resolving conflict when actors have goals that are partially congruent and partially conflicting. If there were complete goal congruency, there would be no need for negotiation and likewise if the goals were completely incongruent, there would be no basis for negotiation.

Managers cannot but not negotiate; however they may negotiate either effectively or ineffectively. As Adler notes, "Negotiating effectively cross culturally is one of the single most important global business skills."[1] The ability to negotiate well is important for a number of different reasons. First and foremost, negotiating effectiveness determines whether (a) the parties are able to *create value* and (b) whether they are able to *maximize value creation*. Beyond this tangible economic benefit there are also *intangibles* that may be equally, if not more important, in the longer run.

Good negotiators not only create value but can also forge *strong interpersonal ties* with their counterparts. They must be able to earn the trust of others while also possessing the ability to trust others. Indeed, the ability to create and maintain relationships has often been cited as a critical skill in doing business internationally.[2] A further observation worth making is that good negotiators also enhance the overall *credibility* and *image* of the organization they are representing. Although it may be difficult to put a monetary value on the intangibles, they are without question, important in determining the effectiveness of the organization in the environment in which it is operating.

Although managers are often aware of the importance of negotiating effectively, their ability to do so may be compromised by the fact that negotiating situations are often *complex*.[3] The complexity of a negotiation stems from a number of different factors. First, there is the inherent tension between strategies designed to *maximize value creation* and strategies designed to *claim value*. The former would encourage information exchange whereas the latter would make managers cautious of sharing information, lest they be exploited.[4] Second, many negotiations unfold in situations of *ambiguity and uncertainty*. As Watkins notes, "When negotiations are complex, involving many parties and-or issues, negotiators may struggle to define simply their own alternatives, interests, and value tradeoffs across complex sets of issues."[5] Negotiating dynamics are also often critically shaped by the first impressions that the negotiators form of each other, and the emergence of a self reinforcing cycle of behavior that may either accentuate the *positive* or the *negative* in the interaction.[6]

Negotiation processes are also subject to a *tipping over effect*, in that once the negotiation process crosses a certain threshold, it is hard to reverse the negotiation process.[7] The complexity of the negotiation process is likely to be further aggravated by the number of actors involved in the negotiation processes and national cultural differences in the negotiating styles of the participants.[8]

Although there are a number of factors that contribute to the complexity of the negotiation processes, the focus of this section will be on the role played by culture, specifically Indian culture, in contributing to the complexity of negotiation processes in India. We begin by briefly outlining the role played by culture in shaping the negotiation process. Next, we look at how the dominant Indian cultural values, as outlined in the earlier chapters, shape Indian negotiating behavior. We conclude by outlining a set of recommendations for the Western expatriate in coping with Indian negotiating behavior.

Culture and Negotiation

The idea that culture influences negotiating behavior has become a commonplace wisdom with both academics and practitioners.[9] Some have argued that there are differences across cultures in the way managers seek to initiate the process of negotiations, make inferences about negotiation processes and outcomes, and manage conflict.[10]

The process of negotiation is broken down into four distinct stages, namely (a) non-task sounding; (b) information exchange; (c) persuasion; and (d) concession making.[11] This framework suggests that the *establishment of a relationship* is an essential prerequisite for making progress in negotiation. Scholars have noted that there are differences at other stages as well. Brett has persuasively argued that the manner in which negotiators exchange information differs across cultures.[12] She suggests that low context negotiators exchange information directly whereas high context negotiators exchange information directly. The latter are deeply concerned about not offending any one, and in particular, not causing the other negotiator to *lose face*. Hence there is a need for indirect communication.

Practitioners and scholars have also highlighted differences in *persuasive styles* as well as in *concession making* patterns across cultures.[13] In some cultures, persuasion is dependent on the use of facts whereas in other cultures emotional appeals play an important role. Likewise, in some cultures the pattern of concession making is reciprocal whereas in other cultures, nothing is settled unless everything is settled. The preferred negotiation strategy, be it *collaboration/problem solving* or *competitive/confrontational/contending*, is also shaped by culture.[14]

Negotiation is also a psychological game in which the negotiators have to form judgments/impressions about their counterparts. How sincere are they? How committed are they to the project that is being considered? What kind of alternatives do they have or might be considering? Is the best "offer," really the very best that they can do? This is by no means an exhaustive list of issues that negotiators have to consider, but it does highlight some *strategically salient issues* on which the negotiators will have to make a judgment. How easily do they make a judgment? How rigid or flexible are they on the judgments that they have made? How extreme or moderate is the judgment that they make?

Kumar has suggested that these *interpretations* are crucial in shaping how negotiations evolve over time, and that *culture* plays an important role in influencing the judgments that are made.[15] In many Asian cultures, for example, negotiators do not make judgments instantaneously. This stands in contrast to Europe and North America where negotiators often feel impelled to make judgments. Similarly, whether or not negotiators make extreme judgments depends on the tightness of the culture and the nature of issue at hand. In other words, in tight cultures judgments are likely to be more extreme.

Judgments involving people may be more extreme in tight as opposed to loose cultures. Conflicts are inevitable but the way conflicts are managed also varies across cultures. Kozan suggests that conflicts are either managed through the use of the *harmony, the confrontational, or the regulative model.*[16] The harmony model is often more concerned with *process* rather than *outcome* insofar as conflict resolution is constrained by the need to save face. By contrast, the confrontational model has the resolution of *substantive issues* as its major concern; and if that makes people unhappy, then so be it. The regulative model focuses on preexisting laws/rules to deal with the conflict.

The divergence in how negotiations proceed, interpretations are made, and conflicts are managed, has a number of important implications. Differences in negotiation styles across cultures imply *differences in expectations*, and it is the *differing set of expectations* that are often at the heart of intercultural conflict.[17] Often, individuals are not even aware that they are acting on the basis of implicitly held expectations.

The implications of *differences in negotiation styles* are profound. These differences can, at the very least, increase the time required to conclude a business deal. The consequences can however also be much more severe. Scholars have noted that differences in expectations can generate negative emotions and mistrust.[18] When negotiators experience emotions such as frustration, anger, tension, or anxiety they may display behaviors that may widen the gulf between the parties. Frustration, most typically, results in an aggressive response and this may manifest itself in negotiators blaming their counterparts for bad faith or lying.

Needless to say, the counterpart may react in a similar manner, and this may accentuate the conflict. When negotiators experience tension or anxiety, they fear that they may be taken advantage of by the other party, and to prevent that from happening may seek to exit the negotiation. Even if some of these dire consequences were not to occur, the *differences in negotiation styles* are, at the very least, likely to engender confusion and disorientation, and this in itself does not provide a good foundation for successful negotiations.

The Indian Negotiating Style

> *On the personal front, however the European interest and respect for other cultures usually get the contacts off to a good start, but the direct, supposedly logical, European approach, can get frustrated with Indian subtleties once one gets down to questions of strategy, agreements, and investments. The European will often have the impression that one issue has been agreed upon but see it return in a different presentation for renegotiation, as to Indians, advantage may be more important than speed.*
>
> C. Wilhelm, *Doing Business in India*

> *In India, the significance of a business arrangement is often determined by the amount of time spent in negotiations.*
>
> M. Kammeyer, *The Other Customs Barrier*

> *Often it seems like they are just so stubborn. Whatever you propose they reject it straight away, without giving it any real consideration. And then you propose something else, and they reject that too. They think that their way is best and will just refuse your suggestions every time.*
>
> Comment of a Danish manager, cited in M. Hughes, *A Theoretical and Empirical Analysis of Indian and Chinese Negotiating Behavior*

> *The Indians are extremely polite. They never want to make the other person feel uncomfortable. They do not push you. You can leave a meeting without knowing whether you have made an agreement. I am still trying to find out what their real intentions are.*
>
> Comment of a Danish manager in a personal interview with the author

These statements made by Western managers and/or westerners, with some experiences in doing business in India, shed some light on the way that Indians seek to approach negotiations. The Indian manager, may or may not see himself/herself from that perspective, and in that sense, it would be fair to say that these perceptions do not constitute any objective reality, but by contrast, only represent a very *subjective lens* employed by Westerners. That said, it is *subjectivity* that shapes human behavior and in particular, the *subjectivity* of the Western managers in shaping their interactions with the Indians. In other words, these reflections made by Western managers reflect their *perceptions* of Indians, and in that sense are important, because *perceptions shape behavior.*

In any event, these comments shed light on how the Indians are *perceived as negotiators*. The remarks suggest that the Indian approach to negotiations is different in many respects from how the Europeans/Americans would approach the negotiations. The Indians, from a Euro-American perspective appear to be both indirect as well as contentious. They also seem to maximize their own self-interest to the highest degree that they can and seem to view time less as a constraint and more as an indicator of what may be at stake in negotiations.

The following paragraphs attempt to shed more light on Indian negotiating behavior by (a) describing in some detail the Indian approach to negotiations; and (b) outlining the reasons for why Indians negotiate in the manner that they do.

(a) Orientation toward Negotiations

The Indian negotiators think of negotiation as a *problem solving* exercise whose success is to be gauged by the negotiator's *cleverness* in designing an ideal solution to the problem.[19] The stress on the ideal solution implies that the Indian negotiators have *high aspiration levels* which they attempt to translate into reality.[20] The high *aspiration levels* with which the Indian negotiators enter into negotiations have a number of different implications.

First of all, the search for the ideal implies that all possibilities have to be explored and the implications of all possible contingencies outlined. This has as its natural consequence that Indian negotiators try to gather and evaluate as much information as is possible. A natural consequence of this is that the negotiation process will slow down. While this may be of some concern to the Westerners, the Indians are less troubled by it as they appear to have a more *elastic view of time.*[21]

High *aspiration levels* also have the associated implication that the Indian negotiators will view the other negotiator's position/situation with a degree of criticality. While a critical perspective is no doubt essential for preventing undesirable outcomes from occurring, an overcritical mind-set may seek to find flaws in just about everything. Overanalysis may at times, have the consequence of leading to a paralysis in "decision making."

The negotiation process may once again be slowed down or alternatively, may make the Western manager rather frustrated, inducing him to exit the negotiation process. There is one other subtle implication of the Indian tendency to search for the ideal solution. The Indian negotiator may become so preoccupied by demonstrating to the other party that his/her method of dealing with issues is indeed the *right* or the *correct* one, that he/she overlooks the larger purpose of the deal that is to create a *mutually profitable transaction.*

Alternatively, the Indian manager may become so *fixated* on his/her imaginary ideals that he becomes divorced from the *constraints of the empirical world.* As a Danish manager commented, "*I would say that most Indians have high expectations, when it comes to negotiations. When I was living in India, I knew of a joint venture company who were trying to increase their sales. They discovered that it is the sales unit where the money comes from and so, they decided to expand their sales team to generate more orders. Naturally, more orders were taken, but they had not thought that they would need to produce more goods to be able to fulfill the orders. Production was unable to cope with the new orders.*"[22]

Another example of the Indian tendency to think in *idealistic* terms comes from an examination of the Indian policy to encourage foreign investors to invest in the Indian energy sector. Following the onset of economic reforms in 1991, the decision makers in the Indian bureaucracy recognized that to accelerate and sustain India's economic growth it was essential that the government encourage more foreign power producers to invest in the country. The Indian government anticipated a need of 10,000 MW of additional capacity but during the period 1991–2000 the net additional expansion was only 2,000 MW.[23] One of the major problems that impeded the ability of the government to attract investment in this sector was the lack of consistency and continuity in governmental policy. They may have had high expectations but their ability to pursue them in this context was very *constrained.*

This does not imply that *an idealistic mode of thinking* is necessarily constraining. It has been pointed out that *high aspiration levels* are often essential for attaining high quality solutions.[24] The problem arises when there is a gap between *high-minded thinking* that may either not be congruent with reality, or the case where high-minded thinking is compromised by poor or ineffective implementation. When properly harnessed, *idealism* can lead to positive outcomes.

(b) Negotiating Strategy

It is known that there is a distinction between the strategies of yielding, problem solving, avoiding, contending.[25] Some have maintained that there is a fifth viable strategy, which may be labeled as "compromise." These strategies have been outlined on the basis that a negotiator has two fundamental concerns, namely a concern about one's outcome and a concern about the other parties' outcome. When both of these concerns are high, the negotiating strategy is called problem solving but when the negotiator is solely concerned about his outcome and shows little concern for the other party's welfare, the strategy is referred to as contending.

These strategies are, as the name indicates, polar opposites of each other. Avoiding implies a situation where concern for oneself and that for one's partner are both low whereas yielding is a situation where one sacrifices one's needs for the other party. Practitioners as well as academic scholars are given to use the terms win–win and win–lose rather often, with the win–win strategy often being considered to be a highly desirable one. In terms of the framework outlined above, the win–win strategy bears strong affinity to a problem solving strategy, whereas a win–lose strategy has strong affinity with the contending strategy.

What reasonable inferences can one draw about the type of strategy that the Indian negotiators are likely to prefer? Although each situation is unique, and the Indian negotiators are likely to be sensitive to the subtle nuances of each specific situation just like any other group of negotiators, the *dominant strategy* that is likely to be characteristic of a typical Indian negotiator can be outlined in broad terms.

Given the preoccupation with obtaining *ideal outcomes*, the Indian negotiators are unlikely to easily make concessions. In the event where arguments take on a strong *moral tone*, the ability of negotiators to engage in making trade offs is diminished even further.[26] The strategy therefore has all of the attributes of what may be perceived to be a *contending strategy*. While the Indian negotiator may not perceive the strategy that he/she is pursuing to be a contending one, the reluctance of the Indian negotiator to easily make concessions may be viewed by the Western counterpart as representing a contending strategy. Indeed as Wilhelm notes, "The European businessman has a more linear 'business-school-like' approach and is usually surprised by the tug of war atmosphere that pervades business dealings in India. It is not uncommon to hear comments during negotiations such as 'are all negotiations as difficult as this'?"[27]

(c) Evaluation of Negotiation Outcomes

It stands to reason that a negotiated agreement that is seen as *fair* is more likely to be durable. The idea that *fairness* plays an important role in negotiations is an axiom that has gained widespread recognition both in the academic as well as in the practitioner oriented community. However, even as concerns of *fairness* are now taking center stage in negotiations, what constitutes fairness is debatable.

Informed observers have now begun to view *fairness* both from the perspective of outcome allocations, as well as from the standpoint of the processes used to generate those outcomes.[28] Outcome allocation has been looked at from the standpoint of three alternative norms, namely *equity, equality*, and *need*.[29] The norm of equity dictates that outcomes be proportional to inputs; the norm of equality that there should be an equal division among the actors; whereas the norm of need dictates that the party that is in greater need should get a greater share of the pie. *Procedural justice*, by contrast, focuses on the processes governing the negotiation. The central questions here are: Do the parties treat each other with respect? Do they refrain from lying and/or engaging in behavior that may be considered questionable? Do they give an opportunity to the other party to make their views and concerns known?

Although, both *distributive* and *procedural justice* are important in India, like elsewhere, it has been pointed out that issues of *distributive justice*, vis-à-vis *procedural justice* have greater resonance in the Indian context.[30] In large part, this may be reflective of the phenomenon of a *poverty syndrome* that has been described by Sinha and Kanungo.[31] Poverty syndrome refers to a situation where people are very afraid of becoming poor and think of themselves as being in a perilous state than may be warranted by objective conditions. This is a condition reflective of a society where historically resources have been scarce.

The saliency of *distributive justice concerns* in the Indian sociocultural context has a number of different implications. First, the Indians will be very sensitive to issues of outcome allocation and may use a variety of strategies to attain their desired outcomes. In a story related to one of the authors when living in Finland, a Finnish manager recalled his negotiations with an Indian company. The manager indicated that the Indians made the argument that because they were from a developing country they could not afford to pay the price for technology that the Finnish company was demanding. They wanted a reduction in price and in this specific instance used *emotional appeals* to put forward their argument.

Of course, this is not the only way that they can express their concerns about outcome allocations. They may attempt to renegotiate the terms or insist on greater effort or contribution from the foreign partner that may not have been originally envisaged. Indeed as Kumar notes, there is "the continual Indian insistence that the foreign partner assist them on a long term basis without getting any equivalent concessions. If this expectation of generosity is not met, Indians develop resentment against their foreign colleagues."[32]

(d) Attitude toward Contracts[33]

For an average Western business person, the success of business efforts are best gauged by the existence of a signed contract. While the use of contracts may be widespread across cultures, the dominant type of contract that is used may well be different. A distinction may be drawn between the transactional, the relational, the ethical, and the ideological forms of contracting. While all contracts contain obligations, they differ in relation to the pervasiveness of obligations, and whether these obligations are codified or not. Transactional contracting reflects a high degree of codification as well as a relatively narrow scope of obligations. At the other end of the spectrum is ideological contracting. This is characterized by a low degree of codification as well as entailing acceptance of a broader set of obligations.

It is transactional contracting, which is the dominant contractual form in the Western world. Transactional contracting provides both *psychological reassurance* as well as *legal safeguards* against any potential contractual breaches. The actors are willing to sue their counterparts if circumstances so dictate. This is not to imply that *legal action* is the preferred mode for resolving disputes; it is only to suggest that there is less of an aversion in relying upon legal solutions to business problems. Increasingly, even in the Western world, companies are relying upon mediation and/or arbitration in resolving disputes, and it would be fair to say that many contractual agreements do incorporate provisions for arbitration as a matter of course.

By contrast, in India, it is ideological contracting that is more prevalent. Although the legal contract is without question of importance even in India, a greater burden is brought to bear on ideological contracting. This is so for a number of reasons. First, the presence of collectivistic tendencies in the Indian populace heightens the importance of relationships in governing exchange transactions. Second, the judicial system with the lengthy delays associated with it, lessens the reliance on legal framework in adjudicating disputes. In other words, social control mechanisms appear to be more effective in controlling opportunistic behavior as opposed to legal mechanisms.

When westerners start doing business in India, they are therefore confronted with an alternative system of regulating exchange transactions. They are often uncomfortable with the more *fluid, ambiguous, relational* ways of coping with uncertainty than a method that relies on the presumed certainty of the contract, although it might be fair to say that the certainty of the contract may be more of an illusion than what the Western businessmen might consider to be the case. Indeed, this fondness, or a preference for relying on transactional contracts is so well exhibited in a statement made by Robert O. Blake, the U.S. Charge de Affaires at a seminar on "Business opportunities in India." As he notes, "If there is one complaint the Mission hears most frequently from American businesses and investors, it is that contractual terms may not be honored in trade disputes or arbitration."

The differing approaches to contracts in India and the West have a number of different implications. The Western perception that contractual terms are not honored may lead to *misperceptions* about their counterpart's intentions. They may come to doubt the sincerity of their counterpart, even though the latter's behavior may only be reflective of an alternative perspective on contracting. From a Western standpoint, it may also call forth additional effort to overcome difficulties of interaction, although it may be fair to say, that the additional effort that is required is itself a product of a transactional approach to contracting. One may also draw the inference that the westerners may get confused and perplexed and may pursue strategies that are likely to exacerbate the situation.

(e) Coping with the Negotiating Challenge: What can the Westerners Do?
The Indian negotiating style does pose a number of challenges for the Western negotiator. The typical Western negotiator is often direct, aggressive, goal oriented, time constrained, and is oriented toward concluding a contractual agreement that is binding. The Indian negotiator combines some of these traits in conjunction with others to develop a more *complex* approach to negotiations.

Complex does not mean either good or bad. The conception of *complexity* only implies that the Indian negotiator adopts a little bit of the Western and a little bit of the Indian approach to negotiations in an environment where *poverty syndrome* is often dominant. This creates an approach to negotiations that, while perfectly understandable from an Indian perspective, may be disorienting for the Western negotiator. How then should a Western negotiator prepare for negotiations with his Indian counterpart? This is the central issue addressed in this section.

(i) Create Incentives for the Indian Negotiators to act Differently. As pointed out earlier in this book, the Indians are often *context sensitive* in their behavioral orientation. This means that they behave differently in different situations. The high aspiration levels of the Indian negotiators in conjunction with their natural suspicion of foreigners, the existence of poverty syndrome, and a strong concern with distributive justice all induce them to pursue a contending negotiating strategy. The Western negotiator, must therefore try to create incentives for the Indians to negotiate differently than what they normally do.

Although there is no magic solution to this problem, the Western negotiators can nevertheless strive to create incentives for altering the behavior of the Indian negotiators. They must try to be as open as possible, within reasonable limits of course. This is not to suggest that the Western negotiator give away the store, only that they not be *unreasonably closed.*

In general, the surmise is that the greater the openness that is displayed by the Western negotiator, the more likely it is that the Indians will reciprocate it. The openness must be supplemented by a behavioral pattern of interaction that is not perceived as being too *aggressive*. As noted, while Indians are by temperament naturally aggressive, they may not respond well to aggressiveness displayed by others, especially by foreigners. To be *humble* may well be a virtue in this environment. It is vital to note here that most Indian business people want to work with people that they be able to call "friends" or even better, a part of their extended family.

The Western businessman would also be well advised to proceed incrementally instead of developing action plans that might suggest that he/she is embarking on an expedition to discover gold. Although none of these actions by themselves may completely alter the behavior of the Indian negotiator, these actions when working together, will create a *climate* that at least to a degree may alter the mind-set of the Indian negotiator.

(ii) Work around the Expectations of the Indian Negotiators. Indians often have high expectations and these expectations may act as a barrier to effective negotiations. The first recommendation is that the Western negotiator should not get involved in *contentious arguments* about how accurate or reasonable these expectations may be. This will lead to nothing but endless debates and confrontations. *Subtlety*, rather than outright combat may be more of a virtue here.

What is essential is that the Western negotiator seek to reframe the terms of the debate surrounding the negotiations. Reframing may occur by bringing in new issues, introducing new information, or by providing a more broader/comparative perspective regarding this project vis-à-vis others. It is, perhaps, also the case that once you earn the trust of Indian negotiators they may view the situation from a different perspective.

(iii) Be Sensitive to Concerns of Fairness. An outcome that is not perceived to be fair, even if guaranteed by an iron clad contract, will not survive the test of time in many countries, of which India is indeed one. The issue of fairness is in some sense seen differently in the West than is often the case in India. From a Western perspective, not adhering to a contract that one has signed may be perceived as a sign of unfairness. While this concern may not be absent in India, it is overshadowed by a larger concern, namely that of arriving at an agreement that guarantees equitable outcomes, notwithstanding the processes or the contracts that might be associated with it.

The issue of fairness becomes even more important in the Indian context when one realizes that in India there are a number of factors over which the business people may have little control, for example, infrastructure, power, political volatility, and the like. This, most clearly, makes outcomes somewhat unpredictable and requires imaginativeness and flexibility to cope with the ongoing challenges. Any sensitivity by the foreign investor to some or all of these issues may be perceived rather favorably by the Indian manager and may further the relationship between them.

Appendices

Sources of Information on India

Foreign Investment
Department of Industrial Policy & Promotion www.dipp.nic.in
Foreign Investment Promotion Board www.fipb.nic.in
Reserve Bank of India www.rbi.org.in
Investment & Trade Promotion Division, Ministry of External Affairs
www.indiainbusiness.nic.in

Foreign Trade
Ministry of Commerce www.commerce.nic.in
Indian Trade Promotion Organization www.indiatradepromotion.org
Export Import Bank www.eximbankindia.com
Directorate General of Foreign Trade http://dgft.delhi.nic.in, //dgftcom.nic.in
Apparel Export Promotion Council www.aepcindia.com
Marine Products Export Development Authority www.mpeda.com
Agricultural and Processed Food Products Export Development Authority www.apeda.com

Industry
Department of Industrial Policy & Promotion www.dipp.nic.in
Ministry of Heavy Industries http://dhi.nic.in
Ministry of Small Scale Industries http://ssi.nic.in

Information Technology
National Association of Software & Service Companies www.nasscom.org
Ministry of Information Technology www.mit.gov.in
Electronics & Computer Software Export Promotion Council www.escindia.org

Economy and Finance
Ministry of Finance www.finmin.nic.in
Center for Monitoring Indian Economy www.cmie.com
Planning Commission. www.planningcommission.nic.in

Industry Chambers
Confederation of Indian Industry (C.I.I.) www.ciionline.org
Federation of Indian Chambers of Commerce and Industry (FICCI) www.ficci.com
FICCI's Business Information Portal www.bisnetworld.net
Associated Chambers of Commerce www.assocham.org
India Brand Equity Foundation www.ibef.org

Miscellaneous

Government of India Portal http://indiaimage.nic.in
Ministry of Power www.powermin.nic.in
Ministry of Non-Conventional Energy Sources http://mnes.nic.in
Directorate General of Hydrocarbons www.dghindia.com
Ministry of Petroleum www.petroleum.nic.in
Department of Biotechnology http://dbtindia.nic.in
Ministry of Shipping http://shipping.nic.in
Department of Company Affairs http://dca.nic.in
Ministry of Environment and Forests http://envfor.nic.in

India Overview

- Located in the southern tip of Asia
- Lies entirely in the northern hemisphere
- Mainland of India (area is seventh largest in the world)
  - North to South 3,200 km
  - East to West 2,900 km
  - Land frontier 15,000 km
  - Coast line 6,100 km
- Population: 1.075 billion
- Climate: Monsoon tropical to mountainous arctic
- Political system: Secular, Socialist, Federal, Democratic
- Structure: 29 Federal States and 6 Union Territories
- Currency: Indian Rupee (INR)
  - Equivalency (December 2004)
    - US$1 = INR 44
    - Euro 1 = INR 58
    - L.Stg. 1 = INR 84
- Per capita GNP: US$545+
- Life expectancy: 66 years
- World's youngest population:
  - Over 65% below 35 years old
  - Over 50% below 20 years old
- Largest producer in world: milk, butter, tractors, polished diamonds, tea, fruits, sugar, movies
- Second largest in world: technical manpower, rice/wheat production, rail network, sponge iron
- Amongst the world leaders in:
  - Space Technology (Moon mission in 2008)
  - Nuclear Technology
  - Super Computers
  - I.T.
  - Biotechnology (335 companies; $1.5 billion turnover, 40% p.a. growth)
  - Missiles and Aircraft
  - Ships, submarines and design of offshore oil platforms

Notes

1 India: A Commercial History Perspective

This chapter has been adapted from a more detailed, to be published, manuscript, scripted by Anand Sethi, a coauthor of this book.

1. Gaurangnath Banerjee (1921). *India as Known to the Ancient World*. Calcutta: Humphrey Press (Reprint, New Delhi AES, 1990).
2. Harprasad Ray. *Trade and Diplomacy in India*. New Delhi: Radiant Publishers.
3. Jacques Pirenne (1962). *The Tides of History*. England: Allen Unwin.
4. C. Rawlinson (1916). *The Intercourse between India and the Western World*. England: Cambridge Press.
5. Xinru Liu (1988). *Ancient India and Ancient China*. Delhi: Oxford University Press.
6. P.C. Bagchi (1971). *India and China—A Thousand Years of Cultural Relations*. Greenwood Press (Reprint).
7. Liu. *Ancient India and Ancient China*.
8. Jawaharlal Nehru (1961). *Discovery of India*. India: Asia Publishing House.
9. Nick Robins. In Search of East India Company. *Down to Earth*. New Delhi: Centre for Science & Environment, Delhi.
10. Ibid.
11. Nehru. *Discovery of India*.
12. Brooke Adams. *The Law of Civilization and Decay*. India: Vintage Books.
13. Nehru. *Discovery of India*.
14. Robins. "In search of East India Company."
15. Peter Ravn Rasmussen (1996). *Tranquebar: The Danish East India Company, 1616–1669*. Essay for University of Copenhagen.
16. Ibid.
17. Ibid.
18. P.N. Agrawala. *A Comprehension History of Business in India*. New Delhi: Vikas Publishing.
19. Francis C. Assisi. *Probing Indian American History* (www.indolink.com).
20. Ibid.
21. Susan S. Bean. *Yankee India*. MAPIN, MA: Peabody Essex Museum.
22. G. Bhagat (1970). *Americans in India*. New York University Press.
23. Gavin Weightman (2003). *The Frozen Water Trade*. Hyperion, U.S.A., January.
24. Federation of Indian Chambers of Commerce and Industry (1999). A Pictorial History of Indian Business. Delhi: Oxford University Press.
25. John Maynard Keynes. *The Economic Journal*, September 1911.
26. Weightman. *Frozen Water Trade*.
27. Agrawala. *Comprehensive History of Business*.
28. Weightman. *Frozen Water Trade*.
29. "The Kirloskar Story"—www.kirloskars.com/html/us/hist.htm
30. Loren Michael. "Kolar Gold Fields Power." Ph.D. Thesis, University of Wisconsin.

31. www.walchand.com/history.htm
32. B.R. Tomlinson. "Foreign Private Investment in India, 1920–1950." *Modern Asian Studies*
33. M.K. Venu. "Bombay Plan to Bombay Club." *Economic Times*, September 9, 2003.
34. Ibid.
35. Abid Hussain. "India's Fifty Years of Economic Development." *India Perspectives*, August 1997.
36. Federation of Indian Chambers of Commerce and Industry. Pictorial History of Indian Business.
37. Ibid.

2 The Rise of India: India and the West—Institutional Contrasts

1. "India stirs," *Financial Times*, August 29, 2002.
2. O. Goswami (2002). "India, 2002–2015: Scenarios for Economic Reforms." Confederation of Indian Industry, New Delhi, 2002.
3. "Indian Economy will Overtake UK, Japan, by 2035: Goldman Sachs," www.rediff.com/money/2003, October 13, 2003.
4. "Nine Indian firms figure in Forbes list of fine corporations," www.domain-b.com/industry/general/20030416_forbes.html, April 16, 2003.
5. N. Forbes (2001). "Doing Business in India: What Has Liberalization Changed?" In A.O. Krueger (Ed.) *Economic Policy Reforms and the Indian Economy*, pp. 130–167. Chicago: University of Chicago Press.
6. *Economist Intelligence Unit*, "Making the Most of India," July 9, 2003.
7. "IBM Buys Indian Call Center Operator," www.msnbc.com/id/4685675, April 7, 2004.
8. www.ficci.com/mca1/business-climate/comp-advantage.htm
9. *International Herald Tribune*, "Adapt to a Changing World Economy," February 5, 2003.
10. A. Sethi (2002). "India: A Commercial History Perspective." Unpublished manuscript.
11. M. Backman and C. Butler (2004). *Big in Asia: 25 Strategies for Business Success*. New York: Palgrave Macmillan.
12. J. Kotkin (1992). *The Tribe: How Race, Religion, and Identity Determine Success in the Global Economy*. New York: Random House.
13. G. Das (2002). *The Elephant Paradigm: India Wrestles with Change*. New Delhi: Penguin Books.
14. Y. Huang and T. Khanna "Can India overtake China," *Foreign Policy*, July/August, 2003.
15. Cited in *Business Today*, January 18, 2004.
16. S.P. Cohen (2001). *Emerging Power: India*. New Delhi: Oxford University Press.
17. S. Khilnani (1997). *The Idea of India*. New Delhi: Penguin Books.
18. Cohen. *Emerging Power: India*.
19. N. Davies (1996). *Europe: A History*. Oxford: Oxford University Press.
20. Khilnani. *The Idea of India*.
21. F.R. Frenkel (1999). "Contextual democracy: Intersections of Society, Culture, and Politics in India." In F.R. Frenkel, Z. Hasan, R. Bhargava, and B. Arora (Eds.) *Transforming India: Social and Political Dynamics of Democracy*, pp. 1–25. New Delhi: Oxford. P.K. Bardhan (2003). "Political Economy and Governance Issues in the Indian Economic Reform Process." *The Australia South Asia Research Centre's K.R. Narayan Oration, March 25, 2003*. Australian National University.
22. E. Luce and Q. Peel (2004). "Reformist Sees Democracy as a Source of India's Strength." *Financial Times*, November 8, p. 5.
23. www.worldbank.org/data/wd 2004
24. World Economic Forum (1999). *Global Competitiveness Report*. Geneva, Switzerland.
25. V. More and S. Narang (2002). "India, 2002–15: Where can Manufacturing Be?" *Confederation of Indian Industry*. New Delhi: India.

26. C. Rufin, U.S. Rangan, and R. Kumar (2003). "The Changing Role of the State in the Electricity Industry in India, China, & Brazil: Differences and Explanations." *American Journal of Economics and Sociology*, 4: 649–675.
27. A.O. Krueger and S. Chinoy (2001). "The Indian Economy in Global context." In A.O. Krueger (Ed.) *Economic Policy Reforms and the Indian Economy,* pp. 10–45. Chicago: University of Chicago Press.
28. T.N. Srinivasan and S.D. Tendulkar (2003). *Reintegrating India with the World Economy.* Washington DC: Institute for International Economics.
29. Krueger and Chinoy. "The Indian Economy in Global Context."
30. Ibid.
31. J. Mukherji (2002). *India's Slow Conversion to Market Economics.* Center for the Advanced Study of India, University of Pennsylvania, Philadelphia, PA.
32. Ibid.
33. Ibid.
34. Krueger and Chinoy "The Indian Economy in Global Context."
35. D. Farrell and A. Zainulbhai (2004). "The Next Steps to Greater Indian Prosperity." *Financial Times*, May 25.
36. Mukherji. *India's Slow Conversion.*
37. Ibid.
38. Asian Development Bank (2001). *Country Economic Review, India.* Manila: Philippines, Asian Development Bank Report.
39. M. Patibandla and B. Petersen (2002). "Role of Transnational Corporations in the Evolution of a High Tech Industry: The Case of India's Software Industry." *World Development*, 30: 1561–1577.
40. N. Bajpai and V. Shastri (1998). *Software Industry in India: A Case Study.* Harvard Institute of International Development: Harvard University Press.
41. A. Singhal (2004). "A Changing India." www.rediff.com/money/2004/feb/21
42. India–U.S. Economic relations. *CRS Report for Congress.* February 25, 2004.
43. www.ficci.com/mca1/business-climate/comp-advantage.htm
44. N. Bajpai and J.D. Sachs (1999). *The Progress of Policy Reform and Variations in Performance at the Sub National Level in India.* Harvard Institute of International Development: Harvard University Press.
45. M. Muller (2000). *India: What Can it Teach Us?* New Delhi: Penguin Books.
46. C. Nakane (1964). "Logic and the Smile: When Japanese Meet Indians." *Japanese Quarterly*, 11(4): 434–438.
47. D. Lal (2001). *Unintended Consequences: The Impact of Factor Endowments, Culture, and Politics on Long Run Economic Performance.* Cambridge, MA: MIT Press.
48. Taeube, F.A. n.d. *Structural Change and Economic Development in India: The Impact of Culture on the Indian Software Industry.* 9th International Conference of Regional Studies Association. Pisa, Italy, April 2003.
49. J.B.P. Sinha (1980). *The Nurturant Task Leader.* New Delhi: Concept Publishing.
50. D. Binstead n.d. *India: History, Succession, and Future of Family-Owned Businesses.* "India Study Program," Global-Trade-Law; GMU School of Public Policy, U.S.A., January 2004.
51. G. Das (1999). The Problem. www.india-seminar.com
52. www.rediff.com, "For Indian Businessmen, Family is the First Choice," February 21, 2003.

3 A Brief History of the Indian Software Industry

1. Jawaharlal Nehru (1961). *Discovery of India.* India: Asia Publishing House.
2. T.R.N. Rao and S. Kak (1998). *Computing in Ancient India.* Lafayette, LA: University of Southern Louisiana.
3. Anand K. Sethi. "Indian Humanware"—A Dimensional Study of India's IT Human Resources in the Context of Denmark's Requirement of IT. A report prepared for the Royal Danish Government.

4. Mrs. Sudha Murthy. *How Infosys was Born—A Reminiscence*. From //roofin.tripod.com/infosys
5. Ibid.
6. Sethi. "Indian Humanware."
7. Prof. Anne Lee Saxenian (September 29, 2000). *Brain Drain or Brain Circulation—The Silicon Valley Asia Connection*. Harvard University Asia Center.
8. "India's Whiz Kids." *Business Week*, International Edition (December 7, 1998).
9. Prof. Anne Lee Saxenian. *Silicon Valley's New Immigrant Entrepreneurs*. Public Policy Institute of California.
10. Sethi. "Indian Humanware."
11. Stuart Whitmore. "Driving Ambition." *Asia Week*, June 1999.
12. Anand K. Sethi (October 2002). "European Semiconductor."

4 Cultural Portrait: Impact of Hinduism on Indian Managerial Behavior

1. C. Storti (1990). *The Art of Crossing Cultures* (p. xiii). Yarmouth, ME: Intercultural Press.
2. G. Hofstede (2001). *Cultures Consequences: Comparing Values, Behaviors, Institutions, and Organizations across Nations*. London: Sage. A. Bird and M.J. Stevens (2003). "Toward an Emergent Global Culture and the Effects of Globalization on Obsolescing National Cultures." *Journal of International Management*, 9: 395–407.
3. Hofstede, p. 10.
4. N.J. Adler. *International Dimensions of Organizational Behavior*. Cincinnati, Ohio: Southwestern Publishing 4th Ed., 2002.
5. Hofstede, p. 9.
6. J.B.P. Sinha (2003). *Multinationals in India: Managing the Interface of Cultures*. New Delhi: Sage.
7. R. Brislin and T. Yoshida (1994). *Intercultural Communication Training: An Introduction*. New Delhi: Sage.
8. P. Mishra (2002). "How the British invented Hinduism." *New Statesman*, August 26, pp. 19–21.
9. "Hinduism." www.msn.com/encyclopedia, June 28, 2004.
10. W. Doniger. "Hinduism." www.kat.gr/kat/history/rel/hinduism.htm from "Encarta" (microsoft) 2001.
11. "Hinduism." www.msn.com/encyclopedia
12. Ibid.
13. Ibid.
14. Monier Williams (1891). *Brahmanism and Hinduism: Religious Thought and Life in India*. London, UK: John Murray Publishers.
15. "Hinduism." www.fact-index.com/h/hi/hindustan.html
16. Doniger. "Hinduism" www.kat.gr/kat/history/rel/hinduism.htm
17. R. Lannoy (1971). *The Speaking Tree: A Study of Indian Society and Culture*. New Delhi: Oxford University Press.
18. Ibid.
19. J.B.P. Sinha (2004). *Facets of Indian Culture*. Unpublished manuscript; Doniger. "Hinduism." www. kat.gr/kat/history/rel/hinduism.htm
20. Lannoy. *The Speaking Tree*.
21. Doniger. "Hinduism."
22. Ibid.
23. A.T. Embree (1989). Brahmanical Ideology and Regional Identities. In M. Jurgensmeyer (Ed.) *Imagining India: Essays on Indian History*, pp. 9–27. London: Oxford University Press; N.C. Jain and E.D. Kussman (1994). Dominant Cultural Patterns of Hindus in India. In L.A. Samovar and E.E. Porter (Eds.) *Intercultural Communication: A Reader* (pp. 95–104). Belmont, CA: R. Inden (1990). *Imagining India*. Oxford: Blackwell.

24. A. Dhand (2002). "The Dharma of Ethics, the Ethics of Dharma: Quizzing the Ideals of Hinduism." *Journal of Religious Ethics*, 30: 347–372.
25. Ibid.
26. Ibid.
27. J.D. White (2000). Harmony and Order in Indian Religious Traditions: Hinduism. In J.B. Gittler and J. Bertram (Eds.) *Research in Human Social Conflict*, pp. 81–102. Connecticut: JAI Press.
28. J.B.P. Sinha. Facets of Indian Culture.
29. D. Gupta (2000). *Interrogating Caste: Understanding Hierarchy and Difference in Indian Society*. New Delhi: Penguin.
30. N. Tarakeshwar, J. Stanton, and K.I. Pargament (2003). "Religion: An Overlooked Dimension in Cross Cultural Psychology." *Journal of Cross Cultural Psychology*, 34: 377–394; R.A. Emmons and R.E. Paloutzian (2003). "The Psychology of Religion." *Annual Review of Psychology*, 54: 377–402.
31. N. Tarakeshwar et al. "Religion."
32. R.A. Emmons and R.E. Paloutzian (2003). "The Psychology of Religion."
33. P. Laungani (1999). "Cultural Influences on Identity and Behavior." In Y.T. Lee, C.R. McCauley, and J.G. Draguns (Eds.) *Personality and Person Perception across Cultures*. pp. 191–212. New Jersey: Lawrence Erlbaum Associates; R. Kumar (2004). "Brahmanical Idealism, Anarchical Individualism and the Dynamics of Indian Negotiating Behavior." *International Journal of Cross Cultural Management*, 4: 39–58; J.B.P. Sinha and R.N. Kanungo (1997). "Context Sensitivity and Balancing in Indian Organizational Behavior." *International Journal of Psychology*, 32: 93–105.
34. F. Kluckhohn and F. Strodtbeck (1961). *Variations in Value Orientations*. Evanston, Il: Row Peterson.
35. S. Gopalan and J.B. Rivera (1997). "Gaining a Perspective on Indian Value Orientations: Implications for Expatriate Managers." *International Journal of Organizational Analysis*, 5: 156–179.
36. J.T. Jones and T. Jackson (2001). Managing People and Change: Comparing Organisations and Management in Australia, China, India, and South Africa. Unpublished manuscript Flinders University of Australia; J.B.P. Sinha and S. Mohanty (2004). *Tata Steel: Becoming World Class*. New Delhi: Sri Ram Centre for Industrial Relations and Human Resources.
37. Ibid.
38. dilbert.iiml.ac.in/mag/panel.htm, Indian vs Western managers. June 14, 2004.
39. S. Stroschneider and D. Guss (1999). "The Fate of the Moros: A Cross Cultural Exploration of Strategies in Complex and Dynamic Decision Making." *International Journal of Psychology*, 34: 235–252.
40. Ibid.
41. J.B.P. Sinha (2004 forthcoming). Glimpses of Indian Culture and Its Impact on Organizational Behavior. In Y.T. Lee, V. Calvez, and A.M. Guenette (Eds.) *Cultural Competence in the World of Globalization: Cultural and Organizational Specificities*.
42. Lannoy. *Speaking Tree*.
43. Kumar. "Brahmanical Idealism." 39–58; H. Nakamura (1964). *Ways of Thinking of Eastern Peoples: India, China, Tibet, and Japan*. Honolulu: East West Center Press.
44. www.managementnext.com, June 2003.
45. Lannoy. *Speaking Tree*.
46. R. Geissbauer and H. Siememsen (1995). *Strategies for the Indian Market: Experiences of Indo-German Joint Ventures*, p. 87. New Delhi: Indo German Chamber of Commerce.
47. P. Laungani (1999). "Cultural Influences on Identity and Behavior."
48. G.W. England, O.P. Dhingra, and N.C. Aggarwal (1974). *The Manager and the Man*. Kent, OH: Kent State University Press; R. Cohen (1997). *Negotiating across Cultures:*

Communication Obstacles in International Diplomacy. Washington DC: US Institute of Peace.

49. H.R. Markus and S. Kitayama (1991). "Culture and the Self: Implications for Cognition, Emotion, and Motivation." *Psychological Review*, 108: 291–310; A. Roland (1988). *In Search of Self in India and Japan: Toward a Cross Cultural Psychology*. Princeton, NJ: Princeton University Press.
50. H.C. Triandis (1994). *Culture and Social Behavior*. New York: McGraw Hill.
51. H.R. Markus and S. Kitayama (1991). "Culture and the self" *Psychological Review*, 98: 224–253.
52. Ibid.
53. R. Kumar (2004). "Culture and Emotions in Intercultural Negotiations." In M. Gelfand and J.M. Brett (Eds.) *Culture and Negotiation: A Reader*, pp. 95–113. Palo Alto: Stanford University Press.
54. J.B.P. Sinha and J. Verma (1987). "Structure of Collectivism." In C. Kagitcibasi (Ed.) *Growth and Progress in Cross Cultural Psychology*, pp. 123–129. Lisse: Swets & Zeitlinger; K. Marriott (Ed.) *India through Hindu Categories*. New Delhi: Sage.
55. J.B.P. Sinha (2005). *Facets of Indian Culture*.
56. H.C. Triandis and D.P.S. Bhawuk (1997). "Culture Theory and the Meaning of Relatedness." In P.C. Earley and M. Erez (Eds.) *New Perspectives in International Industrial Organizational Psychology* (pp. 13–52). San Francisco: New Lexington Press.
57. Sinha. *Facets of Indian Culture*.
58. L. Ericson (2003). Snakes in Bombay: A Case Study of British/Indian Outsourcing Partnership. *The Milestone*, 4: 1–3.
59. Canadian International Development Agency (1994). "Working with an Indian Partner: A Cross Cultural Guide for Effective Working Relationships."
60. J.B.P. Sinha, T.N. Sinha, J. Verma, and R.B.N. Sinha (2001). "Collectivism Coexisting with Individualism: An Indian Scenario." *Asian Journal of Social Psychology*, 4: 133–145.
61. A. Roland. n.d. Multiple Mothering and the Familial Self. Unpublished manuscript.
62. J.B.P. Sinha, N. Vohra, S. Singhal, R.B.N. Sinha, and S. Ushashree (2002). "Normative Predictions of Collectivist-Individualist Intentions and Behaviour of Indians." *International Journal of Psychology*, 37: 309–319.
63. R.K. Gupta (2002). *Towards the Optimal Organisation: Integrating Indian Culture and Management*. New Delhi: Excel Books.
64. R. Gopalakrishnan (2002). Leading diverse teams. www.tata.com, June 29, 2004.
65. C. Chakravarthy (2003). More MNC's Place Faith in Indian Managers. www.economictimes.indiatimes.com, June 15, 2004.
66. A. Panda and R.K. Gupta (2002). "Hi-Tech Communication Limited." *Asian Case Research Journal*, 2: 129–166.
67. Sinha. *Multinationals in India*, p. 154.
68. Ibid., pp. 180–181.
69. P. Laungani (1999). "Cultural Influences on Identity and Behavior," p. 207.
70. Goplan and Rivera. "Gaining a Perspective on India Value Orientation," p. 163.
71. S. Narayan (2000). "Value mind, Indian Mind." www.littleindia.com/India/Feb00/mind.htm
72. J. Harriss (2003). "The Great Tradition Globalizes: Reflections on Two Studies of 'The Industrial Leaders' of Madras." *Modern Asian Studies*, 37: 327–362.
73. Comment of a Danish manager. In M.L. Hughes (2002). *A Theoretical and Empirical Analysis of Chinese and Indian Negotiating Behavior*. Unpublished Masters Thesis, The Aarhus School of Business, Aarhus, Denmark.
74. E.T. Hall (1976). *Beyond Culture*. New York: Doubleday.
75. J.B.P. Sinha and R.N. Kanungo (1997). "Context Sensitivity and Balancing in Indian Organizational Behavior."

76. Sinha. *Glimpses of Indian Culture.*
77. Panda and Gupta. "Hi-Tech Communication Limited."
78. G. Chella (2004). "India's Cultural Competitiveness: The Unfinished Task." *Business Line*, March 5.
79. D.C. McClelland (1975). *Power: The Inner Experience.* New York: Free Press.
80. J.B.P. Sinha (1985). "Psychic Relevance of Work in Indian Culture." *Dynamic Psychiatry*, 18: 134–141.
81. J.B.P. Sinha (1990). *Work Culture in the Indian Context.* New Delhi: Sage.
82. R.K. Gupta (1991). "Employees and Organizations in India: Need for Moving Beyond America and Japan." *Economic and Political Weekly*, XXXVI, M68–M76.
83. J.B.P. Sinha and S. Mohanty (2004). *Tata Steel: Becoming World Class.*
84. Ibid.
85. Ibid.
86. Sinha. *Multinationals in India.*
87. J.B.P. Sinha and S. Mohanty (2004). *Tata Steel: Becoming World Class*, p. 244.
88. Ibid.
89. Gupta. *Towards the Optimal Organization.*
90. R. Gopalakrishnan (2002). "If only India Knew What Indians Know." www.tata.com, April 26.
91. S.V. Prasad (2003). "The Power Motive in the Indian Context: Some Reflections." *Journal of Indian Psychology*, 21: 7–20.
92. T.K. Das (2001). "Training for Changing Managerial Role Behaviour: Experience in a Developing Country." *Journal of Management Development*, 20: 579–603 (p. 585).
93. J.B.P. Sinha (1970). *Development through Behavior Modification.* Bombay: Allied Publishing.
94. Sinha. *Facets of Indian Culture.*
95. A. Roland. n.d. Multiple Mothering and the Familial Self. Unpublished manuscript.
96. Y. Vertzberger (1984). "Bureaucratic-Organizational Politics and Information Processing in a Developing State." *International Studies Quarterly*, 28: 69–95.
97. Sinha. *Facets of Indian Culture.*
98. M.K. Raina (2002). "*Guru–Shisya* Relationship in Indian Culture: The Possibility of a Creative Resilient Framework." *Psychology and Developing Societies*, 14: 167–198.
99. J.B.P. Sinha (1980). *The Nurturant Task Leader.* New Delhi: Concept Publishing.
100. J.B.P. Sinha and S. Mohanty (2004). *Tata Steel: Becoming World Class*, p. 36.
101. Sihna. *Multinationals in India.*
102. J. Gosling and H. Mintzberg (2003). "The Five Minds of a Manager." *Harvard Business Review,* November, pp. 53–63.
103. Ibid., p. 56.
104. R. Kumar (2004). "Brahmanical Idealism, Anarchical Individualism and the Dynamics of Indian Negotiating Behavior."
105. Comment of a Danish manager. In Hughes, *Chinese and Indian Negotiating Behavior*, p. 82.
106. R.E. Nisbett, K. Peng, I. Choi, and A. Norenzayan (2001). "Culture and Systems of Thought: Holistic vs Analytic Cognition." *Psychological Review*, 108: 291–310.
107. R. Kumar (2004). "Brahmanical Idealism, Anarchical Individualism and the Dynamics of Indian Negotiating Behavior," p. 44.
108. R.K. Gupta (2002). "Prospects of Effective Teamwork in India: Some Cautionary Conjectures from a Cross Cultural Perspective." *Indian Journal of Industrial Relations*, 38: 211–229.
109. R. Kumar (2004). "Brahmanical Idealism, Anarchical Individualism and the Dynamics of Indian Negotiating Behavior."
110. Panda and Gupta. "Hi-Tech Communication Limited."
111. Hughes. *Chinese and Indian Negotiating Behavior.*
112. Cited in Sinha. *Multinationals in India.*

5 Understanding India

1. Pavan K. Varma (2004). *Being Indian.* India: Penguin/Viking.
2. Shashi Tharoor (2005). "A Culture of Diversity." *Resurgence* Magazine, 8 March.
3. Varma. *Being Indian.*
4. Ibid.
5. Sudip Talukdar. "Makeshift Miracles." *Times of India*, January 1, 2004.
6. Shashi Tharoor. "Culture of Diversity."
7. N.Vittal. "Corruption is Eating the Very Core of the Nation." Paper presented at the Rotary District Conference, New Delhi, January 2002.
8. Ibid.

6 Strategizing Success in India

1. C.A. Bartlett and S. Ghoshal (2000). *Transnational Management.* New York: McGraw Hill.
2. Economist Intelligence Unit (2000). "Selling to India." March, pp. 1–2.
3. Ibid.
4. G. Shukla (2004). "Global Winners, Indian Losers." www.rediff.com/money/2004/nov/09spec.htm
5. Ibid. p. 5.
6. A. Andres, S. Bernberg, G. Jindal, G. Ritwik, M.S. Bhatia, P. Swapnil, and S. Namit (2004). *Taming the Elephant: Turnaround of Mercedez-Benz India Ltd.* Vallendar, Germany: Otto Beisheim Graduate School of Management.
7. Ibid., p. 7.
8. Shukla. "Global Winners, Indian Losers."
9. Ibid.
10. S.D. Gupta (2004). "Korean Chaebols Rule Indian Markets." www.rediff.com/money/2004/jul/spec.htm
11. D.N. Mukherjea and R. Dubey (2003). "The Koreans." *BusinessWorld*, September 15, pp. 37–42.
12. Ibid.
13. Ibid.
14. Gupta. "Korean Chaebols," p. 3.
15. W. Pinckney (2004). "Indians Want Quality and Will Pay for It." www.agencyfaqs.com/www1/news/interviews/pinckney.html
16. Ibid.
17. Ibid., p. 1
18. Cited in D. Keskar (2001). "When in India, Do as Indians Do." http://web23.epnet.com/citation.asp? p. 1.
19. S. Ramchander (2002). "Make Sure Your Product is Special." www.hindubusinessline.com/bline/catalyst/2002/06/13/stories/20020613000
20. Ibid., p. 5.
21. Cited in R. Bhushan (2003). "It Takes Time to Understand the Indian Market." www.blonnet.com/catalyst/2003/05/08/stories/2003050800040100.htm
22. Mukherjea and Dubey. "The Koreans," p. 41.
23. C.K. Prahalad and A. Hammond (2002). "Serving the World's Poor, Profitably." *Harvard Business Review*, September, pp. 4–11.
24. J.B.P. Sinha (2004). *Multinationals in India: Managing the Interface of Cultures.* New Delhi: Sage.
25. C.K. Prahalad and K. Lieberthal (1998). "The End of Corporate Imperialism." *Harvard Business Review*, July–August, pp. 69–79.
26. Sinha. *Multinationals in India.*
27. Prahalad and Lieberthal. "End of Corporate Imperialism."
28. Ibid.

29. R. Goffee and G. Jones (1996). "What Holds the Modern Company Together?" *Harvard Business Review*, November–December, pp. 133–148.
30. R.A. Ostrander (1995). "Subcontinental Telecommunications Solutions." Palo Alto, CA: Graduate School of Business, Stanford University.
31. P.L. Fagan, M.Y. Yoshino, and C.A. Bartlett (2003). *Silvio Napoli at Schindler India* (A). Cambridge, MA: Harvard Business School Press.
32. M.Y. Yoshino and P.L. Fagan (2002). *Silvio Napoli at Schindler India* (B). Cambridge, MA: Harvard Business School Press.
33. Ibid.
34. Sinha. *Multinationals in India.*
35. Cited in Yoshino and Fagan. Schindler India (B).
36. Cited in R. Kumar (1996). "Order Amid Chaos: Doing Business in India." *Wall Street Journal*, May 28.
37. J.S. Black, M. Mendenhall, and G. Oddou (1991). "Toward a Comprehensive Model of International Adjustment: An Integration of Multiple Theoretical Perspectives." *Academy of Management Review*, April, pp. 291–317.
38. R.M. Hodgetts and F. Luthans (2000). *International Management: Culture, Strategy, and Behavior*. New York: McGraw Hill.
39. A.E. Fantini. n.d. *A Central Concern: Developing Intercultural Competence*. www.sit.edu/publications/docs/competence.pdf
40. D.A. Griffith (2002). "The Role of Communication Competencies in International Business Relationship Development." *Journal of World Business*, 37: 256–265.
41. S.L-O'Sullivan (1999). "The Distinction Between Stable and Dynamic Cross Cultural Competencies: Implications for Expatriate Trainability." *Journal of International Business Studies*, 30: 709–725.
42. P.C. Earley and R.S. Peterson (2004). "The Elusive Cultural Chameleon: Cultural Intelligence as a New Approach to Intercultural Training for the Global Manager." *Academy of Management Learning and Education*, 3: 100–115.
43. Cited in P.C. Earley and E. Mosakowski (2004). "Cultural Intelligence." *Harvard Business Review*, October, pp. 139–146.
44. Ibid.
45. R. Brislin and T. Yoshida (1994). *Intercultural Communication Training: An Introduction.* London: Sage.
46. P. Petzal (2004). "India and Outsourcing: Beyond the Cost Savings." www.mce.be/knowledge/430/35
47. A. Meisler (2004). "Global Companies Weigh the Cost of Offering a Helping Hand to the Expats." www.workforce.com
48. R. Bennett, A. Aston, and T. Colquhoun (2000). "Cross Cultural Training: A Critical Step in Ensuring the Success of International Assignments." *Human Resource Management*, 39: 239–250.
49. Brislin and Yoshida. *Intercultural Communication Training.*
50. Boston Consulting Group (2004). "Ten Tips from Successful European Companies in India": A report for the Confederation of Indian Industry.

7 Communicating with Indians

The epigraphs in this chapter are drawn from: W.B. Gudykunst and Y.Y. Kim (1992). *Communicating with Strangers: An Approach to Intercultural Communication* pp. 41,89. C. Storti (1990). *The Art of Crossing Cultures.* Maine: Intercultural Press; D.C. Thomas (2002). *Essentials of International Management: A Cross Cultural Perspective.* Thousand Oaks, CA: Sage.

1. Cited in W.B. Gudykunst and Y.Y. Kim (1992). *Communicating with Strangers: An Approach to Intercultural Communication.* New York: McGraw Hill (p. 41).

2. M. Guirdham (1999). *Communicating across Cultures*. Hampshire, UK: Palgrave Macmillan.
3. H.W. Lane, J.J. DiStefano, and M.L. Maznevski (1998). *International Management Behavior*. Oxford, UK: Blackwell Publishers.
4. S.T. Fiske and S.E. Taylor (1991). *Social Cognition*. New York: McGraw Hill; L. Thompson (2003). *The Mind and Heart of the Negotiator*. New York: Prentice Hall.
5. E.Schein (1985). *Organizational Culture and Leadership*. San Francisco: Jossey-Bass.
6. M. Guirdham. *Communicating across Cultures*, p. 175.
7. "Doing business in India: A Cultural Perspective." Stylusinc.com/business/India/business_india.htm, February 8, 2004.
8. Fiske and Taylor. *Social Cognition*.
9. Dr. Zareen Karani Lam de Araoz. "When Cultures Collide: Professionals in Transition." www.siliconindia.com/startup/detail.asp, February 8, 2004.
10. R. Brislin, K. Cushner, C. Cherrie, and M. Young (1986). *Intercultural Interactions*. Beverly Hills, CA: Sage.
11. C. Storti (1990). *The Art of Crossing Cultures*. Yarmouth, ME: Intercultural Press.
12. G. Mandler (1975). *Mind and Emotion*. New York: John Wiley.
13. L. Berkowitz (1989). "Frustration–Aggression Hypothesis: A Reformulation." *Psychological Bulletin*, 106: 59–73.
14. Cited in www.siliconindia.com/magazine/MayJune98mating.html
15. Guirdham. *Communicating across Culture*.
16. T.A. Chandler, D.D. Shama, F.M. Wolf, and S.K. Planchard (1981). "Multiattributional Causality: A Study of Five Cross-National Samples." *Journal of Cross Cultural Psychology*, 12: 207–221.
17. R.M. Kramer and D.M. Messick (1998). "Getting by with a Little Help from our Enemies: Collective Paranoia and Its Role in Intergroup Relations." In C. Sedikides (Ed.) *Intergroup Cognition and Intergroup Behavior*, pp. 233–255. Mahwah, NJ: Lawrence Erlbaum Associates.
18. M. Williams (2001). "In Whom We Trust: Group Membership as an Affective Context for Trust Development." *Academy of Management Review*, 26, 377–396.
19. H.C. Triandis (1995). *Culture and Social Behavior*. New York: McGraw Hill.
20. Ibid.
21. Ibid.
22. Ibid.
23. E.T. Hall and M.R. Hall (1995). *Understanding Cultural Differences: Germans, French, and Americans*. Yarmouth, ME: Intercultural Press.
24. Ibid., p. 6.
25. R.M. Hodgetts and F. Luthans (2000). *International Management: Culture, Strategy, and Behavior*. New York: McGraw Hill.
26. A.M. Francesco and B.A. Gold (1998). *International Organizational Behavior*. Upper Saddle River, NJ: Prentice Hall.
27. Canadian International Development Agency (1994). "Working With An Indian Partner: A Cross Cultural Guide for Effective Working Relationships"; P. Hobbs (2002). "The Complexity of India." *New Zealand Business*, November, pp. 12–13; R. Gopalakrishnan (2002). "If only India Knew what Indians Know." www.tata.com/tata_sons/articles/20020426_gopalkrishnan_2.htm
28. M. Jayashankar. "Building Outsourcing Bridges: Change Management Teams Help US Clients and Indian Firms Understand how to Work Together." www.businessworldindia.com/june21st,2004./indepth02.asp
29. Kramer and Messick. "Little Help from Our Enemies."
30. R. Gibson. "Intercultural Communication: A Passage to India." Interview with Sujata Bannerjee. www.business-spotlight.de/doc/13053?PHPSESSID, May 2003.
31. Araoz. "When Cultures Collide."
32. Cited in J.B.P. Sinha (2003). *Multinationals in India: Interface of Cultures*. New Delhi: Sage.

33. Cited in Ibid., p.144.
34. Hodgetts and Luthans. *International Management.*
35. R. Cohen (1997). *Negotiating across Cultures: Communication Obstacles in International Diplomacy.* Washington, DC: United States Institute of Peace.
36. H.C. Triandis (1995). *Culture and Social Behavior* (p. 193). New York: McGraw Hill.
37. A. Perry. "An Eternally Faltering Flame: Despite Its Billion-Plus Population, India is Always an Also-Ran at the Olympics." www.time.com/asia/magazine/article/0,13673, 501040823-682346,00.html, February 9, 2004.
38. Triandis. *Culture and Social Behavior.*
39. Ibid.
40. R. Fisher and W. Ury (1991). *Getting to Yes.* Boston: Houghton Mifflin.
41. Cited in J.B.P. Sinha (2003). *Tata Steel: Becoming World Class.* New Delhi: Sri Ram Center for Industrial Relations and Human Resources.
42. L. Beamer and I. Varner (2001). *Intercultural Communication in the Workplace.* New York: McGraw Hill.
43. L. Copeland and L. Griggs (1985). *Going International: How to Make Friends and Deal Effectively in the Global Marketplace.* New York: Random House.
44. R.R. Gesteland (1999). *Cross Cultural Business Behavior: Marketing, Negotiating, and Managing across Cultures.* Copenhagen: Copenhagen Business School Press.
45. Ibid., p. 71.
46. Canadian International Development Agency (1994). "Working with an Indian Partner: A Cross Cultural Guide for Effective Working Relationships," p. 16.
47. A. Viswanathan. "Indian Companies are Adding Western Flavour." www.wipro.com/ newsroom/newsitem/newstory288.htm, July 28, 2004.
48. Jayashankar. "Building Outsourcing Bridges."
49. P. Jasrotia. "IT Pros Find it Harder to Work in Europe." www.expressitpeople.com/ 20011029/cover1.htm, October 29, 2001.
50. Cited in A. Ben Ze-'ev (2000). *The Subtlety of Emotions.* Cambridge, MA: MIT Press.
51. Sinha. *Multinationals in India,* p. 139.

8 Managing Relationships with the Indian Government: The Critical Challenges for Multinational Firms

1. R. Vernon (1971). *Sovereignty at Bay: The Multinational Spread of US Enterprises.* New York: Basic books.
2. Ibid.
3. S. Kobrin (1987). "Testing the Bargaining Hypothesis in the Manufacturing Sector in Developing Countries." *International Organization,* 41: 609–638.
4. R. Narula and J.H. Dunning (2000). "Industrial Development, Globalization, and Multinational Enterprises: New Realities for Developing Countries." *Oxford Development Studies,* 28: 141–167.
5. Y. Luo (2001). "Toward a Cooperative View of MNC–Host Government Relations: Building Blocks and Performance Implications." *Journal of International Business Studies,* 32: 401–419; R. Vernon (1998). *In the Hurricane's Eye: The Troubled Prospects of Multinational Enterprises.* Cambridge, MA: Harvard University Press.
6. Ibid.
7. L.T. Wells. Jr. (1998). "Multinationals and Developing Countries." *Journal of International Business Studies,* 29: 101–114.
8. L. Eden, S. Lenway, and D.A. Schuler (2004). "From the Obsolescing Bargain to the Political Bargaining Model." Paper presented at the workshop "International Business and Government Relations in the 21st Century," Thunderbird, Phoenix, Arizona, January 5, 2004.
9. R. Ramamurti (2001). "The Obsolescing 'Bargain Model'? MNC–Host Developing Country Relations Revisited." *Journal of International Business Studies,* 32: 23–39.

10. D. Farrell, J.K. Remes, and H. Schulz (2004). "The Truth about Foreign Direct Investment in Emerging Markets." *McKinsey Quarterly*, March 1.
11. K.E. Meyer (2004). "Perspectives on Multinational Enterprises in Emerging Economies." *Journal of International Business Studies*, 35: 259–276.
12. Ibid.
13. L. Alfaro (2002). *Foreign Direct Investment*. Cambridge, MA: Harvard Business School Press.
14. Ibid.
15. M. Koennig-Archibugi (2004). "Transnational Corporations and Public Accountability." *Government and Opposition*, pp. 234–259.
16. R.E. Kennedy and R.D. Tella (2001). *Corruption in International Business (B)*. Cambridge, MA: Harvard Business School Press.
17. Ibid.
18. T.J. Palley (2002). "The Child Labor Problem and the Need for International Labour Standards." *Journal of Economic Issues*, 36: 601–615.
19. Farrell, Remes, and Schulz. "Truth about Foreign Direct Investment."
20. Ibid.
21. M. Patibandla and B. Petersen (2002). "Role of Transnational Corporations in the Evolution of a High Tech Industry: The Case of India's Software Industry." *World Development*, 30: 1561–1577.
22. I. Ivarsson and C.G. Alvstam (2004). "International Technology Transfer to Local Suppliers by Volvo Trucks in India." *Tijdschrift voor Economische en Sociale Geografie*, 95: 27–43.
23. Wells. "Multinationals and Developing Countries," p. 102.
24. D.J. Encarnation (1989). *Dislodging Multinationals: India's Strategy in Comparative Perspective*. Ithaca, NY: Cornell University Press.
25. Ibid., p. 181.
26. J.B.P. Sinha (2004). *Multinationals in India: Managing the Interface of Cultures*. New Delhi: Sage.
27. Ibid.
28. Encarnation. *Dislodging Multinationals*.
29. Ibid.
30. Sinha. *Multinationals in India*, p. 20.
31. Ibid., p. 21.
32. T.U-M. Nazki (2004). "Business Confidence for FDI in India." Hyderabad, India: ICFAI Business School Case Development Center.
33. Cited in A. Perry (2004). "An Eternally Faltering Flame: Despite its Billion-Plus Population, India is always an Also-Ran at the Olympics. August 16. www.time.com/asia/magazine/article/0
34. N. Bardhan and P. Patwardhan (2004). "Multinational Corporations and Public Relations in a Historically Resistant Host Culture." *Journal of Communication Management*, 8: 246–263.
35. Cited in R.H.K. Vietor and E.J. Thompson (2004). *India on the Move*. Cambridge, MA: Harvard Business School Press.
36. V.K. Rangan and A. McCaffrey (2004). *Stakeholder Analysis: Enron and the Dabhol Power Project in India*. Cambridge, MA: Harvard Business School Press.
37. Ibid.
38. Ibid., p. 5.
39. R. Kumar, U.S. Rangan, and C. Rufin (2004). "Negotiating Complexity and Legitimacy in Independent Power Development." Manuscript forthcoming in *Journal of World Business* (2005).
40. P. Dittakavi (2003). "Coke and Pepsi in India: Pesticides in Carbonated Beverages." Hyderabad, ICFAI Knowledge Center.
41. Ibid.
42. Ibid.

43. G. Bhatia (2003). "Multinational corporations: Pro or Con?" *Outlook India*, October 29.
44. N. Assanie, Y.P. Woo, M.A. Jans, and J. Purves (2003). *Emerging India: Canadian Business Perceptions on Trade and Investment* (p. 15). Vancouver: Asia Pacific Foundation of Canada.
45. R. Kumar (2000). "Confucian Pragmatism vs Brahmanical Idealism: Understanding the Divergent Roots of Indian and Chinese Economic Performance." *Journal of Asian Business*, 16: 49–69; B.S. Raghvan (2002). "Nettle that Nobody Grasps—Bureaucratic Cobwebs Defy Brooms." *Businessline*. March 26.
46. G. Das (2002). *The Elephant Paradigm: India Wrestles With Change*. (p. 62) New Delhi: Penguin Books.
47. E. Luce (2004). "India's Tragic Comedy of Civil Disservice." *Financial Times*, November 10, p. 13.
48. Das. *The Elephant Paradigm*.
49. C. Rufin, U.S. Rangan, and R. Kumar (2003). "The Changing Role of the Electricity Industry in India, China, & Brazil: Differences and Explanations." *American Journal of Economics and Sociology*, 62: 649–675.
50. Cited in Assanie, Woo, Jans, and Purves. *Emerging India*.
51. R.E. Kennedy and R.D. Tella (2001). *Corruption in International Business (A)*. Cambridge, MA: Harvard Business School Press.
52. K. Elliott. "Corruption as an International Policy Problem: Overview and Recommendations." In K. Elliot (Ed.) *Corruption and the Global Economy*. Washington, DC: Institute of International Economics.
53. Kennedy and Tella. *Corruption in International Business (A)*.
54. P. Eigen (2002). "Multinationals Bribery goes Unpunished." *International Herald Tribune*, November 12.
55. J.P. Doh, P. Rodriguez, K. Uhlenbruck, J. Collins, and L. Eden (2003). "Coping with Corruption in Foreign Markets." *Academy of Management Executive*, 17: 114–127.
56. Ibid.
57. M. Habib and L. Zurawicki (2002). "Corruption and Foreign Direct Investment." *Journal of International Business Studies*, 33: 291–307.
58. Doh, Rodriguez, Uhlenbruck, Collins, and Eden. "Coping with Corruption."
59. Ibid., p. 118.
60. www.transparency.org/cpi/2003/cpi2003.en.html
61. K.K. Tummala (2002). "Corruption in India: Control Measures and Consequences." *Asian Journal of Political Science,* 10: 43–69 (p. 51).
62. Ibid.
63. Doh, Rodriguez, Uhlenbruck, Collins, and Eden. "Coping with Corruption."
64. J.E. Campos, D. Lien, and S. Pradhan (1999). "The Impact of Corruption On Investment: Predictability Matters." *World Development*, 27: 1059–1067.
65. A. Karnani (1996). *Competing for the Local Market: Local Firms vs MNCs*. New Delhi: Indian Institute of Foreign Trade.
66. "Should 'press note 18' be scrapped?" www.rediff.com/money/2003/apr/09debate.htm
67. "Disinvest mantris: The best way to PSU reform is to say 'No minister.' " //timesofindia.indiatimes.com/articleshow/858772.cms
68. Ibid.
69. A. Jethmalani. "Travails of joint ventures." www.economictimes.indiatimes.com/articlesshow/msid-863830 September 26, 2004.
70. T. Kostova and S. Zaheer (1999). "Organizational Legitimacy under Conditions of Complexity: The Case of the Multinational Enterprise." *Academy of Management Review*, 24: 64–81.
71. R.Kumar (2004). "Interpretative Performance and the Management of Legitimacy in Emerging Market Economies: Lessons from India." *Business and Society Review*, 109: 363–388.
72. Bardhan and Patwardhan. "Multinational corporations."
73. Ibid.

74. D. Dunn and K. Yamashita (2003). "Microcapitalism and the Megacorporation." *Harvard Business Review*, August: 1–9.
75. Ibid., p. 1.
76. C.K. Prahalad and K. Lieberthal (1998). "The end of corporate imperialism." *Harvard Business Review*, July–August: 69–79.
77. Ibid.
78. C.K. Prahalad and A. Hammond (2002). "Serving the World's Poor, Profitably." *Harvard Business Review*, September 4–11, 80: 9.
79. E. Szwajkowski (2000). "Simplifying the Principles of Stakeholder Management: The Three Most Important Principles." *Business and Society*, 39: 379–396.
80. M. Yaziji (2004). "Turning Gadflies into Allies." *Harvard Business Review*. February: 1–8.
81. P. Ghandikota (2002). When "Power Failures" Undermine International Business Negotiations: A Negotiation Analysis of the Dabhol Power Project. Mald Thesis, Boston, MA: Fletcher School of Law and Diplomacy.
82. Cited in Ghandikota. " 'Power Failures' Undermine."
83. Ibid.

9 Negotiating and Resolving Conflicts in India

The epigraphs in this chapter are drawn from Henry Ford. Cited in G.R. Shell (1999). *Bargaining for Advantage: Negotiation Strategies for Reasonable People,* p. 76. New York: Penguin; cited in W. Mastenbroek (1999). "Negotiating as Emotion Management," p. 49. *Theory, Culture, and Society*, 16: 49–73; C. Wilhelm (2002). "Part 3: Doing Business in India." *Asia Times*, February 20; M. Kammeyer (2001). The other customs barrier. *Export America*, April, pp. 32–33; Comment of a Danish manager. Cited in M. Hughes (2002). *A Theoretical and Empirical Analysis of Chinese and Indian Negotiating Behavior.* Unpublished Masters thesis, Aarhus School of Business, Denmark; Comment of a Danish manager in a personal interview with one of the authors.

1. N.J. Adler (2002). *International Dimensions of Organizational Behavior*, p. 210. Cincinnati, OH: Southwestern Publishing Company.
2. L. Copeland and L. Griggs (1985). *Going International: How to Make Friends and Deal Effectively in the Global Market Place*. New York: Random House.
3. M. Watkins (1999). "Negotiating in a Complex World." *Negotiation Journal*, July, pp. 245–270; S. Weiss (1993). "Analysis of Complex Negotiations in International Business: The RBC perspective." *Organization Science*, 4: 269–300.
4. D.A. Lax and J.K. Sebenius (1986). *The Manager as a Negotiator*. New York: Free Press.
5. M. Watkins (1999). "Negotiating in a Complex World," p. 250.
6. Ibid.
7. Ibid.
8. J.K. Sebenius (2002). "The Hidden Challenge of Cross Border Negotiations." *Harvard Business Review*, March: 76–85.
9. J.W. Salacuse (2003).*The Global Negotiator: Making, Managing, and Mending Deals around the World in the Twenty-First Century*. New York: Palgrave-Macmillan; J.M. Brett, W. Adair, A. Lempereur, T. Okumura, P. Shikhirev, C. Tinsley, and A. Lyttle (1998). "Culture and Joint Gains in Negotiation." *Negotiation Journal*, January: 61–85; J.L. Graham and N.M. Lam (2003). *The Chinese Negotiation*, October 1, 2003. R. Kumar (1999). "A Script Theoretical Analysis of International Negotiating Behavior." In R.J. Bies, R.J. Lewicki, and B.H. Sheppard (Eds.) *Research on Negotiation in Organizations*, Vol. 7, (pp. 285–311). CT: JAI Press.
10. Kumar. "Script Theoretical Analysis."
11. J.L. Graham and Y. Sano (1984). *Smart Bargaining: Doing Business with the Japanese.* New York: Harper Business.

12. J.M. Brett (2000). "Culture and Negotiation." *International Journal of Psychology*, 35: 97–104.
13. E.S. Glenn, D. Witmeyer, and K.A. Stevensen (1977). "Cultural Styles of Persuasion." *International Journal of Intercultural Relations*, 1: 52–66; Adler. *International Dimensions*.
14. J.W. Salacuse (2003). *The Global Negotiator*, J.M. Brett et al. (1998), "Culture and Joint Gains in Negotiation," R. Kumar (1999), "A Script Theoretical Analysis."
15. Kumar. "Script Theoretical Analysis."
16. M.K. Kozan (1997). "Culture and Conflict Management. A Theoretical Framework." *International Journal of Conflict Management*, 8: 338–360.
17. R. Brislin, K. Cushner, C. Cherrie, and M. Young (1986). *Intercultural Interactions: A Practical Guide*. Newbury Park, CA: Sage.
18. R. Kumar (1999). "Communicative Conflict in Intercultural Negotiations: The Case of American and Japanese Business Negotiations." *International Negotiation Journal*, 4: 63–78.
19. R. Kumar (2004). "Brahmanical Idealism, Anarchical Individualism, and the Dynamics of Indian Negotiating Behavior." *International Journal of Cross Cultural Management*, 4: 39–58.
20. Ibid.
21. R. Cohen (1997). *Negotiating across Cultures: Communication Obstacles in International Diplomacy*. Washington, DC: United States Institute of Peace Press.
22. Comment of a Danish manager. Cited in Hughes. *Chinese and Indian Negotiating Behavior*.
23. C. Rufin, U.S. Rangan, and R. Kumar (2003). "The Changing Role of the State in the Electricity Industry in India, China, & Brazil: Differences and Explanations." *American Journal of Economics and Sociology*, 62: 649–675.
24. A.C. Filley (1975). *Interpersonal Conflict Resolution*. Glenview, IL: Scott Foresman.
25. J.Z. Rubin, D.G. Pruitt, and S.H. Kim (1994). *Social Conflict: Escalation, Stalemate, and Settlement*. New York: McGraw Hill.
26. R. Kumar and V. Worm (2005). "Institutional Dynamics and the Negotiation Process: Comparing India and China." Forthcoming in *International Journal of Conflict Management*.
27. C. Wilhelm (2002). "Part 3: Doing Business in India." *Asia Times*, February 20.
28. J. Brockner and B.M. Wiesenfield (1996). "An Integrative Framework, for Explaining Reaction to Decisions." *Psychological Bulletin*, 120: 189–211.
29. M. Deutsch (1975). "Equity, Equality, and Need: What Determines Which Value Will be Used as a Basis for Distributive Justice?" *Journal of Social Issues*, 31: 137–149.
30. R. Pillai, E.S. Williams, and J.J. Tan (2001). "Are the Scales Tipped in Favor of Procedural or Distributive Justice? 'An investigation of, the US, India, Germany, and Hong Kong.' " *International Journal of Conflict Management*, 12: 312–332.
31. J.B.P. Sinha and R.N. Kanungo (1997). "Context Sensitivity and Balancing in Indian Organizational Behavior." *International Journal of Psychology*, 32: 92–105.
32. R. Kumar (1996). "Order Amid Chaos: Doing Business in India." *Asian Wall Street Journal*, May 23: 23.
33. R. Kumar (2005). "Contracts and the Dynamics of Exchange Relationships in India." In R. Ajami, C.E. Arrington, F. Mitchell, and H. Norreklit (Eds.) *Globalization, Management Control, and Ideology* (pp. 99–111). Copenhagen: Djof Publishing.

INDEX